The Best American
Spiritual Writing 2006

The Best American
Spiritual Writing 2006

EDITED BY *Philip Zaleski*

INTRODUCTION BY *Peter J. Gomes*

HOUGHTON MIFFLIN COMPANY
BOSTON · NEW YORK   2006

ISSN: 1555-7820
ISBN-13: 978-0-618-58644-8   ISBN-10: 0-618-58644-x
ISBN-13: 978-0-618-58645-5 (pbk.)   ISBN-10: 0-618-58645-8 (pbk.)

Printed in the United States of America

MP 10 9 8 7 6 5 4 3 2 1

Contents

Contents

Foreword

THE GREATEST ART considers the human being *sub specie aeternitatis,* in the light of eternity. In doing so, it discloses both our meanness and our majesty, in keeping with Pascal's dictum that we dwell between two abysses, the Infinite and the Nothing, that every person is a "nothing in comparison with the infinite, an all in comparison with the nothing, a mean between nothing and everything." Art that sustains this transcendent perspective, perceiving in us both angel and beast — I am thinking here of art as diverse as the *Iliad,* Beethoven's *Late Quartets,* or *Thus Spake Zarathustra* — offers us, each time we stand before it, more truth about ourselves, about the cosmos, and about the relation of the one to the other. On rare occasions, it may even hand us the keys to our existence.

Everyone has, or should have, one or two such works to cherish through a lifetime. C. S. Lewis, young and old, sought wisdom in George MacDonald's fantasies, while Gabriel Betteredge, the unforgettable house steward in Wilkie Collins's *The Moonstone,* relies upon the miraculous powers of *Robinson Crusoe:*

> Such a book as *Robinson Crusoe* never was written, and never will be written again. I have tried that book for years — generally in combination with a pipe of tobacco — and I have found it my friend in need in all the necessities of this mortal life. When my spirits are bad — *Robinson Crusoe.* When I want advice — *Robinson Crusoe.* In past times when my wife plagued me; in present times when I have had a drop too much — *Robinson Crusoe.* I have worn out six stout *Robinson Crusoes* with hard work in my service. On my lady's last birthday she gave me a seventh. I took a drop too much on the strength of it; and *Robinson Crusoe* put me right again.

It may occur to you that the Bible or some other sacred writing fulfills, for many people, the role of Betteredge's *Robinson Crusoe;* but I mean a work other than Scripture. Holy texts, at least for those who take them seriously, are inspired by God; they exhale the breath of divinity into a profane world. They may invite kisses, tears, song, even dancing as with the Hasidim, but they maintain a disquieting otherness — they are revelation first, art second. When I speak of art to treasure through the decades, I mean a work, no matter how great its wisdom, shot through with flaws; something brewed from flesh and blood rather than pure spirit; human work aspiring toward the divine, not divine work condescending to our level. I mean a creation that might have been fashioned not by the Olympians or their human amanuenses, but by a good gifted friend at the height of his powers, at the dawn of his very best day; an art that, in its all too human genius, still informs, guides, cheers, solaces, upbraids, goads, infuriates, and delights.

For many years now, my choice for this mode of art has been the *Commedia* of Dante Alighieri. I do not intend to describe here my relationship to the *Commedia,* its nearly indispensable role in the snail-like progress of my soul, so I will merely cite, to indicate this poem's exceptional nature, two remarks from people who possess the authority to speak. T. S. Eliot writes that "the majority of poems one outgrows and outlives, as one outgrows and outlives the majority of human passions: Dante's is one of those which one can only just hope to grow up to at the end of life." Erich Auerbach, emphasizing the *Commedia*'s supernatural perspective, says that Dante "leads all men into a realm apart, where the air is not that of our everyday earth. Not that the reality of life has vanished; it has grown doubly plain and tangible."

I have spent many hours in Dante's company, traveling alongside the poet from his first encounter with Beatrice Portinari when he was eight and she was nine to his terrifying plunge into Hell, his ascent of Mount Purgatory, and his beatific tour of the empyrean, culminating in the *Commedia*'s final canto, which Eliot acclaims as "the highest point that poetry has ever reached or ever can reach." High praise indeed! But not unfitting, both because it may be true and because Dante's work is always a quest for heights, not only in images but in morals, feeling, and intellect, and above all, for the zenith where these categories of human experiences converge. This point, according to Dante, is located beyond death, past pur-

gation and purification, in the beatific vision, the face-to-face encounter with God. He describes the beatific vision as "living light,"
"eternal light," "light supreme," light that is revealed, in the canto's
parting epiphany, as "the love that moves the sun and the other
stars."

Dante mastered the heights of vision; he also displays, throughout his oeuvre, a profoundly practical turn of mind. His grasp of
human psychology is keen, his ability to portray empathetically a
panorama of characters unmatched by anyone but Shakespeare.
He knows much about politics, theology, art. In particular — and
this is why I write about him here — he has much of interest to say
about the subject of this annual collection: about writing, about
writers, and about their relationship to the soul.

Dante takes words very seriously indeed. Language is what makes
us human, he argues in *De vulgari eloquentia*, composed just a few
years before he began the *Commedia*. All other beings possess intrinsic modes of communication, angels through "spiritual reflection," animals through instinct. Only humans need to devise tools
or "signals" based on reason and sense perception organized
through grammar and syntax to present ideas. Even Adam had
such a language, and his first communication was not a primitive
grunt but an elegant religious gesture, proclaiming the name of
God. As for Adam's children, particularly that small but exalted
tribe known as poets, Dante asserts in the *Convivio* that their words
— and, by extrapolation, those of all serious writers — carry, or
at least should carry, four levels of meaning: literal, allegorical,
moral, and anagogical or spiritual (so that the literal meaning also
"signifies . . . a part of the supernal things of eternal glory"). To
speak, be it with tongue or pen, is thus to generate a hierarchy of
meanings. The writer's ultimate task is to present these manifold
levels of meaning in light of the great cosmic drama of sin and salvation, for the good of humankind and the glory of God. Dante,
while composing the *Commedia*, always kept this view in mind. "The
aim of the whole," he wrote in a letter to his patron Can Grande,
"is to remove those living in this life from a state of misery and
to guide them to a state of happiness." In other words — and we
may flinch at the poet's audacity — what God does through grace,
Dante Alighieri will do through art.

It follows that Dante has an extremely high regard for writers. As
Thomas Macauley puts it in *Miscellaneous Writings,*

Every reader of the Divine Comedy must be struck by the veneration which Dante expresses for writers far inferior to himself. He will not lift up his eyes from the ground in the presence of Brunetto, all of whose works are not worth the worst of his own hundred cantos. He does not venture to walk in the same line with the bombastic Statius. His admiration of Virgil is absolute idolatry.

Reading Macauley's assessment, it occurred to me that in an effort to gauge as precisely as possible Dante's attitude toward his fellow wordsmiths, it would be both amusing and instructive to catalog the writers who appear in the *Commedia* and see where Dante places them within the tripartite Catholic afterlife that provides the poem's superstructure. Of the more than six hundred people whom Dante mentions by name, a considerable number — at least 5 percent, probably closer to 10 percent — achieved fame through their pens. Would these authors, or the bulk of them, in keeping with Macauley's presumption of favoritism, wind up in Paradise or at least on the upper rungs of Purgatory? Not so. I discovered, to my great surprise, that Dante's Hell is packed with poets. At first glance this seems to contradict Macauley's view, but a closer look proves otherwise. For the writer-inmates of the *Inferno* stand apart from other damned souls. Fire, sting, scourge, these and other hellish torments pass them by. Almost all the damned literati dwell in Hell's outermost suburbs, a benign region known as Limbo, where they divide their time among a majestic castle, forest glades, and verdant meadows that encourage conversations that Dante calls "tuneful sweet." Their sole punishment is to yearn eternally for a beatific vision that can never be theirs. Dante admires his fellow poets, he celebrates and salutes them; indeed, while wishing to avoid their infernal fate, he longs to be counted among them. In *Inferno* IV: 97–102 his wish is granted, as the five poetic geniuses of classical Greece and Rome — Homer, Horace, Lucan, Ovid, and Virgil (Dante's "Master") — welcome him into their company:

> When they together had discoursed somewhat,
> They turned to me with signs of salutation,
> And on beholding this, my Master smiled.
>
> And more of honor still, much more, they did me,
> In that they made me one of their own band,
> So that the sixth was I, 'mid so much wit.

These pagan poets, along with their prose-writing counterparts such as Thales, Heraclitus, Plato, and Aristotle, languish in Limbo because they lived and died before the Christian revelation, were never baptized, and thus, in the understanding of salvation in Dante's day (and, it is worth noting, no longer held by the Catholic Church), found the gates of paradise forever closed. Dante's sympathies are clear, however: if these pagans had lived in the Christian era, they would most likely be arrayed around the celestial throne.

Writers living in Purgatory, by contrast, however heinous their past crimes, do possess assurance that eventually they will meet God face to face. Here we find most of Dante's poetic contemporaries, such as Bonagiunta, from the city of Lucca, assigned to Purgatory's sixth circle for his gluttony, and Arnaut Daniel, cited in *De vulgari eloquentia* as the preeminent poet of love, placed in the seventh circle among the lustful. Also in this circle filled with flames (an appropriate purgation for inflamed passions) is Guido Guinicelli, whose work foreshadowed *dolce stil nolvo*, the poetic school to which Dante belonged in youth. Dante's response, upon learning that Guinicelli is in Purgatory, confirms his high regard for his fellows. Stricken, he proclaims Guinicelli "the father / Of me and of my betters, who had ever / Practiced the sweet and gracious rhymes of love" and his poetry "those dulcet lays of yours / Which, long as shall endure our modern fashion / Shall make forever dear their very ink!" One can say, in general, that Dante's attitude toward those in Purgatory is: hate the sin, love the sinner, love him all the more if he wields a pen.

And what of heaven? Dante sprinkles a healthy number of writers throughout the Paradiso, all of whom led exemplary lives and all of whom he holds in high esteem. But what is the source of this regard? Do their writings have any bearing, as inspiration or impediment, upon their final salvation? Here it may be useful to recall the work of another first-rate author, Søren Kierkegaard, who famously erected a hierarchy of modes of being, which ascend from the aesthetic to the ethical to the religious. Kierkegaard suggests, in line with Plato, that the highest life entails the rejection of the aesthetic, that conjuror's game of illusion and deceit. Dante's heavenly population, upon first impression, buttresses this view, for the only poet of renown permitted into Paradise is Folquet de Marseille, a troubadour who, in the midst of an acclaimed career, aban-

doned the refinements of courtly love and amorous verse for the
cloister, becoming first a friar, then an abbot, and finally the bishop
of Toulouse. Only by turning his back on art, it seems, did Folquet
turn his face toward God. To become a saint, Dante apparently
suggests, one must lay aside poetry and other unworthy pastimes.

But is this all Dante had to say on the matter? Is there no way off
the collision course between art and holiness? Let us note that
Saints Thomas Aquinas, Francis of Assisi, Anselm of Canterbury,
and Augustine of Hippo also inhabit Paradise. Each of these holy
men wrote hymns, canticles, verse, or religious prose poems as well
as philosophical treatises. In some cases, such as Saint Francis's
Canticle of the Sun or Saint Thomas's hymns for the feast of Corpus Christi, these works rank with the finest religious art of their
age. Notice too, with this in mind, that Dante locates Folquet in
Paradise's sphere of Venus, the home of love, and Folquet declares that

> Folco that people called me unto whom
> My name was known; and now with me this heaven
> Imprints itself, as I did once with it.

Less cryptically, Folquet is saying that while on earth, love im-
printed itself upon him (that is, he was a troubadour), and now
that he is in Paradise, he imprints himself upon love (that is, he
lives within the sphere of love, or Venus). He will always be a lover:
on earth first of women and song, then of charity and poverty. All
along, but especially in death, he remains a lover of God. His voca-
tion is love, and its youthful manifestation in the courtly poetry of
love has not been abandoned but subsumed into his eternal mission.

For Dante, then — and this is the crux of the matter — art may
lead one astray, as it did in the case of Francesca da Rimini and
Paolo Malatesta, the celebrated lovers of the *Inferno* who fell into
adultery while reading a romance of Lancelot and Guinevere;
or art may prove irrelevant to one's fate, as with Bonagiunta or
Guinicelli in the *Purgatorio;* or art may be an intrinsic part of the
path to goodness, a vital element in one's capacity to see God face
to face, as with Folquet. The most important evidence for the
superiority of this third path, in which art nurtures sanctity and
sanctity fulfills art, lies with Dante himself. The *Commedia* is that evidence. God is the supreme artist and the created cosmos his work,

"the Master's art, who in himself so loves it / That never does his eye depart therefrom." All Paradise responds to God's art with art of its own, praising the Creator through prayer and song. And so too the *Commedia*, in its own appropriate register of thirteenth-century vernacular poetry, is a hymn of praise to God, a work of holy service, to give glory to the Creator and bring salvation to his creation ("to remove those living in this life from a state of misery and to guide them to a state of happiness").

Dante's magnificent achievement, unparalleled in literature, is a summons to all who write or read — all who love words — to place that love in the service of eternity.

As always, submissions are encouraged for future volumes of this series. Only essays and poems previously published in an American periodical are eligible. Please send submissions (with a self-addressed stamped envelope) to Philip Zaleski, 138 Elm Street, Smith College, Northampton, Massachusetts 01063. The best way for a periodical to ensure that its contents will be read and considered for future volumes is to add the *Best American Spiritual Writing* series, at the above address, to its subscription list.

I would like to thank all who contributed to this year's volume, including Professor Peter J. Gomes; Anton Mueller, Sasha Zoueva, and all the great folks at Houghton Mifflin; my wonderful agents, Kim Witherspoon and David Forrer of InkWell Management; and, as always, my beloved Carol, John, and Andy, who are for me the earthly representatives of what Dante termed, in the last line of his incomparable poem, *l'amor che move il sole et l'altre stelle.*

PHILIP ZALESKI

Introduction

THE SPIRITUAL DIMENSION of the American experience continues to be a source of amazement, with our neighbors around the world wondering what it is about it that seems so much a part of the American identity. Here we are, a country with no official religious establishment, whose constitutional origins might appear to be indifferent, if not hostile, to religious interests, and yet anyone who fails to see the power of the religious life in America runs the serious risk of failing to see an essential aspect of the American experience. No politician hopeful of election would ever suggest that religion has no role to play in American life, and yet the doctrine of the separation of church and state — an extraconstitutional principle not found in any of the founding documents — is understood by many to be the basis of the relationship between secular and religious interests.

Early American religionists, such as Roger Williams, the Baptist who founded the colony of Rhode Island and Providence Plantation, argued that the church needed protection from the state and thus "state" religion would inevitably put at risk true religion. His experience was with the English establishment and the risks to nonconformity, and he had experienced the same sense of a religious state in the Puritan establishment of the Massachusetts Bay Colony, where dissent was hardly more tolerated than in England. When the Founding Fathers decided on the essential ingredients of their new nation-state, they were determined not to replicate the errors of Roman Catholic Europe, Anglican England, and Puritan New England, for the nation as a whole would not permit an establishment of religion, although the various states could maintain such establishments at the pleasure of their voters. In Massachusetts, ministers of the Congregational Church were supported by taxes until the 1820s; disestablishment came not through a lack of interest in religion but through the inability of the tax rate to support the clergy of other denominations whose growth indicated an increase rather than a decrease of public piety. The irony here is that the state got out of the religion business because the state could not afford an equitable support of all the clergy, without whom neither the civil nor the ecclesiastical life of society could be expected to flourish.

This is the stuff of legal, constitutional, and ecclesiastical history, and does not speak to the fact that religion in all its permutations continues to be an enterprise at the heart of the contemporary American experience. Perhaps it could be said that religion is hardwired into the American cultural brain and part of the American DNA, and that once upon a time it could have been rather easily defined. Before the great rounds of nineteenth-century immigration, for example, religion in America was essentially Protestant; with the arrival of Roman Catholics it became Christian; and while Jews contributed to the Jewish-Christian identity of the culture, it was not until the modern immigration acts of the late twentieth century that religion in America would become truly diverse, with Muslims, Buddhists, and Hindus, among others, taking their place in the American spectrum. As Europe debates the historic role of Christianity in its formation and defines itself as essentially a secular and pluralist amalgam of states, the vivid continuities of old Christian establishments notwithstanding, America is probably more religious now, albeit in significantly different ways, than at any point in its history.

We might well ask what makes this possible. If America is a place of self-invention, a culture where it is possible to conform to the prevailing mores and redefine those aspects of one's past that are essential for survival and prosperity in a new and demanding environment, then perhaps we can see what role religion plays in the self-invention of Americans. It is thus that we explore the phenomena of "freedom from" and "freedom for."

"Freedom from" means that each new generation of immigrants defines itself in its liberation from its past. Cultural baggage can be discarded, and one is no longer bound by the circumstances of one's birth or the geography of one's ancestors. Ellis Island not only gave new names to people, often out of ignorance and bureaucratic "efficiency," it also afforded new opportunities. Freedom from the past was often the greatest opportunity provided by the New World, a phenomenon as old as the landing in 1620 of the Pilgrims at Plymouth.

There was also "freedom for," a chance not only to reinvent but to reappropriate and, for many in the case of religion, to rediscover. The power of ethnic churches in such places as nineteenth-century New York City and Chicago suggests that religion was one of the keys to the maintenance of an old identity and the establishment of a new. Irish, German, and Polish churches were not simply nostalgic institutions of the old country; they became the means to the establishment of a new and increasingly powerful identity in the new country. The Catholics in Boston, New York City, and Chicago gradually found themselves more powerful, and therefore more cultivated, in the political realm as well as in the cultural, than they ever would have in their old countries of Ireland, Germany, Italy, or Poland.

In the so-called new immigration from Asia in the late twentieth century, a new religious phenomenon would be at work when many of the first generations of arrivals faced some of the same cultural issues of assimilation and success as had their predecessors from Europe. It would be their children born in America, however, who would affect a rediscovery of the religion of the old country within the cultural context of the new. The young people, the college-age students of immigrants, would study the religions of their ancestors in the growing religious studies programs in American universities. They were no less American than their predecessors, but, unlike many of their parents and immigrant predecessors, they were interested not in religious assimilation into the American "Christian" culture, but in the correlation of their newly discovered religious heritage with the demands and opportunities of their experience in America. They were able to tap into the American religious experience on their own terms and in their own ways, and while there may be fewer Presbyterians and Episcopalians than there were a hundred years ago, America's religious experience grows and intensifies because people relatively new to the culture invest their own religious identities into it.

My experience of more than thirty-five years at Harvard allows me to observe that probably more people today are engaged in some regular form of religious practice at Harvard than at any point since the American Revolution. The practice and the practitioners are very different from those white Anglo-Saxon Protestants of a century ago, but because there is more cultural diversity present in the college than in the past, there is also more religious practice. Diversity has broken the cultural tension between the religious and the secular, for where there are wider options and experiences, people are not forced to fight the nineteenth-century European battles of belief versus unbelief, but are able to take advantage of what the far-seeing William James once called the "varieties of religious experience."

America allows people to be religious in ways previously not available to them in other countries. Freedom presupposes choice, and the exercise of freedom allows people to be religious or not religious, as the case may be, and in different ways, one of which is what we call "spirituality." How often have we heard a person say, "I'm not religious, but I'm spiritual"? The argument suggests that religion imposes a set of doctrinal beliefs and the ethical behaviors that spring from it: conviction leads to conduct, belief influences behavior. An ingredient in most religious practice is the conviction that the practices and beliefs of that particular tradition are the only valid ones, and this can lead to an arrogance of opinion based on absolute and exclusive truth claims. When these claims conflict, as they must in a pluralistic world, there appears to be a choice only between a demoralizing relativism and a fundamental conflict with the "other" that leads either to conversion or to extinction. When people speak of religion as the source of all serious trouble in the world, they usually have this rather grim scenario in mind, and, alas, the history of the world and its political and cultural conflicts tend to confirm this pessimistic view of religion's role in human affairs.

To some, the only answer to this is a denigration of religion itself and the passions it ignites. Atheism, agnosticism, and secular humanism all tend to see religion as part of the problem, and not part of the solution in the conflicts between human beings. Spirituality, however, is not seen by those who embrace it as essentially anti-religion; spirituality is often described as more than religion, and in some cases as beyond religion. The appeal of spirituality in the postmodern age is that it offers an experience of the divine within the realm of the human in the place of doctrines, creeds, and beliefs. An old Buddhist aphorism puts it this way: "Seek not to follow in the footsteps of the men of old; seek what they sought." Rather than cherish a tradition one belongs to by birth, culture, or affinity, one seeks the essence of that to which religion aspires: a transcending of the human limits, and an experience that makes the transcendent possible.

For many, the old religious categories are too limiting and even atrophied, and they find themselves frozen into the time frame of those who had formulated a theological position. Thus, for example, Christians are always trying to reinsert themselves into the formative period of primitive Christianity, and Protestants are trying to be what Luther was, to understand what Calvin meant, and to see themselves as consistent with whatever previous experience their tradition claims as normative. The appeal of spirituality is the notion that the freedom others found is also available to those who seek it now and is not dependent on the experience of others.

When the Dalai Lama deprecates a comparison with the pope and with a merry laugh tells people that he is "not God," he knows that the apparent contradiction of his own spiritual authority — with an appeal to people to follow not him but as he follows — will both confuse and appeal. It is no accident that the Dalai Lama enjoys enormous popularity in the West, particularly in the United States, for his personal and moral charisma suggests that he has access to a wisdom, a degree of insight, that is extra-institutional and available to every person with the wit and the will to pursue it.

Critics of spirituality say that its appeal lies in its essential individualism, its suspicion of institutional authority, and in the degree of personal improvisation it inspires. Such criticism may be justified on the part of those who see the practices of spirituality as dangerous to the maintenance of institutional solidarity and identity, and who see religion as an essentially collectivist or corporate enterprise. After all, spirituality is often invoked as an excuse on the part of people too lazy or indifferent to undergo the rigors and duties of their religious obligations, which invariably involve more than mere personal satisfaction. The invocation of spirituality can be an excuse to opt out of lives that put the autonomy of the individual in submission to the well-being of the group.

This brings to mind a conversation I had a while back at the breakfast table of a respectable British bed-and-breakfast one Sunday morning. I asked my companions if they were going to church, and, "Oh, we're not religious!" they replied. "We're Church of England." Today they might say, "We're not religious. We're spiritual," and with that distinction communicate that adherence to a set of rules of a cultural hegemony was not for them.

Spirituality, however, as represented by the writings in this collection, is by no means simply antireligion or "not" religion, and the appetite for whatever it may be continues to grow both among those who engage in some regular form of religious practice and among those for whom such practice is inconceivable. Although it is quite wrong to suggest that religion is antithetical to the arts, sciences, and humanities, and that it has no aesthetic, many are prepared to make that claim. They do so, alas, in the ignorance of the historic relationships, particularly in the West, between religion and aesthetics, the human experience, and the appeals to reason and beyond reason with which religion has more frequently than not been engaged.

Yet, a case can be made for the fact that spiritual truth, that is, spiritual "atonement," can be found in the aesthetic and emotive experiences mediated by religion. A conventional religious person hearing Mozart's *Requiem* may hear a mere setting of the words of the Roman Mass, a magnificent setting but a setting nonetheless in the service of a set of creedal propositions. A nonreligious person, not necessarily a nonbeliever, may well not hear the Mass but may very well connect with the inner soul of the piece and hear it at a level that neither musicians nor believers may fully appreciate. A friend once told me that she believed in nothing, but when she sang in a professional chorus that specialized in the cantatas of Bach and Schutz, she found a dimension of herself that was released and connected with something more than a mere religious or aesthetic experience. It was this moment of submissive transcendence that came to define what she called her "spirituality."

Ours has been called a "throw-away" culture, and by that is meant that we are conditioned to save only until something better comes along; and as it is the business of the culture to produce something better all the time, where would industry, entertainment, and advertising be without the insistent demand for something new and better? Thus, the permanent suggests a lack of imagination, and continuity a failure of nerve. We resist this caricature of ourselves and of our time, and we are even tempted to laugh at ourselves when we think about it, yet, for many, the alternatives are not attractive. The current popularity of what, for lack of a better term, is called "traditional values," or "conservatism," suggests that at some place and point in the past there was a better moment than this one, and that if we could only recapture that moment, or its policies or habits, or support those who promise they will do it for us, all will be well. So far, all we have been able to generate in this regard is a tinny patriotism and a religion of self-indulgent retrospection. The present is irritating to everyone, it seems, and thus the only alternatives are either a selective nostalgia or the anticipations of Armageddon and the apocalypse. When the "Rapture" comes, the chosen are removed from the irritating present and everyone else is left behind to suffer; and for many, this grim and self-serving scenario passes for religion.

To many others, however, and perhaps to those who will take some satisfying pleasure from much that is to be found in this collection, more is required and expected than just nostalgia or anticipation. Standing in the living present, "memory and hope between," as the hymn writer puts it, such people wish to be able to see beyond that which naked analysis affords, and to feel that which points beyond reason and emotion. Not only do they wish to experience these things for themselves, they wish to share in those experiences with like-minded souls, both past and present, and together cultivate an experience and not simply an explanation. In short, these are people who propose cultivating the interior life as a means not of escaping from the world but of coping with it and beyond it, and those who speak to these issues have already won a large and discerning audience. Fortunately, poets, essayists, dramatists, artists, and the occasional public intellectual serve to guide our thoughts in that realm, which transcends both religion and culture.

While the clergy of sixteenth- and seventeenth-century England were obsessed with the wars of religion, William Shakespeare was speaking to the hearts and minds of those for whom sermons and political manifestos no longer spoke. T. S. Eliot, for whom religion was no easy way out, wrote of the curse of the man of excellent intention and impure heart; and who knows whose voice today offers something substantial to sate the ravenous appetite of the interior life? All that can be said is that the search for something both substantial and spiritual is not likely to end any time soon, and it is clear that the honest pilgrim will have to be wary of quacks and fakes who, in times of spiritual hunger, flourish like flies on carrion. As a religious man, I am aware that authentic religion and authentic spirituality have nothing to fear from one another. To be religious is to follow a path that one's tradition provides, but the end — the object — of the journey is to know the place perhaps for the first time.

PETER J. GOMES

RICK BASS

A Fitting Desire

FROM *Orion*

IN JULY, as the fields and meadows begin to bloom with the white blossoms of yarrow, clusters of pearly everlasting, and oxeye daisies, the deer fawns, similarly spotted, lie in these same fields, camouflaged within the season, calibrated almost to the day, perhaps even to the hour.

It is a finely tuned sameness, this tendency, predisposition, even yearning for one thing to follow the lead of another, like the wheeling of an entire flock of birds — each giving itself over surely to no considered forethought but instead pivoting on some invisible point in the sky deflecting the flight of a hundred individuals as one being with not even a whisper or rustling of wings.

What is the name for it, the way deer and elk antlers look exactly like the limbs and branches of the same forest thicket in which they take refuge?

The yellow sulphurs dance and skitter across the fields from one buttery dandelion to the next, from the similarly yellow blossoms of one heartleaf arnica to another. Watching them stir, you think at first the blossom itself has suddenly unfolded and taken flight — and it all seems like a kind of inaudible orchestra, the movements and order like the score and composition for beautiful sheet music that we cannot hear, can instead only see.

How secure — or tenuous — is this ancient collaboration, now, in a time grown so frighteningly reckless? To cant our weather and seasons by five or ten degrees Fahrenheit, as if striving to tip the world over on its side with some huge pry bar — how will that listing, that destruction, affect all the invisible angles and hard-gotten, beautiful negotiations of the earth, and the rightness of things?

As the olive-sided flycatchers perch high in the branches of coni-
fers, a vertical tide of the day's warming currents lifts summer
insects — lacy wings glittering and whirling diaphanous — up toward the waiting birds. Meanwhile, water pipits hop along on the
ground just below the whistling flycatchers, gleaning from snow-
melt puddles and patches of ice the remains of those insects that
perished overnight in the alpine chill. Having evaded the acro-
batic swoops and pursuits of the olive-sided flycatchers, the bugs
find themselves stranded nonetheless, and stipple the ice the next
morning in dark flecks and nuggets upon the snow.

It seems to me, from a poetic perspective, that such specialization — such fit — speaks at least as much to a notion of gentle cooperation and gracefulness in nature as it does to the old hammer-
and-tong model of scrabbling competition. This is not to suggest
that nature is anything less than fiercely clamant, with every individual scrambling hourly for tooth-and-claw survival, and for the
continuance of each being's genes and names. But upon closer examination, it might seem that there are always two worlds, one
overlaid upon the other — two worlds at right angles to one another, perhaps — the savage, competitive world and the gentle, co-
operative world. And that to a careful observer, there is evidence
everywhere of a pattern and sophistry beyond the random: evidence of wild nature's, or God's, or gods' desire to fill the world
with beauty and order — with full elegance, so that every niche is
miraculously and intricately occupied.

What is the name for this desire of fit? Would it be different in
different seasons, different weather, different landscapes? Would
an adult have a different word for it than a child, and a man a different term than a woman? Perhaps we need to make up a name
for it, to help draw more attention to it, in order that we might be
more respectful of it — this fittedness, this elegance in which we
rarely participate, but which we have been entrusted to notice, and
safeguard.

WENDELL BERRY

Renewing Husbandry

FROM *Orion*

I REMEMBER WELL a summer morning in about 1950 when my father sent a hired man with a McCormick High Gear No. 9 mowing machine and a team of mules to the field I was mowing with our nearly new Farmall A. That memory is a landmark in my mind and my history. I had been born into the way of farming represented by the mule team, and I loved it. I knew irresistibly that the mules were good ones. They were stepping along beautifully at a rate of speed in fact only a little slower than mine. But now I saw them suddenly from the vantage point of the tractor, and I remember how fiercely I resented their slowness. I saw them as "in my way." For those who have had no similar experience, I was feeling exactly the outrage and the low-grade superiority of a hot-rodder caught behind an aged dawdler in urban traffic.

This is not an exceptional or a remarkably dramatic bit of history. I recite it to confirm that the industrialization of agriculture is a part of my familiar experience. I don't have the privilege of looking at it as an outsider.

We were mowing that morning, the teamster with his mules and I with the tractor, in the field behind the barn on my father's home place, where he and before him his father had been born, and where his father had died in February of 1946. The old way of farming was intact in my grandfather's mind until the day he died at eighty-two. He had worked mules all his life, understood them thoroughly, and loved the good ones passionately. He knew tractors only from a distance, he had seen only a few of them, and he rejected them out of hand because he thought, correctly, that they compacted the soil.

Even so, four years after his death his grandson's sudden resentment of the "slow" mule team foretold what history would bear out:
the tractor would stay and the mules would go. Year after year, agriculture would be adapted more and more to the technology and
the processes of industry and to the rule of industrial economics.
This transformation occurred with astonishing speed because, by
the measures it set for itself, it was wonderfully successful. It "saved
labor," it conferred the prestige of modernity, and it was highly productive.

Though I never entirely departed from farming or at least from
thoughts of farming, and my affection for my homeland remained
strong, during the fourteen years after 1950 I was much away from
home.

In 1964 my family and I returned to Kentucky and in a year were
settled on a hillside farm in my native community, where we have
continued to live. Perhaps because I was a returned traveler intending to stay, I now saw the place more clearly than before. I saw it
critically, too, for it was evident at once that the human life of the
place, the life of the farms and the farming community, was in decline. The old self-sufficient way of farming was passing away. The
economic prosperity that had visited the farmers briefly during
World War II and for a few years afterward had ended. The little
towns that once had been social and economic centers, thronged
with country people on Saturdays and Saturday nights, were losing
out to the bigger towns and the cities. The rural neighborhoods,
once held together by common memories, common work, and the
sharing of help, had begun to dissolve. There were no longer local
markets for chickens or eggs or cream. The spring lamb industry,
once a staple of the region, was gone. The tractors and other mechanical devices certainly were saving the labor of the farmers and
farmhands who had moved away, but those who had stayed were
working harder and longer than ever.

Because I remembered with affection and respect my grandparents and other country people of their generation, and because I
had admirable friends and neighbors with whom I was again farming, I began to ask what was happening, and why. I began to ask
what would be the effects on the land, on the community, on the
natural world, and on the art of farming. And these questions have
occupied me steadily ever since.

The effects of this process of industrialization have become so apparent, so numerous, so favorable to the agribusiness corporations, and so unfavorable to everything else, that by now the questions troubling me and a few others in the 1960s and 1970s are being asked everywhere. It has become increasingly clear that the way we farm affects the local community, and that the economy of the local community affects the way we farm; that the way we farm affects the health and integrity of the local ecosystem, and that the farm is intricately dependent, even economically, upon the health of the local ecosystem. We can no longer pretend that agriculture is a sort of economic machine with interchangeable parts, the same everywhere, determined by "market forces" and independent of everything else. We are not farming in a specialist capsule or a professionalist department; we are farming in the world, in a webwork of dependences and influences probably more intricate than we will ever understand. It has become clear, in short, that we have been running our fundamental economic enterprise by the wrong rules. We were wrong to assume that agriculture could be adequately defined by reductionist science and determinist economics.

It is no longer possible to deny that context exists and is an issue. If you can keep the context narrow enough (and the accounting period short enough), then the industrial criteria of labor saving and high productivity seem to work well. But the old rules of ecological coherence and of community life have remained in effect. The costs of ignoring them have accumulated, until now the boundaries of our reductive and mechanical explanations have collapsed. Their collapse reveals, plainly enough for all to see, the ecological and social damages they were meant to conceal. It will seem paradoxical to some that the national and global corporate economies have narrowed the context for thinking about agriculture, but it is merely the truth. Those large economies, in their understanding and in their accounting, have excluded any concern for the land and the people. Now, in the midst of so much unnecessary human and ecological destruction, we are facing the necessity of a new start in agriculture.

And so it is not possible to look back at the tableau of team and tractor on that morning in 1950 and see it as I saw it then. That is not because I have changed, though obviously I have; it is because,

in the fifty-five years since then, history and the law of consequence
have widened the context of the scene as circles widen on water
around a thrown stone.

My impatience at the slowness of the mules, I think, was a fairly
representative emotion. I thought I was witnessing a contest of machine against organism, which the machine was bound to win. I did
not see that the team arrived at the field that morning from the history of farming and from the farm itself, whereas the tractor arrived from almost an opposite history, and by means of a process
reaching a long way beyond that farm or any farm. It took me a
long time to understand that the team belonged to the farm and
was directly supportable by it, whereas the tractor belonged to an
economy that would remain alien to agriculture, functioning entirely by means of distant supplies and long supply lines. The tractor's arrival had signaled, among other things, agriculture's shift
from an almost exclusive dependence on free solar energy to a total dependence on costly fossil fuel. But in 1950, like most people
at that time, I was years away from the first inkling of the limits of
the supply of cheap fuel.

We had entered an era of limitlessness, or the illusion thereof,
and this in itself is a sort of wonder. My grandfather lived a life
of limits, both suffered and strictly observed, in a world of limits.
I learned much of that world from him and others, and then I
changed; I entered the world of labor-saving machines and of limitless cheap fossil fuel. It would take me years of reading, thought,
and experience to learn again that in this world limits are not only
inescapable but indispensable.

My purpose here is not to disturb the question of the use of draft
animals in agriculture — though I doubt that it will sleep indefi-
nitely. I want instead to talk about the tractor as an influence. The
means we use to do our work almost certainly affect the way we
look at the world. Brought up as a teamster but now driving a tractor, a boy almost suddenly, almost perforce, sees the farm in a different way: as ground to be got over by a means entirely different,
at an entirely different cost. The team, like the boy, would grow
weary, but that weariness has all at once been subtracted, and the
boy is now divided from the ground by the absence of a living connection that enforces sympathy as a practical good. The tractor can

work at maximum speed hour after hour without tiring. There is no longer a reason to remember the shady spots where it was good to stop and rest. Tirelessness and speed enforce a second, more perilous change in the way the boy sees the farm: seeing it as ground to be got over as fast as possible and, ideally, without stopping, he has taken on the psychology of a traveler by interstate highway or by air. The focus of attention has shifted from the place to the technology.

Mechanical farming makes it easy to think mechanically about the land and its creatures. It makes it easy to think mechanically even about oneself, and the tirelessness of tractors brought a new depth of weariness into human experience, at a cost to health and family life that has not been fully accounted.

Once one's farm and one's thoughts have been sufficiently mechanized, industrial agriculture's focus on production, as opposed to maintenance or stewardship, becomes merely logical. And here the trouble completes itself. The almost exclusive emphasis on production permits the way of working to be determined not by the nature and character of the farm in its ecosystem and in its human community, but rather by the national or the global economy and the available or affordable technology. The farm and all concerns not immediately associated with production have in effect disappeared from sight. The farmer too in effect has vanished. He is no longer working as an independent and loyal agent of his place, his family, and his community, but instead as the agent of an economy that is fundamentally adverse to him and to all that he ought to stand for.

After mechanization it is certainly possible for a farmer to maintain a proper creaturely and stewardly awareness of the lives in her keeping. If you look, you can still find farmers who are farming well on mechanized farms. After mechanization, however, to maintain this kind of awareness requires a distinct effort of will. And if we ask what are the cultural resources that can inform and sustain such an effort, I believe that we will find them gathered under the heading of *husbandry.*

The word "husbandry" is the name of a connection. In its original sense, it is the name of the work of a domestic man, a man who has accepted a bondage to the household. Husbandry connects the farm to the household. It is an art wedded to the art of housewifery. To husband is to use with care, to keep, to save, to make last, to conserve. Old usage tells us that there is a husbandry also of the land, of the soil, of the domestic plants and animals — obviously because of the importance of these things to the household. And there have been times, one of which is now, when some people have tried to practice a proper human husbandry of the nondomestic creatures, in recognition of the dependence of our households and domestic life upon the wild world. Husbandry is the name of all the practices that sustain life by connecting us conservingly to our places and our world; it is the art of keeping tied all the strands in the living network that sustains us.

Most and perhaps all of industrial agriculture's manifest failures appear to be the result of an attempt to make the land produce without husbandry. The attempt to remake agriculture as a science and an industry has excluded from it the age-old husbandry which was central and essential to it.

This effort had its initial and probably its most radical success in separating farming from the economy of subsistence. Through World War II, farm life in my region (and, I think, nearly everywhere) rested solidly upon the garden, dairy, poultry flock, and meat animals that fed the farm's family. Especially in hard times farm families, and their farms too, survived by means of their subsistence economy. This was the husbandry and the housewifery by which the farm lived. The industrial program, on the contrary, suggested that it was "uneconomic" for a farm family to produce its own food; the effort and the land would be better applied to commercial production. The result is utterly strange in human experience: farm families that buy everything they eat at the store.

An intention to replace husbandry with science was made explicit in the renaming of disciplines in the colleges of agriculture. "Soil husbandry" became "soil science," and "animal husbandry" became "animal science." This change is worth lingering over because of what it tells us about our susceptibility to poppycock. Purporting to increase the sophistication of the humble art of farming, this change in fact brutally oversimplifies it.

"Soil science," as practiced by soil scientists, and even more as it has been handed down to farmers, has tended to treat the soil as a lifeless matrix in which "soil chemistry" takes place and "nutrients" are "made available." And this, in turn, has made farming increasingly shallow — literally so — in its understanding of the soil. The modern farm is understood as a surface on which various mechanical operations are performed, and to which various chemicals are applied. The undersurface reality of organisms and roots is mostly ignored.

"Soil husbandry" is a different kind of study, involving a different kind of mind. Soil husbandry leads, in the words of Sir Albert Howard, to understanding "health in soil, plant, animal, and man as one great subject." We apply the word "health" only to living creatures, and to soil husbandry a healthy soil is a wilderness, mostly unstudied and unknown, but teemingly alive. The soil is at once a living community of creatures and their habitat. The farm's husband, its family, its crops and animals, all are members of the soil community; all belong to the character and identity of the place. To rate the farm family merely as "labor" and its domestic plants and animals merely as "production" is thus an oversimplification, both radical and destructive.

"Science" is too simple a word to name the complex of relationships and connections that compose a healthy farm — a farm that is a full membership of the soil community. If we propose not the reductive science we generally have, but a science of complexity, that too will be inadequate, for any complexity that science can comprehend is going to be necessarily a human construct, and therefore too simple.

The husbandry of mere humans, of course, cannot be complex enough either. But husbandry always has understood that what is husbanded is ultimately a mystery. A farmer, as one of his farmer correspondents once wrote to Liberty Hyde Bailey, is "a dispenser of the 'Mysteries of God.'" The mothering instinct of animals, for example, is a mystery that husbandry must use and trust mostly without understanding. The husband, unlike the "manager" or the would-be objective scientist, belongs inherently to the complexity and the mystery that is to be husbanded, and so the husbanding mind is both careful and humble. Husbandry originates precautionary sayings like "Don't put all your eggs into one basket" and "Don't count your chickens before they hatch." It does not boast of technological feats that will "feed the world."

Husbandry, which is not replaceable by science, nevertheless uses science, and corrects it too. It is the more comprehensive discipline. To reduce husbandry to science, in practice, is to transform agricultural "wastes" into pollutants, and to subtract perennials and grazing animals from the rotation of crops. Without husbandry, the agriculture of science and industry has served too well the purpose of the industrial economy in reducing the number of landowners and the self-employed. It has transformed the United States from a country of many owners to a country of many employees.

Without husbandry, "soil science" too easily ignores the community of creatures that live in and from, that make and are made by, the soil. Similarly, "animal science" without husbandry forgets, almost as a requirement, the sympathy by which we recognize ourselves as fellow creatures of the animals. It forgets that animals are so called because we once believed them to be endowed with souls. Animal science has led us away from that belief or any such belief in the sanctity of animals. It has led us instead to the animal factory which, like the concentration camp, is a vision of hell. Animal husbandry, on the contrary, comes from and again leads to the psalmist's vision of good grass, good water, and the husbandry of God.

Agriculture must mediate between nature and the human community, with ties and obligations in both directions. To farm well requires an elaborate courtesy toward all creatures, animate and inanimate. It is sympathy that most appropriately enlarges the context of human work. Contexts become wrong by being too small — too small, that is, to contain the scientist or the farmer or the farm family or the local ecosystem or the local community — and this is crucial. "Out of context," as Wes Jackson has said, "the best minds do the worst damage."

Looking for a way to give an exact sense of this necessary sympathy, the feeling of husbandry at work, I found it in a book titled *Feed My Sheep* by Terry Cummins. Mr. Cummins is a man of about my age, who grew up farming with his grandfather in Pendleton County, Kentucky, in the 1940s and early 1950s. In the following sentences he is remembering himself at the age of thirteen, in about 1947:

When you see that you're making the other things feel good, it gives you a good feeling, too.

The feeling inside sort of just happens, and you can't say this did it or that did it. It's the many little things. It doesn't seem that taking sweat-soaked harnesses off tired, hot horses would be something that would make you notice. Opening a barn door for the sheep standing out in a cold rain, or throwing a few grains of corn to the chickens are small things, but these little things begin to add up in you, and you can begin to understand that you're important. . . . I do think about myself a lot when I'm alone way back on the place bringing in the cows or sitting on a mowing machine all day. But when I start thinking about how our animals and crops and fields and woods and gardens sort of all fit together, then I get that good feeling inside and don't worry much about what will happen to me.

This passage goes to the heart of farming as I have known it. Mr. Cummins describes an experience regrettably and perhaps dangerously missing now from the childhood of most children. He also describes the communion between the farmer as husband and the well-husbanded farm. This communion is a cultural force that can exist only by becoming personal. To see it so described is to understand at once how necessary and how threatened it now is.

Two paramount accomplishments of husbandry to which I think we will have to pay more deliberate attention, in our present circumstances, are local adaptation and local coherence of form. It is strange that a science of agriculture founded on evolutionary biology, with its practical emphasis on survival, would exempt the human species from these concerns.

True husbandry, as its first strategy of survival, has always striven to fit the farming to the farm and to the field, to the needs and abilities of the farm's family, and to the local economy. Every wild creature is the product of such an adaptive process. The same process once was a dominant influence on agriculture, for the cost of ignoring it was hunger. One striking and well-known example of local adaptation in agriculture is the number and diversity of British sheep breeds, most of which are named for the localities in which they were developed. But local adaptation must be even more refined than this example suggests, for it involves consideration of the individuality of every farm and every field.

Our recent focus upon productivity, genetic and technological uniformity, and global trade — all supported by supposedly limitless supplies of fuel, water, and soil — has obscured the necessity for local adaptation. But our circumstances are changing rapidly now, and this requirement will be forced upon us again by terrorism and other kinds of political violence, by chemical pollution, by increasing energy costs, by depleted soils, aquifers, and streams, and by the spread of exotic weeds, pests, and diseases. We are going to have to return to the old questions about local nature, local carrying capacities, and local needs. And we are going to have to resume the breeding of plants and animals to fit the region and the farm.

The same obsessions and extravagances that have caused us to ignore the issue of local adaptation have caused us to ignore the issue of form. These two issues are so closely related that it is difficult to talk about one without talking about the other. During the half century and more of our neglect of local adaptation, we have subjected our farms to a radical oversimplification of form. The diversified and reasonably self-sufficient farms of my region and of many other regions have been conglomerated into larger farms with larger fields, increasingly specialized, and subjected increasingly to the strict, unnatural linearity of the production line.

But the first requirement of a form is that it must be comprehensive; it must not leave out something that essentially belongs within it. The farm that Terry Cummins remembers was remarkably comprehensive, and it was not any one of its several enterprises alone that made him feel good, but rather "how our animals and crops and fields and woods and gardens sort of all fit together."

The form of the farm must answer to the farmer's feeling for the place, its creatures, and its work. It is a never-ending effort of fitting together many diverse things. It must incorporate the lifecycle and the fertility cycles of animals. It must bring crops and livestock into balance and mutual support. It must be a pattern on the ground and in the mind. It must be at once ecological, agricultural, economic, familial, and neighborly. It must be inclusive enough, complex enough, coherent, intelligible, and durable. It must have within its limits the completeness of an organism or an ecosystem.

The making of a form begins in the recognition and acceptance of limits. The farm is limited by its topography, its climate, its ecosystem, its human neighborhood and local economy, and of course by the larger economies, and by the preferences and abilities of the farmer. The true husbandman shapes the farm within an assured sense of what it cannot be and what it should not be. And thus the problem of form returns us to that of local adaptation.

Soon the majority of the world's people will be living in cities. We are now obliged to think of so many people demanding the means of life from the land, to which they will no longer have a practical connection, and of which they will have little knowledge. We are obliged also to think of the consequences of any attempt to meet this demand by large-scale, expensive, petroleum-dependent technological schemes that will ignore local conditions and local needs. The problem of renewing husbandry, and the need to promote a general awareness of everybody's agricultural responsibilities, thus becomes urgent.

How are we to do this? How can we restore a competent husbandry to the minds of the world's producers and consumers?

For a start we can recognize that this effort is already in progress on many farms and in many urban consumer groups scattered across our country and the world. But we must recognize too that this effort needs an authorizing focus and force that would grant it a new legitimacy, intellectual rigor, scientific respectability, and responsible teaching. There are many reasons to hope that this might be supplied by our colleges of agriculture.

With that hope in mind, I want to return to the precaution that I mentioned earlier. The effort of husbandry is partly scientific but it is entirely cultural, and a cultural initiative can exist only by becoming personal. It will become increasingly clear, I believe, that agricultural scientists will need to work as indwelling members of agricultural communities or of consumer communities. Their scientific work will need to accept the limits and the influence of that membership. It is not irrational to propose that a significant number of these scientists should be farmers, and so subject their scientific work, and that of their colleagues, to the influence of a farmer's practical circumstances. Along with the rest of us, they will need to accept all the imperatives of husbandry as the context of their work. We cannot keep things from falling apart in our society if they do not cohere in our minds and in our lives.

PETER J. BOYER

The Big Tent

FROM *The New Yorker*

BILLY GRAHAM'S FINAL CRUSADE had reached the midway point, on a sweltering evening last June in Flushing Meadows, when things took an unexpected turn. Graham, now eighty-six and using a walker, had slowly made his way to the pulpit, aided by his oldest son, Franklin. As the crowd of eighty thousand, seated on folding chairs, awaited his sermon (on the subject of making bad choices), Graham glanced across the platform and acknowledged his special guests, Bill and Hillary Clinton. "They're a great couple," Graham told the crowd. He then recalled a remark he'd once made about the Clintons when they were in the White House. "I felt when he left the Presidency he should be an evangelist, because he has all the gifts — and he'd leave his wife to run the country." At this, Hillary turned to her husband and slapped him a high five.

Bill Clinton joined Graham at the pulpit, and, taking his hand, he said, "What an honor it is to be here as a person of faith with a man I love and whom I have followed. He is about the only person I know who I've never seen fail to live his faith."

Clinton then told a story from his childhood, about attending a Graham crusade with his Sunday-school class in Little Rock. It was during a time of racial disharmony, and Graham had refused the suggestion by some city leaders to segregate his revivals. "I was just a little boy," Clinton said, "and I never forgot it, and I've loved him ever since."

There was, certainly, an element of politics to the moment. Evangelicals are not a known component of the Clinton base, and a blessing from Graham before eighty thousand worshippers has value, but Clinton is convincing on the subject of Billy Graham. We had talked a few days earlier, and the former president recollected that Graham's long-ago stand on race had occurred at a moment when young Clinton, a Southern Baptist, was questioning his own faith. "When he gave the call — amid all the civil-rights trouble, to see blacks and whites coming down the aisle together at the football stadium, which is the scene, of course, of our great football rivalries and all that meant to people in Arkansas — it was an amazing, amazing thing," he said. "If you weren't there, and if you're not a Southerner, and if you didn't live through it, it's hard to explain. It made an enormous impression on me. I was at that age where kids question everything, you know? And all of a sudden I said, 'This guy has got to be real, because he did this when he didn't have to.'" Over the years, Clinton formed a bond with Graham — friend of Nixon, Reagan, and the Bushes — and when Clinton's personal troubles emerged Graham publicly counselled forgiveness. "He took sin seriously," Clinton told me. "But he took redemption seriously. And it was incredibly powerful, the way he did it."

For Franklin Graham, sitting next to Hillary on that hot evening in Flushing Meadows, hearing his father and the former president exchanging praise must have stirred some discomfort. He had unreservedly condemned Clinton's liaison with Monica Lewinsky, summoning the Old Testament example of David's carrying on with Bathsheba, and the wrath of God it had produced. "Mr. Clinton's months-long extramarital sexual behavior in the Oval Office now concerns him and the rest of the world, not just his immediate family," Franklin wrote in a 1998 opinion article published by the *Wall Street Journal.* "If he will lie to or mislead his wife and daughter, those with whom he is most intimate, what will prevent him from doing the same to the American public?"

In addition to the family religious enterprise, the Billy Graham Evangelistic Association, which has some five hundred employees worldwide, a hundred-million-dollar operating budget, and a fifteen-hundred-acre training center in North Carolina, Franklin Graham has inherited his father's chiselled features and his deep Carolina timbre, but politically and theologically the son wields a much sharper sword. Billy Graham has steadfastly avoided pronouncing judgments as he nears his own end (writing that "sincere Christians may differ on whether or not abortion is ever justified," and telling Larry King that God loves even Satan), but Franklin is quite willing to voice what he deems harsh truths. Just that morning, he had told me that the United Nations will fail, because it is a godless enterprise. Abortion is murder, he said, and homosexuality is a sin in the eyes of God. After the attacks of September 11, Franklin declared that as a religion Islam was "wicked, violent, and not of the same God" — an assertion from which he has hardly retreated.

Predictably, Billy Graham's praise of Bill Clinton and his apparent endorsement of Hillary Clinton's political aspirations excited dismay among evangelicals. Several days later, when the Graham organization issued a "clarification," it was in the name of Franklin Graham. His father had only been joking about Bill Clinton becoming an evangelist, Franklin said. "President Clinton has the charisma, personality, and communication skills, but an evangelist has to have the call of God, which President Clinton obviously does not have, and my father understands that." As for Hillary Clinton, Graham continued, his father "certainly did not intend for his comments to be an endorsement for Senator Hillary Clinton."

Yet it was fitting that Bill Clinton played a part in Billy Graham's last crusade. The two men share a real, if not obvious, kinship, an intuitive communion. Long before Clinton fashioned a "third way" in politics, Graham had figured out how to triangulate American Protestant Christianity.

Graham consolidated that effort nearly fifty years ago, when he opened his first New York crusade, on the evening of May 15, 1957, at the old Madison Square Garden, at Forty-ninth Street and Eighth Avenue. He described himself that night as "fearful," and, indeed, there was much at stake. It wasn't a question of Graham's establishing himself as a national religious figure; he'd already been on the cover of *Time,* had preached to Queen Elizabeth, and had become a pen pal of President Eisenhower. Graham and his team had every reason to expect a successful crusade. The organization's fabled promotional machine was fully operational, as evidenced by the extensive coverage accorded the crusade by the New York press. The *Herald Tribune* let Graham write a daily column on his reflections on the revival. Nearly a third of the campaign's initial budget, of a million dollars, was allotted to advertising and publicity, and the old Garden filled to capacity every night. What was at stake for Graham in that first New York crusade was the evangelist's final break from the fundamentalist wing that had formed him, and his hope of advancing a new evangelicalism that would survive, even thrive, in the cultural mainstream.

The events that brought Graham to that moment, and to a subsequent bittersweet triumph in New York, had huge consequences, including the marginalization of fundamentalists and the steady withering of the mainline denominations. It is largely because of Graham's bold course that evangelicalism — a heterogeneous multidenominational movement estimated to number more than fifty million born-again followers, with best-selling books (the "Left Behind" series), megachurches, and the nation's president, George W. Bush — has attained its current place in American culture as the center of gravity of Protestant Christianity.

In 1918, when Graham was born, to a moderately prosperous Presbyterian farm family in North Carolina, American Protestantism had been a unified faith for fifty years. There were doctrinal differences among Baptists and Methodists and Presbyterians, but the mainline denominations, to which most Americans belonged, shared an orthodoxy that, in contemporary terms, might be called fundamentalist. Most professing Christians believed in the divine inspiration and literal truth of the Bible; the divinity of the Virginborn Jesus Christ; the vicarious atonement by Jesus at the Cross for a fallen mankind; Christ's bodily resurrection; and the validity of biblical miracles. There once was, in that sense, such a thing as the Christian nation, for which some religious conservatives still pine.

But the fin de siècle had brought a growing acceptance among educated people of Darwin's theory of evolution, which challenged providential creation; the discipline of "higher criticism" asserted human authorship of Scripture; scholars investigating the "historical Jesus" emphasized Christ's humanity rather than his supposed divinity. In 1907, Henry Adams, recalling the era of his childhood, wrote that "in essentials like religion, ethics, philosophy; in history, literature, art; in the concepts of all science, except perhaps mathematics, the American boy of 1854 stood nearer the year 1 than to the year 1900."

Some theologians, first in Europe, then in American seminaries, assimilated the new thinking and reinterpreted Christianity

accordingly. Central to the "modernist" theology was the imma-
nence of God; that is, the notion that the divine will of God could
be seen in the progress of man on earth. In this view — the moral-
spiritual companion to evolution — mankind was essentially good
and wholly perfectible, and would eventually progress to the
achievement of God's kingdom on earth. At first, most American
Protestants were only vaguely aware of the modernists, and within
the denominations, especially the Presbyterians and the Baptists,
they were aggressively opposed to modernism. An influential series
of books called "The Fundamentals," published between 1910 and
1915, laid out the case for Christian orthodoxy, and provided a
body of argument for the opponents of modernism — who came
to be called fundamentalists.

The fundamentalists succeeded for a time, but by the 1920s the
modernists, though a distinct minority, had gained influence in
the schools and the ecclesiastical machinery of the denominations.
As Kevin Bauder, a fundamentalist theologian and the president of
the Central Baptist Theological Seminary, in Minneapolis, puts it,
"The result was, for a period of about twenty years, there was all-out
war in most of the major Protestant denominations."

In the course of that "war," a Manhattan preacher named Harry
Emerson Fosdick delivered one of the most consequential sermons
ever preached from an American pulpit. Fosdick, a Baptist minister
raised in the old orthodoxy, found his faith transformed by a study
of the orthodoxy's hindrance to the progress of mankind. Fosdick
was hired as the preacher at the First Presbyterian Church on West
Twelfth Street, and on May 21, 1922, he delivered his defense of
the modernist case. Liberal Christians, he said,

> have assimilated as part of the divine revelation the exhilarating insight
> which these recent generations have given to us, that development is
> God's way of working out His will. They see that the most desirable ele-
> ments in human life have come through the method of development.
> Man's music has developed from the rhythmic noise of beaten sticks un-
> til we have in melody and harmony possibilities once undreamed. Man's
> painting has developed from the crude outlines of the cavemen until in
> line and color we have achieved unforeseen results and possess latent
> beauties yet unfolded. Man's architecture has developed from the crude
> huts of primitive men until our cathedrals and business buildings reveal
> alike an incalculable advance and an unimaginable future. Develop-
> ment does seem to be the way in which God works. And these Christians,

when they say that Christ is coming, mean that, slowly it may be, but surely, His will and principles will be worked out by God's grace in human life and institutions.

Fosdick's sermon, which he titled "Shall the Fundamentalists Win?," posited that "multitudes of reverent Christians," among whom he counted himself, saw the Bible as a human record of the progressive unfolding of God's will, not as the literal Word of God. On the "vexed and mooted question of the virgin birth," Fosdick explained, it was "one of the familiar ways in which the ancient world was accustomed to account for unusual superiority" of a "great personality." The doctrine of the Second Coming of Christ, Fosdick said, was an artifact of early Christian hope, explained by the fact that "no one in the ancient world had ever thought, as we do, of development, progress, gradual change, as God's way of working out His will in human life and institutions."

To the fundamentalists, Fosdick was guilty of rank apostasy, and the following year J. Gresham Machen, a young theologian at the Princeton Theological Seminary, the citadel of Presbyterian orthodoxy, published a book called *Christianity and Liberalism,* in which he argued that a theology that denied Christ's divinity and doubted the Bible wasn't Christianity at all but, rather, a distinct and separate religion. As such, Machen argued, liberal theology had no proper place in the Christian seminary or in the Christian pulpit. That reasoning became the defining logic of the fundamentalist movement, and prompted an effort by the Church's national body to force the New York Presbytery to affirm the fundamentals of the faith from its pulpits. The issue was bitterly disputed at the national convention, with Machen's position being argued by the bedrock fundamentalist William Jennings Bryan. One of Fosdick's fiercest allies was the liberal pastor Henry Sloane Coffin, of Madison Avenue Presbyterian Church. The resolution was passed, Fosdick left First Presbyterian, and John D. Rockefeller, Jr., built him a new place in which to preach: the Riverside Church, in Morningside Heights, completed in 1930, which became the home cathedral of liberal theology and social activism.

Machen's formulation — that liberal theology represented a false religion that could not coexist with the true faith — had a scriptural basis in the Apostle Paul's warning to the new Christians in Corinth to steer clear of apostates. ("Come out from among them, and be ye separate, saith the Lord.") This separatist impulse, however, carried the risk of schism and eventual marginalization. At the Princeton Theological Seminary, the faculty was soundly orthodox through the 1920s, but it was divided on the question of whether the Church should accept liberals in its midst or turn them out, as Machen insisted. In 1929, after Princeton added members to its board who were sympathetic to the liberal movement, Machen left, and founded a new school — Westminster Theological Seminary, in Philadelphia.

The "modernist controversy" soon roiled the missionary field, where Christian missionaries like Pearl Buck were confirming the redemptive promise of other faiths. Machen lost the battle to purify the missions, and he left the Presbyterian Church in 1936 to begin a new, militantly orthodox Presbyterian church. Among hard-line fundamentalists, separatism itself became a doctrine of faith, which required "second-degree" separation even from those Christians who held to the traditional orthodoxy but declined to leave their error-stained churches. Once fundamentalists parted from the mainstream, there was nowhere to search for error but among themselves, where much error was found. (One Baptist group separated on the doctrine that only the King James translation of the Bible contained God's pure word.) Within months of its founding, even Machen's new church suffered its own schism, as, eventually, did the new splinter sect.

In the midst of these convulsions, the 1925 prosecution, in Dayton, Tennessee, of the biology instructor John Scopes for teaching evolution actually served to put fundamentalism on trial. Clarence Darrow's ridicule and humiliation of the aging William Jennings Bryan was so effective that fundamentalism, born in theological counterrevolt in Princeton, New Jersey, gained a lasting image of Dogpatch theology. By 1940, it had become an uprooted, disputatious, and contracting faith.

With the Protestant establishment now solidly liberal — more liberal than its congregations — and fundamentalists ever more strident and fractured, there remained a vast body of believers who were faithful to the traditional orthodoxy but felt increasingly untethered. By the 1940s, a group of churchmen had emerged who were the theological kinsmen of the fundamentalists but who were embarrassed by the movement's excesses. They did not share the obsession with separation, and many wished to remain loyal to their denominations and to fight the modernists and liberals from within. Among these was Harold Ockenga, the pastor of the Congregationalist Park Street Church, in Boston. Ockenga had been a student of Machen's at Princeton, and he had followed when Machen established his own school. But Ockenga became one of fundamentalism's severest critics, castigating its self-created impotence. "Fundamentalism has lost every major ecclesiastical battle for twenty years," Ockenga said in a sermon. "Their plan is division in every denomination and every church where Modernism or error appears. The absurdity of division ad infinitum has become apparent."

Ockenga and other like-minded Protestant conservatives undertook the hard work of forging a new movement, which they called the New Evangelicalism. They built seminaries that prized intellectual rigor, where coherent apologetics could be written and young ministers formed in the conservative theology.

The New Evangelicals saw no reason that the work of social justice should be abandoned to the preachers of the "social gospel" in the liberal churches. In *The Uneasy Conscience of Modern Fundamentalism* (1947), one of the new movement's founding figures, Carl F. H. Henry, excoriated fundamentalism's failure to address the world's social and intellectual needs. A key reason for this failure was the widely held belief among conservative Protestants in the doctrine of premillennial dispensation, which holds that the present age ("dispensation") might well be the last before Christ's return to establish a thousand-year reign on earth. This glorious culmination would be signaled by the "rapture" — the lifting up into the clouds of Christ's living faithful — and a seven-year period of tribulation endured by those left behind. The terrible trials of humankind, in this view, might well portend the joyous conclusion of God's long drama of humanity.

The New Evangelicals didn't reject premillennialism or abandon the core tenet of traditional Protestantism — salvation by faith alone. Rather, they proposed that Christians should undertake good works, as evidence of their faith, and engage the secular culture.

By the end of the World War II, which had effectively demolished Harry Emerson Fosdick's assurances about the perfectibility of man, the two camps within Protestantism's conservative wing stood ready to contend for the spiritually hungry. What was needed was some force to galvanize revival, some new voice to renew the mighty faith.

The vessel into which both the fundamentalists and the New Evangelicals ultimately poured their hopes was Billy Graham. His faith, enunciated in that singular Carolina stage English, was unlined by the doctrinal boundaries that might have excluded either wing. "I didn't know one theological position from another," he recently told me in New York. "I just knew that I had come to know the Lord as my Savior."

Graham was raised on a dairy farm near Charlotte amid flinty Presbyterians who held firmly to the tenets of the old faith, and as he made his way to his calling, and then swiftly to the first rank of evangelists, the men who influenced him were fundamentalists.

Graham's own salvation was achieved in November of 1934, on the eve of his sixteenth birthday, when he heard an itinerant preacher named Mordecai Ham, whose hellfire revival, in a wooden-roofed tabernacle, was well into its second month. When Graham speaks of Ham now, he is careful to assert that "there are things I don't agree with today that he said and did," an apparent reference to the fact that Ham harbored delusions of a conspiratorial world Jewry. But those delusions would not have stood out in that particular milieu, certainly not to the young man who answered the altar call that night as a choir concluded singing "Just as I Am." Graham was fixed on the preacher's accusing stare, which had so unnerved him on previous evenings that he tried moving into the choir to avoid it, before finally submitting and coming forward to accept Christ.

Graham's parents rejoiced in his decision, and when he graduated from high school they prevailed upon him to put aside hopes of attending the University of North Carolina, and to enroll instead at the small Christian college run by the fundamentalist Bob Jones, in Greenville, South Carolina. To Graham, the place seemed like a reform school, with rules against speaking to girls or dallying in hallways, and curfews that were fiercely enforced by the autocratic Jones. Graham was so unhappy there that he became ill, and withdrew after one term. But, looking back, he attributes his own preaching style to what he learned from Jones during his chapel talks at school. "They were so simple, almost juvenile," Graham recalls. "But he had a power of the Lord through him."

Simplicity was the key, Graham realized, and as he began his own preaching, taking a pulpit wherever he could as he made his way through the Florida Bible Institute and then through Wheaton College, in Illinois, he seldom burdened his sermons with nuance or layers of subtext. You're a sinner, Graham preached, but God so loves you that he's given you a way to save yourself, if you'll only say yes. A Billy Graham sermon was not, in itself, the feature that distinguished his ministry; what set him apart was his uncanny ability to achieve conversions at such a consistently high rate. He'd spent a summer as a door-to-door Fuller Brush salesman, and outsold every other Fuller man in two states. Evangelism is measured in won souls, and Graham's productivity at the altar call was unmatched.

At Wheaton, Graham met his future wife, Ruth Bell, who had grown up in China as the daughter of missionaries and would become his most trusted adviser. Within a year of graduating, he had been given a church pastorship in Chicago and a weekly local radio broadcast, both of which he surrendered in order to become the chief evangelist of a nationwide movement called Youth for Christ, founded by a Chicago pastor to minister to servicemen and young people. In 1947, Graham was summoned to Minneapolis by one of fundamentalism's pioneers, William Bell Riley, who made a deathbed plea that Graham agree to take over Riley's Northwestern Schools, a complex that included a Bible college, a seminary, and a four-year liberal-arts college (now Northwestern College, in St. Paul). And so Graham became, at twenty-nine, the youngest college president in America.

Graham, whose theology doctorates are honorary, has always claimed that his greatest regret is his lack of higher education, and when he found himself in a learned forum he would routinely protest, "I'm not a theologian." That demurral was perhaps justified. The one time that Graham undertook a serious theological inquiry, it nearly took his faith.

The source of his crisis was his close friend and fellow Youth for Christ evangelist Charles Templeton, whom Graham has characterized as one of the very few men he loved. Graham met Chuck, as he called him, onstage at a Chicago rally, and they quickly became the organization's dynamic personalities. The two young men were very different; Graham, with his raw-boned amiability, was the essence of country-boy ingenuousness. Templeton seemed to have already lived a full life; a high-school dropout from a broken home in Toronto, he had made his way on his own, starting a successful career as a newspaper cartoonist while he was a teenager. Templeton was Graham's equal, if not his better, as a sermonizer, though he couldn't match Graham's conviction and his power at the altar. As preachers, and as friends, they were perfect complements; they roomed together on an evangelistic tour of Europe, swanking around the war-devastated Continent in their loud suits and hand-painted ties, lifted by the promise of their shared gift.

Templeton had a burning intellectual curiosity, which played at Graham's one insecurity, his middling intellectual firepower. For Templeton, however, that searching began to have a corrosive effect on his faith, and he hoped for resolution by applying for admission to the Princeton Theological Seminary. Despite his incomplete education, Templeton was admitted there in 1948. The skeptical ethos of the school, which by then had become firmly liberal, pulled at Templeton's uncertainty, and gradually his faith began to unravel.

In the winter of 1948–49,Templeton and Graham often met at the Taft Hotel in New York, and for hours Templeton would bombard him with the new hermeneutics he'd learned at Princeton, needling him about his simple certainty. Graham would listen, and try to argue, eventually falling back on his default position — he was no theologian. As Templeton later recalled, Graham told him, "Chuck, look, I haven't a good enough mind to settle these questions. The finest minds in the world have looked and come down on both sides of these questions."

But Graham began to have his own doubts. Modernism had given way to neo-orthodoxy in fashionable theology, and Graham started to read the leading neo-orthodox thinkers — people like Karl Barth and Reinhold Niebuhr — with their new definitions of the divine "inspiration" of the Bible. It was a critical moment in Graham's career, because the biggest campaign of his life, a 1949 revival in Los Angeles, was looming.

On the eve of that campaign, Graham attended a fundamentalist retreat in the mountains near Los Angeles, and among the young preachers there was Chuck Templeton. He told Graham, "Billy, you're fifty years out of date. People no longer accept the Bible as being inspired the way you do."

"He said, 'I'm not even sure I believe in God,'" Graham recalls.

Graham's gathering doubt was tormenting him. "I just began to doubt certain passages in the Bible that I couldn't reconcile in my mind," he told me.

Graham knew that he couldn't conduct a revival on such an unsteady spiritual premise, and that he probably shouldn't be heading a Christian school or seminary if he didn't believe what it proclaimed. In crisis, he grabbed his Bible one night, and headed into the woods.

"I had my Bible, and I opened it on the tree stump," he says. "I opened it, and I said, 'Lord, I don't understand all of this Bible. But I accept it all by faith. I accept it.' And at that moment I just had a tremendous conviction, and faith."

The Los Angeles revival was a triumph, helped by a series of fortuitous events. Among the seekers who came forward at Graham's invitation inside the six-thousand-seat revival tent ("the Canvas Cathedral," he called it) was the radio star Stuart Hamblen, who began touting Graham's revival on his broadcast (he also lost a cigarette sponsor by urging listeners to quit tobacco). Another convert was an associate of the mobster Mickey Cohen. William Randolph Hearst, for reasons that he never explained, gave the order to "puff Graham," and his two dailies played the Graham crusade for every angle.

The Los Angeles campaign made Graham a national figure, and was followed by a similar success the following year, in Boston. There, one of his sponsoring churches was the Park Street Church, whose pastor was Harold Ockenga, the father of the New Evangelicalism. Ockenga had nursed doubts about Graham and mass evangelism, but Graham's success in New England convinced him that the movement had found its voice.

One afternoon in the summer of 1955, as Graham was playing golf with the Duke of Windsor on a course near Versailles, he received a telegram from George Champion, the executive vice-president of Chase Manhattan Bank, asking him to hold a crusade in New York in 1957. Accepting the invitation, as Graham did, meant forcing the issue between the New Evangelicals and the fundamentalists once and for all. Champion represented the New York Protestant Council, the defining institution of the liberal establishment Church. The council's sponsorship of the crusade meant Graham's cooperation with liberal churchmen who not only purveyed adventurous theology but, in some cases, denied the very fundamentals of Christian orthodoxy.

Graham accepted the invitation precisely for that reason. He liked the New Evangelical program of engaging the culture, and, especially, of ecumenical fellowship with Christians with whose doctrines he disagreed — even including Catholics. Associating with Rome was, for Protestant conservatives, an error of the most serious kind, for reasons that were foundational to the Reformation: evangelicals believe in *sola fide,* salvation by faith alone, and in *sola scriptura,* that the Bible is the lone source of authority for Christians. But, in the years after the Los Angeles campaign, Graham had gradually decided that doctrinal differences weren't that important among Christians. "I just loved all those people whoever they were," Graham recalls. "They reached out for me. And I responded. I didn't say to them, but I felt, I love these people. They're people of God."

There was, of course, great practical value in Graham's ecumenism. His evangelistic enterprise, based in Minnesota, had branched into publishing, broadcasting, even films, but the core of it all was the crusades, and mass evangelism, as Graham practiced it, required a broad base of local support. "Because Bill was true to his conviction, and didn't criticize people who maybe didn't believe theologically like the others did, but he accepted them all with love, there was a greater willingness to cooperate together," Cliff Barrows, who has been Graham's music director and master of ceremonies since the organization was started, says. "We wouldn't have had some of these great citywide meetings that we've had if he hadn't done that." It was an arrangement that benefited all parties. Typically, the Graham people would send an advance team to stay in the city a year before the event, and they would persuade local churches to promote and help organize the crusade. In return, Graham's organization would assiduously direct harvested souls into the local churches.

In New York, the Protestant churches were in urgent need of new life, which is why the council had extended its invitation to Graham, despite much reluctance in the liberal establishment. Reinhold Niebuhr, dean of the Union Theological Seminary and the most prominent theologian in the United States, actively opposed the Graham crusade in New York. Graham's message, Niebuhr wrote in *Life,* tended to "negate all the achievements of Christian historical scholarship." Niebuhr worried about "life's many ambiguities," and concluded that Graham's message — Jesus as the answer to life's problems — was "rather too simple in any age, but particularly so in a nuclear one with its great moral perplexities."

Graham, still seeking intellectual respectability, tried to meet with Niebuhr, certain that he could change the theologian's mind, or, at least, temper his criticism. Niebuhr refused to see him. "I had such great respect for him," Graham says now.

Graham's 1957 Madison Square Garden campaign, which had been scheduled to run for two months, lasted nearly the entire summer, culminating in a rally in Times Square, in September, before a crowd the size of a New Year's Eve throng. Later that year, Harold Ockenga declared that the new moderate movement had indeed found its voice — "Billy Graham, who on the mass level is the spokesman of the convictions and ideals of the New Evangelicalism."

To the fundamentalists, however, Graham had become Belial, an Old Testament term embodying godless evil. One fundamentalist has written that Graham, in meeting with the liberal church leaders, "was actually locking himself into a room with the Devil, because these men were certainly the Devil's ministers." Key fundamentalist leaders, such as John R. Rice, the publisher of the fundamentalist periodical *Sword of the Lord,* had kept their claim on Graham until his New York "compromise," as the conservatives called it. "It was an obscuring of the very boundary of Christianity itself," says Kevin Bauder, of the Central Baptist Theological Seminary (the descendant of the seminary that Graham once headed at Northwestern Schools). "What he was doing, from a fundamentalist point of view — from my point of view — was taking religious leaders who had no legitimate claim, properly, to the name Christian, and he was saying to the world, 'These men are good Chris-

tian leaders.' And, in doing that, what he was doing, I think, was obscuring the importance of the very Gospel that he was at that time
preaching. I think that what Dr. Graham did, and what the Neo-
Evangelicals did, is the worst thing a Christian can do."

Graham was deeply troubled by such criticism at the time, but
looking back he says, "It doesn't bother me too much anymore." In
fact, he had begun to redefine himself as "a theological conservative but a social liberal," as he terms it now. The social liberalism of
the New Evangelicalism appealed to Graham, and even Niebuhr allowed that Graham had "sound personal views on racial segrega-
tion and other social issues of our time." At that New York crusade,
Graham invited Martin Luther King, Jr., to the platform to lead an
opening prayer, introducing him as a leader of "a great social revolution going on in the United States today."

Such gestures alienated many conservatives. "Dr. Graham has declared emphatically that he would not hold a meeting anywhere,
North or South, where the colored people and the white people
would be segregated in the auditorium," Bob Jones said, "and I do
not think anytime in the foreseeable future the good Christian colored people and the good Christian white people would want to set
aside an old established social and religious custom."

Graham had embarked on a long, inexorable march to the middle, from which he never retreated, and through the years he has
progressively softened his views, even on matters touching on core
doctrine. As early as his 1949 Los Angeles campaign, when he'd
emerged from his battle with doubt, he had decided that hell was
not necessarily a bottomless pit of fire and brimstone but the everlasting punishment of "separation from God." He has stopped wor-
rying about whether pagans are cut off from salvation, and has
even come close to syncretism, suggesting that devout believers of
other faiths have found ways of "saying yes to God."

Dogmatic fundamentalism had been consigned to the margins,
and, with the culture wars and the eruption of international terrorism, the very word became anathema. Even Bob Jones III, the president of the university founded by his grandfather, suggested in
2002 that fundamentalism drop the name. "Instead of 'Fundamentalism' defining us as steadfast Bible believers, the term now carries
overtones of radicalism and terrorism," he wrote. "'Fundamental-

ist' evokes fear, suspicion, and other repulsive connotations in its current usage. Many of us who are separated unto Christ feel it is appropriate to find a new label that will define us more positively and appropriately." Jones's suggestion was "preservationist," a term that, so far, has failed to catch on.

Liberal establishment Protestantism, meanwhile, has found itself riven by flashpoint social issues like same-sex marriage and the ordination of homosexuals. Even as overall church membership in the United States continues to grow — by fully one-third since 1960 — the mainline churches have seen their numbers shrink by 21 percent. The trend is noticeably evident in New York City. The First Presbyterian Church continues its ministry in the liberal tradition of Harry Emerson Fosdick, but the most vital Presbyterian church in New York is an evangelical church, Redeemer Presbyterian, that was founded in 1989 and meets in rented spaces, such as the auditorium at Hunter College. Redeemer Presbyterian was begun by Timothy Keller, a graduate of Machen's Westminster Seminary, as a ministry for evangelical city professionals, and has grown so prodigiously that the church actively shuns publicity for fear of overgrowth and an influx of "church tourists." Its Sunday meetings at Hunter attract a capacity congregation of twenty-eight hundred worshippers, and that is just one of Redeemer's three Sunday services. The church has spun off more than a score of "plant" churches in the city and elsewhere, including one, the evangelical Emmanuel Church, that holds its weekly services in the James Chapel at the Union Theological Seminary — formerly presided over by Reinhold Niebuhr.

Evangelical churches and organizations have experienced remarkable growth — owing, in large part, evangelicals say, to the doctrinal latitude and character of moderation established by Graham and the New Evangelicals. "I think it put a friendly face on what was thought of as fundamentalism," Greg Laurie, the senior pastor of the megachurch Harvest Christian Fellowship, in Riverside, California, and a member of the Graham association board, says. "It was appealing, it was engaging, there was a cultural connection. Yet, at the same time, it did not compromise the essential Gospel message, or the Biblical emphasis."

It is telling that Graham, for his final crusade, chose as his New York chairman Dr. A. R. Bernard, of the Christian Cultural

Center, in Brooklyn. Bernard, a former Black Muslim, began his ministry with a storefront church that has grown into a Texas-size megachurch (with a restaurant, fish ponds, and gardens) that is attended by twenty thousand worshippers each week. "We hold to Christian orthodoxy," Bernard says. "We hold to the authority of Scripture, and we're very conservative in our views. But we're not antagonistic to the culture. We believe that we can be a prophetic voice in that culture, understanding that culture, adjusting to it, without compromising our convictions. For too long, Christians tended to speak in a language that only other Christians could understand."

Endorsement of the New York event was hardly unanimous among black church leaders. A few weeks before the crusade, Dr. Calvin Butts, the pastor of Abyssinian Baptist Church in Harlem, said that he'd heard several complaints from his parishioners about Graham's promotional effort in Harlem, which included a huge billboard on 125th Street. "I believe he has the right to come to New York and preach the Gospel — we do have religious freedom in this country," Butts told me. "Having said that, I personally believe that he's been an apologist for political right-wingers his whole career."

Although Graham came to avoid political pronouncements, his orientation early on reflected the conservatism of his native region. His particular closeness with Richard Nixon stained his reputation, not least because of tape transcripts recounting a White House conversation in which Graham denigrated Jews (for which he has apologized, often and abjectly, offering to crawl on his knees for forgiveness). Yet Graham, a longtime registered Democrat, did not cultivate only Republican political leaders. When the first president of his acquaintance, Harry Truman, shunned him at a 1952 crusade in Washington, dismissing him as just another religious huckster, Graham importuned him (unsuccessfully) with flattering pleas. Through the years, Graham assiduously pursued the favor of men of high office, winning his way into the presidential circle with his Fuller Brush salesman's cheery persistence. He golfed with president-elect Jack Kennedy in Palm Beach and with former president Gerald Ford in Palm Springs — and prayed with every president. For politicians, association with Graham brought a very particular sort of public endorsement, as well as the private solace proffered in low moments, such as those endured by Lyndon Johnson and Nixon. For Graham, his association with world leaders satisfied his need to be seen as "somebody who stood in the circle of other somebodys," as his biographer William Martin phrased it.

But Graham also achieved another purpose in becoming the preacher to presidents. He became the symbol of Protestant Christianity in America — in effect, branding evangelicalism as the mainstream American faith. The feat made him welcome not only in Nixon's White House but in Kennebunkport, Maine, in the high Episcopal home of George H. W. Bush. It was on a 1985 visit to that vacation home that Graham, walking on the beach with Bush's prodigal son, George W., posed the question, Are you right with God? For the younger Bush, it was a life-altering moment. ("Billy Graham didn't make you feel guilty," Bush later wrote. "He made you feel loved.") Graham had found a soul perfectly suited to the simple faith.

William Franklin Graham III was also, through much of his young life, a devoted heller — the embodiment of "preacher's kid" syndrome, magnified by the fact that his daddy wasn't just any preacher. Franklin smoked, drank, rode motorcycles, and once led the local police in a car chase, safely escaping at the last moment by dodging through the Graham estate's electronic gates. (His father let the police in, and Franklin was warned that he'd go to jail next time.) He wanted to fly, and got a pilot's license, and then crashed a plane while making an ill-advised landing. He was urged to leave two Christian schools, where he was inclined to fighting and breaking the rules, and as for church he says, "I found it kind of boring."

When he was twenty-two, his father approached him one day and, as Franklin recalls it, said, "I sense there's a battle for the soul of your life. You're going to have to make a choice — either to accept what Jesus Christ did on Calvary's Cross, or reject it. You can't ride the fence. You, Franklin, are going to have to make a decision. And I want you to know that your mother and I are praying for you, that you'll make the right decision." Franklin says that he got on his knees that night, threw away his cigarettes, and surrendered his life to God.

In the space of a few weeks that summer, Franklin graduated from a local two-year college, married his boyhood sweetheart, Jane Austin Cunningham, and took up studies at a Bible college in Colorado. At his wedding, he had publicly vowed to devote his life to God's service, but he was determined to avoid any calling that might invite comparison to his father. This became the central tension of his new life; yet, a year later, in the summer of 1975, he and his wife were living with his parents and the only work he had was helping in his father's crusades. A way out appeared one day when Franklin received a phone call from an evangelist named Bob Pierce, who was, by nature and by calling, something like an anti-Billy Graham.

Pierce had been a contemporary of Billy's at the beginning, another young evangelist in the wartime Youth for Christ movement. It was a boom time for evangelism, but somehow Pierce, who had attended a small religious college in California, struggled in his ministry even as Graham and Chuck Templeton soared. (Templeton eventually left the ministry and returned to Canada, where he took up journalism and rose to become managing editor of the *Toronto Star.*) Pierce showed up one day at the Youth for Christ Chicago headquarters in a deep gloom, determined to quit the pulpit; but the organization sent him to the West Coast, and eventually to Asia, where he found his calling. In China, Pierce encountered social disorder, poverty, and human misery of a magnitude he could scarcely register; but there was also a deep spiritual hunger amid that squalor, and the combined effect was strangely exhilarating. He wrote home that, after his experience in Asia, he couldn't imagine a return to preaching in America again, "to just go through the motions of evangelizing."

One day, a missionary thrust a Chinese girl into Pierce's arms, saying that the child had been beaten and thrown into the streets by her father, who was angered by the attentions she'd received from the Christian missionaries. Pierce immediately handed over all the cash in his pocket, and vowed that he would personally see that the child's education was paid for. It was a rash promise that Pierce had no rational expectation of keeping, but China had somehow tilted his senses. When the Maoist triumph brought the eviction of Christian evangelists, in 1949, Pierce found other locales, and new exhilarations. Making rash promises became his standard mode of operation; yet he also began to make good on such promises. On trips back home, he toured churches and Christian organizations, showing movies of the distant sorrows he'd promised to ease, and the central feature was almost always a hungry child. People responded beyond Pierce's hopes, and through the 1950s he built an organization, World Vision, that became the largest Christian aid enterprise in the world.

Pierce was driven in his mission by a kind of reckless zeal, praying for the ability to personally experience God's own heartbreak for his most broken people, to take on their suffering — and then gambling that God would somehow make good on Bob Pierce's promises to them. The method exacted a toll. Pierce was given to bursts of pique, followed by remorse, and, as World Vision grew, his personality and operating style unsettled the Christian enterprise. After a bitter dispute with the World Vision board in 1967, he was forced to resign from the organization. His personal life was no less unsettled. He suffered a mental breakdown, and was undergoing insulin shock treatments. A few years later, he learned that he had leukemia.

It was in this low period that Pierce came to believe that there was something of himself in Billy Graham's prodigal boy, Franklin. He knew that Franklin was newly married and at loose ends, and in that phone call he invited Franklin to take an Asian tour with him that would be nothing like the overseas journeys Franklin had experienced with his father. Franklin agreed, and over the next two months the dying Pierce pitched Franklin Graham on the great adventure of doing God's work, but on an entrepreneurial level. Pierce had built a small aid organization, Samaritan's Purse, whose mission was to fly into the world's emergency zones, assess the need, and then somehow raise the money that Pierce invariably had committed. In one particularly fitting episode on the trip, the small entourage, in a Cessna 185, landed on a narrow strip cut into a mountain in the jungle of Borneo, halting at the edge of a steep ravine. Pierce's thrill-ride evangelism spoke to Franklin, and he took over Samaritan's Purse shortly after Pierce died, in 1978.

One of Franklin's early aid trips took him to a remote missionary hospital in Kenya, an overtaxed facility where patients were treated two to a bed. Before leaving, Graham promised to try to raise the four hundred thousand dollars needed to build a new wing. He told the story of the hospital on Jim and Tammy Faye Bakker's *Praise the Lord* television broadcast, raised four hundred and nine thousand dollars, and then later returned the extra nine thousand to Bakker. Graham wanted Samaritan's Purse to be unlike any other organization, and certainly distinct from a Christian aid bureaucracy, and his ideas were sometimes impractical or misbegotten. He once tried to transform the compound at Jonestown, Guyana, where in 1978 hundreds of religious cultists died in a mass suicide, into a resettlement camp for Southeast Asian boat people. During the first Gulf War, he sent thousands of Bibles, translated into Arabic, to American soldiers encamped in Saudi Arabia — a move that infuriated the commanding general, Norman Schwarzkopf, who said that it threatened to unravel the fragile coalition.

But Graham began to apply a disciplined hand and sound practices to Samaritan's Purse, and the organization has become a highly regarded two-hundred-and-fifty-million-dollar enterprise. (Less than 4 percent of its annual revenues go to fund-raising expenses.) It carries out substantial relief operations in more than a hundred countries, including Iraq, India, and Sudan. Preoccupied with his work, Franklin stoutly resisted any suggestion that he take up the pulpit. "I was afraid that if I did preach, people would compare me to my father," he says. "I'm not my dad."

In his way, Franklin Graham had at last answered one of his father's severest critics, Reinhold Niebuhr, who had long ago written that the trouble with Billy Graham was that he talked the talk of social progress but his simple ministry of soul conversion did little to help the wretched of the world. "I believe that my father has been called to the big stadiums of this world," Franklin told an interviewer. "God has called me to the ditches and to the gutters along life's road."

Franklin's resolve not to preach began to weaken in the nineties, as his father started to grow infirm. He finally received the divine call to preach, although he concedes that God's beckoning to him was more clearly heard by others (including his mother) than by him. He started out shakily. "There was a tentativeness," says Anne Graham Lotz, Franklin's older sister, who is also a preacher (deemed the best in the family by her father, though she had no desire to succeed him). "He hadn't got the delivery, and the style, and all of that down. He was a little uncomfortable. But you could hear his heart. And I believe he has a heart for the Gospel."

Franklin's decision to preach did not settle the issue of succession at the Billy Graham Evangelistic Association, and in some ways complicated it. Franklin, who is fifty-three, says that some in the organization questioned his commitment before he took over as C.E.O., in 2000. "There were a lot of internal struggles," he says. "There were people at that time who did not want me doing it. It was a challenge. . . . They had legitimate concerns and questions." Part of the difficulty was Billy himself, who had always ran the organization with a light hand, ruling by consensus, and he did not want to appear to be steering the enterprise toward his son. He wonders now, he says, whether Franklin thinks he didn't do enough. "I feel sometimes he may be disappointed because I don't intervene," Billy says. "I haven't talked to anybody about him, to try to get something for him in the organization." Franklin's management style is more direct than his father's, and he is less inclined to consensus. He has consolidated the workforce and moved the organization's headquarters from Minneapolis, where it had been since Billy Graham's days at the Northwestern Schools, to Charlotte, where the Grahams live. (Samaritan's Purse, which he still runs, is also headquartered in North Carolina.)

Although Franklin's preaching style is cooler and more conversational than his father's, he is much less willing to smooth the edges of the faith. If Billy's theme, especially in his later years, was the saving grace of God's love, Franklin's is more elemental. "My message is very focused," he says. "My message is to call on people to repent their sins." Franklin believes in a sulfurous hell, and has no doubt about who is going to be there. "The Bible says every knee under the earth, every knee that's in hell, one day is going to bow," he says. "And every tongue is going to confess Him as Lord one day. Now, either you're going to do it voluntarily and submit your heart to the Lord Jesus Christ, or you're going to be forced. And when you're forced it's going to be too late then."

Franklin Graham's strongest trait is certitude, which extends to the divisive issues that Billy chose to avoid. Regarding Islam, Franklin says, "The global war on terrorism, let's give it the name — it's Islamic. That's who we're fighting. We're not fighting the Maoists. We're not fighting the Hindus or the Buddhists. It's Islamic." As to the refrain that a peaceful religion has been "hijacked by terrorists" — a refrain sounded even by his friend the president — Franklin scoffs. "They haven't hijacked it at all. I think that's what people are wishing. And listen, there are millions of Muslims out there who are good people, who do want to live in peace. But you have to look at the government of Saudi Arabia; this is what true Islam is. There is no tolerance of other religions or other faiths. True Islam, just look at Saudi Arabia, that's it. Or look at the Taliban, that's it. Or Sudan. That's what this is all about."

Abortion, Franklin asserts, is not about a woman's reproductive choice. "I believe that abortion is murder," he says. "Now, that has nothing to do with politics, left wing, right wing. I believe that when a woman's right to choose takes the life of another person, that's a sin against God. The state says you can do this, it's legal. OK. It's still a sin against God. And that blood of that child, God will hold you accountable. That blood is on your hands." Homosexuality is likewise a sin against God in the younger Graham's system of faith, and he disputed the justification that homosexuals are created that way by God. "Listen, sin is sin, OK? The Bible says that we're all sinners. We're born with it. We all have this desire to sin, to disobey God. Now, we try to make excuses as a society. . . . For the gay, I mean, it's 'Well, I have no choice. I was born this way.' Well, we were all born sinners, with the desire to sin."

Such pronouncements have led some people to dismiss Franklin Graham as just another right-wing Jeremiah. Yet he may well emerge as the most important political figure in the evangelical sphere. In his aid work, he is as tough and insistent as he is in running the Graham organization, or in laying out his theology. Some on the left see a neocolonial missionary impulse in his motivations, and Graham is unrepentant about the fact that his do-gooding is solely a means of bringing people to Christ. One of his inspirations was to put wells on church property in a parched zone of India: "Have people come to church to get their water. Why not?"

But it was Franklin Graham who brought Christian zeal to the struggle against the world AIDS pandemic. Samaritan's Purse had become deeply involved in trying to stop the slaughter of Christians and animists in Sudan, and in the course of this political effort Franklin had awakened to the realization that fighting AIDS was also God's will. He began to sound the alarm among evangelicals, chastening Christians for their past reluctance to fight against a scourge that somehow offended their moral piety.

For the last three years, Richard Holbrooke, Bill Clinton's former ambassador to the United Nations, has asked Franklin Graham to speak at the annual fundraiser for the Global Business Coalition on HIV/AIDS. There was some awkwardness on the first occasion, in 2002, because Graham was seated at a table with Secretary-General Kofi Annan and Bill Clinton. Holbrooke recalls telephoning Clinton before the event and asking if he thought it would be all right. "Sure," the former president said. "It's a smart thing to do."

At that event, Graham offered the benediction, praying, as he always does at public events, in the name of Jesus. And, as always happens at public events, some people complained. "I'm not going to betray the blood of Jesus Christ for political correctness," Graham says.

But Holbrooke counseled forbearance. "Some people were upset," Holbrooke recalls. "They said, 'Why do you have that guy there?' And I said, 'If we want to beat AIDS, we need to build bridges to people in areas that we agree on.'"

Holbrooke says that Graham has been "enormously important" in the fight against AIDS abroad. "Samaritan's Purse created one of the most important new developments in American foreign policy in the last generation — the entry of Christian conservatives into American foreign policy as pro-foreign-aid people."

Billy Graham says that he approves of Franklin's public stands, theological and political. He adds that, even if he doesn't agree with his son, "he's strong."

It is, perhaps, a case of the son finding his own way to a middle ground. Franklin Graham has managed to win the admiration of a former Clinton administration official, even while his public positions have some old-line fundamentalists listening, hopefully, for the return of an evangelist Graham to their fold. "He intrigues me," the hard-line theologian Kevin Bauder acknowledged recently. Though he still condemns the elder Graham's 1957 "compromise" as "the worst thing a Christian could do," Bauder said, "I think we're still getting to know Franklin Graham. I don't think we've quite figured out who he is yet. But I'm very interested to find out. Franklin, every time he says something publicly, my ears pick up. I want to chart this guy. I want to see where he's going."

SCOTT CAIRNS

On Making The Martyrdom of Saint Polycarp: *Writing the True Icon*

FROM *Image*

WHEN A FRIEND ASKED if I'd mind his passing my contact information along to a J.A.C. Redford, he explained that J.A.C. was looking for a librettist for an oratorio on the life of Saint Polycarp. My
first — unuttered — response was something like "Sheesh, good
luck with that." In a subsequent e-mail, my friend outlined the project, wised me up about J.A.C.'s many prior successes, and got me
thinking about the possibility of giving this new genre a shot. He
warned me that J.A.C. would call me soon to talk it over.

In the meantime, I began attending to my own ignorance regarding Saint Polycarp, his life, and his martyrdom. As I pored over
the few extant documents from the period — primarily Polycarp's
epistle to the Philippians and Markion's epistle to Smyrna — and
several more contemporary accounts cobbled together from those
historical accounts, I felt chastened for my previous ignorance and
exhilarated by what I was reading. In particular, these famous
words of his caught me immediately and brought me to sudden
tears: "For eighty-six years I have served Jesus Christ, and he has
never done me wrong. How can you expect me to betray and blas-
pheme my king who has saved me?"

The accounts provided other words from the saint during this
time of trial, words that continued to resound with calm, unwavering faith and, most importantly, charity for those around him, even

and especially those who sought his death. Also, subtly laced within these phrases were traces of wit, of generous, even playful, humor. On one occasion, in the midst of the crowd, the proconsul encouraged Saint Polycarp to say, ostensibly in condemnation of the Christians, "Away with the blasphemers"; Polycarp, gesturing toward the mob instead, says boldly, "Away with the blasphemers." I would cling to these traces of personality later on, as the project developed, and I sought to find what I would call a *true icon* of his voice, his person.

When J.A.C. called the following week, I was immediately struck by his warmth and wit, by his candor, and by his willingness not only to tolerate but to participate in my inveterate fondness for puns (or what my wife calls "half-witticisms"). That is to say, we hit it off.

To be absolutely candid, I was unsure about accepting the commission. I was eager to attempt it but anxious that I would fail, letting down J.A.C., our mutual friend, *and* Saint Polycarp. In the past, I had read with pleasure verse libretti by Auden, Ashbery, and Wilbur, among others, but had never imagined attempting one myself. Still, as J.A.C. talked me through his vision of the structure (citing the various scenes he'd already glimpsed as necessary moments), I too experienced — even as he spoke over the phone — a developing vision of how my beginning with individual, discrete lyrics — dramatic monologues, actually — might at least get me started in the right direction. I didn't know beans about writing libretti, but I knew how to make a lyric poem. As J.A.C. continued to describe the scenes, I began imagining the individual lyric utterances that might occur within those scenes.

Fortunately, J.A.C.'s composition habit — when working with lyrics — is to settle on the words first and develop the music thereafter. I wouldn't have been able to work the other way round. For me also, words come first; in my experience, meaning is spoken (or written) into being.

Among my long-established habits of composition, several proved to be ideal preparation for this challenge. Since my earliest work in poetry — including many of the poems that comprised my early books — I had been drawn to, had even come to depend upon, the unique freedom of writing dramatically, of writing monologues in the voice of another.

Even today, one of the first lessons I try to teach my beginning students is to resist the notion that poetry is a documentary enterprise, to resist the error of thinking that poems are about the poet. Most young writers come to the task loaded up with misunderstandings about what poems are, misunderstandings about what poems do. Most arrive in class absolutely convinced that poems are the means by which poets communicate their experiences and their received wisdom to the masses. There are at least a couple errors in that notion: 1) that a poem is a vehicle for some prior understanding the poet has arrived at, and 2) that the masses give a damn.

In my case, the dramatic monologue has become — both in my own work and in my pedagogy — an invaluable means for skirting the liabilities of the personal mode and its attendant, terminal ennui.

In the past, the "others" speaking in my poems were sometimes mythic or historical figures, oftentimes scriptural characters, and, on occasion, purely fictional constructions of my imagination. In each case, the inevitable tilting of the head that occasions the adoption of a mask, the imaginative move of speaking in another's voice, brings with it an exhilarating liberty, a freedom from the more narrow concerns of the self. For this project, I would be more than willing to surrender — as much as I was able — my own personality in the search for Saint Polycarp's voice.

Another long-established habit — that of working off prior texts in the manner of rabbinic midrashim — had also prepared me for leaning into the spare and fragmentary documents regarding Saint Polycarp in order to press them imaginatively for subsequent development and coherence. In this business, gaps are good; they are, in fact, opportunities. Of the many epistles Saint Polycarp is supposed to have written as bishop of Smyrna, only his letter to the Philippians survives. Virtually the only other matter that witnesses to the voice and manner of the saint is the better-known epistle to Smyrna, attributed to a certain Markion, and providing the account of the saint's last days and martyrdom.

The rabbinic disposition toward sacred texts — that they are the beginning of the story, rather than the end of it — is one that has come to infuse all my creative work, my reading, *and* my writing. It is a disposition that, on the one hand, witnesses to the generative power, the life and agency of the word, and, on the other hand, effects a level of attention, concentration, and meditation in the reader, so much so that the reader attains a collaborative relationship with those words as meaning is made.

Finally, a third habit proved invaluable: while I am no iconographer, I had come to appreciate the seriousness and humility with which the "writers" of icons approach their sacred undertaking. Their rules are these:

1. As you approach the work, make the sign of the cross, and pray silently to forgive all who have offended you.
2. Work deliberately, taking care with every detail of the image, as if the Lord himself stood with you, for he does in fact stand with you.
3. Keep praying, to strengthen yourself physically and spiritually, avoiding useless words, honoring silence, into which you must enter.
4. Pray especially to the saint whose image you are writing. If you keep your mind from distractions, the saint will assist you toward a true likeness.
5. When choosing a color, stretch your hands *within,* seeking to touch the Christ who lives in your heart, and ask for his leading.
6. Do not covet your neighbor's work, but rejoice in it: his success is your success, too, and the Lord's as well.
7. When your icon is done, offer sincere thanksgiving to God for his mercy in granting you the grace to write the holy images.
8. Bring your icon to be blessed, putting it on the altar, as the first to pray before it before passing it to others.
9. Never forget the joy of spreading holy images in the world, the joy of laboring in icon-writing, the joy of using your accomplishments to offer each saint the ability to shine through his icon, nor the joy of being in union and communion with the saint whose face you are writing.

These rules have become part of my daily work in poetry, especially when I am working — as now I most often do — on meditative verse or prose regarding one aspect or another of scriptural or theological enigma. My purpose, in these cases, is to press the language into yielding further, speculative insight. In the case of Saint Polycarp's oratorio, my purpose was to find a voice, a demeanor, a character that was, on the one hand, available and engaging for the audience; this challenge is always in mind for any dramatic lyric, but for Saint Polycarp, I was cognizant of an overriding *other hand:*

the voice, demeanor, and character had to constitute a true icon of the blessed saint. I didn't want to make him up; I didn't want to create a man in my own image, being no saint.

So I prayed the iconographer's prayers, followed — as much as I was able — the iconographer's rule. I read, and reread, and read yet again (and daily) the existing documents, focusing primarily upon the words attributed to the saint, listening for any subtleties of character that I might embrace and develop.

As it happened, much of this was immediately preceded by the events of September 11, 2001. On the morning of that tragedy, I met with a pastor friend, as I regularly did. Most often he and I would compare notes on matters of theology, poetry, and fiction; we would discuss matters of the contemporary church; we would swap books.

On that day, we landed, in a state of bewildered numbness, in our familiar corner of the Coffee Zone. Stunned, with almost nothing to say to each other, we nevertheless decided to stay put, to hang out together, if only for moral support, working in silence toward some articulation — he working on his sermon and I working on scraps of verse — of what we were feeling. Rather, I'd say now that we were turning to language in order *to find* feeling.

In retrospect, I realize that I was again, as if by default, trusting in the rabbinic approach of midrashim as a way to proceed through enigma. In the case of actual midrashic text, the *darshan* (the writer of midrashim), confronted by a *dark saying* — an enigmatic passage with which he is at a loss to deal — will have recourse to another text, *a verse from afar,* which is able to supply some sense to the apparently senseless matter before him. In this case, the events of 9/11 were my dark saying, and miraculously my verse from afar, Exodus 13:21–22, came to the rescue:

> And the Lord went before them by day in a pillar of cloud to lead them along the way, and by night in a pillar of fire to give them light, that they might travel by day and by night; the pillar of cloud by day and the pillar of fire by night did not depart from before the people.

Over the course of that hour, I didn't come up with much, just these eight lines — two squat quatrains, like columns lying down.

> According to the promise, we had known
> We would be led, and that the ancient God

Would deign to make His hidden presence shown
By column of fire, and pillar of cloud.

We had come to suspect what fierce demand
Our translation to another land might bode,
But had not guessed He would insist our own
Brief flesh should bear the flame, become the cloud.

Weeks later, as I read about Saint Polycarp's dream of a flaming pillow, a flaming bed, as I read his subsequent words to his friends, "I must be burned alive," and as I read the account of his willingness to receive the martyr's flame untethered, my own words returned to me as being germane to the heart of the matter, as being suggestive of the heart of Saint Polycarp, whose image I was hoping to find.

I am often telling my students that the key to strong writing is strong reading. We talk, most often, about how essential it is that they develop a curious, conversational attitude toward prior works of literature, learning to take the cues for their performances from the language of those who precede them to the stage, as it were. Less often, we talk about developing a similar disposition to our own, prior words. It is nonetheless an invaluable lesson. If we can approach *any* prior text — the work of another *or* our own work — as if it were being witnessed for the first time, we can glimpse much that we hadn't anticipated, much that can then lead us into further making.

In the case of my quatrains, I found a disposition — a resigned, if baffled, willingness — that would continue to serve my finding the right tenor for Saint Polycarp's voice. He would become for me — as, I trust, he *was* — not so much predetermined as faithful, trusting, willing to see what would come of his honoring God, of his saying yes to whatever befell him. I began to understand that the unfailing courage he exhibited at the end of his life was not a static perfection, previously attained, nor a miraculous trumping of personality by an omnipotent God with heavy thumbs, but was a maturity that the bishop of Smyrna had grown into. His serious questioning of what God would have him do became, for me, absolutely essential to that growth, and I was determined to honor this gradual development over the course of successive soliloquies.

Equipped with this hint of his voice, prepared with the prayers of the iconographer, I focused next upon the words of the saint that have been retained in the historical accounts — in particular, the two epistles mentioned above. In the case of Polycarp's own epistle to the Philippians, I learned a great deal about the saint's character from what might seem the *absence* of character; the letter is virtually a pastiche of Pauline or Johannine exhortation, with hardly a word of modification, hardly a word that might be helpful in *revealing* Polycarp — or so it seemed. The more I read that letter, the more I realized how beautifully the saint's humility showed through his unwillingness to spin the message. I'd say it like this: his *personality* shows through those immediate, spoken moments recorded by Markion, and his *character* shows through his humble retreat into the language of his teachers.

And as I moved from scene to scene, I came to think that I knew the man, and was therefore able to imagine some of the interior struggle he might have undergone, including his concerns for his people, his church. I imagined that, among his concerns, he would be cautious about what sort of witness he was being, cautious about what sort of sacrifice he was asking his flock to accept. I believe, as the documents suggest, that Saint Polycarp received mystical assurances from our Lord, but I developed a strong sense that these assurances did not come all at once, but were the increasingly complete answers to many hours of concentrated prayer.

Finally, when most of the lyric moments — the dramatic monologues in the voices of the various personae — had been finished, I was at a complete loss as to how to supply the connective tissue that would avail a coherent narrative. J.A.C. came to the rescue here.

He was the one to seize upon the existing narrative shape of the historical letter, adopting Markion himself as the narrator of the oratorio, adapting portions of the letter to supply the story. This was an absolute blessing. Once the challenge of producing the narrative thread was solved, I was all the more free to pursue revisions — subsequent drafts — of the monologues without the burden of narration. To my ear, the monologues immediately improved, becoming purer, lighter, more suggestively poetic.

And so, as I sent the more-or-less final drafts to J.A.C. in early 2003, I felt my part in the process had been completed. J.A.C. and I continued to visit off and on by phone or by the occasional e-mail, tweaking a line here or there, modifying a minor character now and again, but, to be honest, I turned my attention to other tasks.

It wasn't until the spring of 2004, as I was making preparations to attend the premier, that I became reengaged in the project. I listened to some of the synthesized tracks J.A.C. had sent me, looked over the scores he'd been sending in intervals; I even tried picking out some of the melody lines on the keyboard, but my ineptitude pretty much kept me from appreciating what J.A.C. had accomplished until I sat in on my first rehearsal.

J.A.C. had told me how he'd altered — for what I would call matters of rhetorical concern — the solo narration of Markion into sections of recitative by a children's choir, but until I heard the result I didn't fathom its effects. In the letter of Markion, certain miraculous events are attested to, in particular the way the flame of the pyre surrounded, but did not harm, the saint, and the presence of a dove flying from the saint's body as he is pierced by a lance. While Christians who are familiar with hagiography would not have blinked at these elements, J.A.C. feared that an audience comprised of evangelical Christians might be put off by these assertions; his solution was brilliant: he established the voices of children as delivering this narration, effectively mitigating resistance in an audience uncomfortable with mystery and miracle. But more than this: the added texture of the children's choir — sometimes reciting, sometimes intoning, sometimes singing connecting elements of Markion's narrative — brought a deliciously fresh aspect to the overall composition.

As we worked with the university choir and with the children's choir in rehearsal, we continued to fiddle with wording and with presentation, even as final rehearsals were under way. This part of the process was absolutely new to me. As a poet, working in solitude — with no collaborator and with, frankly, hardly an audience — I had never before experienced the excitement of working with others to bring a complicated production together. New or not, it was delicious, thrilling.

I stayed away from the orchestra rehearsals, so when the actual premier rolled around, I was as new to the complete production as anyone there. To say I was moved is a paltry understatement. I was shaken. J.A.C.'s orchestrations were soul-stirring, the performers were astonishingly accomplished, and to be honest, the words became what they were all along: someone else's.

MICHAEL CHABON

After Strange Gods

FROM *The New York Review of Books*

I WAS IN THE THIRD GRADE when I first read *D'Aulaires' Book of Norse Myths* and already suffering the changes, the horns, wings, and tusks that grow on your imagination when you thrive on a steady diet of myths and fairy tales. I had read the predecessor, *D'Aulaires' Book of Greek Myths* (1961), and I knew my Old Testament pretty well, from the Creation more or less down to Ruth. There were rape and murder in those other books, revenge, cannibalism, folly, madness, incest, and deceit. And I thought all that was great stuff. Joseph's brothers, enslaving him to some Ishmaelites and then soaking his florid coat in animal blood to horrify their father. Orpheus' head, torn off by a raving pack of women, continuing to sing as it floats down the Hebrus River to the sea: that was great stuff, too. (Maybe that says something about me, or about eight-year-old boys generally. I don't really care either way.) Every splendor in those tales had its shadow; every blessing its curse. In those shadows and curses I first encountered the primal darkness of the world, in some of our earliest attempts to explain and understand it.

I was drawn to that darkness. I was repelled by it, too, but as the stories were presented I knew that I was supposed to be only repelled by the darkness and also, somehow, to blame myself for it. Doom and decay, crime and folly, sin and punishment, the imperative to work and sweat and struggle and suffer the Furies, these had entered the world with humankind: we brought them on ourselves. In the Bible it had all started out with a happy couple in the Garden of Eden; in the Greek myths, after a brief eon of divine patricide and child-devouring and a couple of wars in heaven, there came a long and peaceful Golden Age. In both cases, we were meant to understand, the world had begun with light and been spoiled. Thousands of years of moralizers, preceptors, dramatists, hypocrites, and scolds had been at work on this material, with their dogma, and their hang-ups, and their refined sense of tragedy.

The original darkness was still there in the stories, and it was still very dark indeed. But it had been engineered, like a fetid swamp by the Army Corps, rationalized, bricked up, rechanneled, given a dazzling white coat of cement. It had been turned to the advantage of people trying to make a point to recalcitrant listeners. What remained was a darkness that, while you recognized it in your own heart, obliged you all the same to recognize its disadvantage, its impoliteness, its unacceptability, its being *wrong*, particularly for eight-year-old boys.

In the world of the Northmen, it was a different story.

As the d'Aulaires told it (in their book, originally titled *Norse Gods and Giants*), there was something in Scandinavian mythology that went beyond the straightforward appeal of violence, monstrosity, feats of arms, sibling rivalry, and ripping yarns. Here the darkness was not solely the fault of humans, the inevitable product of their unfitness, their inherent inferiority to a God or gods who — quite cruelly under the circumstances — had created them.

The world of Norse gods and men and giants, which the d'Aulaires depicted, in a stunning series of lithographs, with such loving and whimsical and brutal delicacy, begins in darkness, and ends in darkness, and is veined like a fire with darkness that forks and branches. It is a world conjured *against* darkness, in its lee, so to speak; around a fire, in a camp at the edges of a continent-sized forest, under a sky black with snow clouds, with nothing to the north but nothingness and flickering ice. It assumes darkness, and its only conclusion is darkness (apart from a transparently tacked-on post-Christian postlude). Those veins of calamity and violence and ruin that structure it, like the forking of a fire or of the plot of a story, serve to make more vivid the magical glint of goodness that light and color represent. (Everything that is beautiful, in the Norse world, is something that glints: sparks from ringing hammers, stars, gold and gems, the aurora borealis, tooled swords and helmets and armbands, fire, a woman's hair, wine and mead in a golden cup.)

Here the gods themselves are no better or worse, in the moral sense, than humans. They have the glint of courage, of truthfulness, loyalty, wit, and in them maybe it shines a little brighter, as their darkness throws deeper shadows. The morality encoded in these stories is a fundamental one of hospitality and revenge, gift-giving and life-taking, oaths sworn, dooms pronounced, cruel and unforgettable pranks. Moreover (and to my eight-year-old imagination this more than anything endeared them to me) the Norse gods are *mortal*. Sure, you probably knew that already, but think about it again for a minute or two. *Mortal gods.* Gods whose flaws of character — pride, unfaithfulness, cruelty, deception, seduction — while no worse than those of Jehovah or the Olympians, will one day, *and they know this,* prove their undoing.

Start anywhere; start with Odin. First he murders the gigantic, hideous monster who whelped his father, and slaughters him to make the universe. Then he plucks out his own right eyeball and trades it to an ice giant for a sip — a sip! — of water from the well of secret knowledge. Next he hangs himself, from a tree, for nine days and nine nights, and in a trance of divine asphyxia devises the runes. Then he opens a vein in his arm and lets his blood commingle with that of Loki, the worst (and most appealing) creature who ever lived, thus setting in motion the chain of events that will lead to the extinction of himself, everyone he loves, and all the nine worlds (beautifully mapped on the book's endpapers) that he himself once shaped from the skull, lungs, heart, bones, teeth, and blood of his grandfather.

The d'Aulaires capture all of this, reporting it in a straightforward, fustian-free, magical-realist prose that never stops to shake its head or gape at marvels and freaks and disasters, making them seem somehow all the stranger, and more believable. Their spectacular and quirky illustrations (a pair of adjectives appropriate to few illustrators that I can think of offhand) never found a more appropriate subject than the Norse world, with its odd blend of gorgeousness and violence, its wild prodigies and grim humor.

What makes the book such a powerful feat of visual storytelling is the way in which the prose and the pictures (reflecting, perhaps, the marriage and lifelong partnership of the authors, a Norwegian and a Swiss who lived in Connecticut and collaborated on picture books from the 1930s to the late 1960s) complement each other, advance each other's agenda. Almost every page that is not taken up by a giant bursting lithograph of stars and monsters is ornamented, with a smaller drawing, or with one of the curious, cryptic, twisted little margin-men, those human curlicues of fire, that so disquieted me as a kid and continue, to this day, to freak out and delight my own kids.

Through this intricate gallery of marvels and filigree the text walks with calm assurance, gazing calmly into every abyss, letting the art do the work of bedazzlement while seeing to it that the remarkable facts — the powers and shortcomings of Thor's hammer, Mjolnir, which always returned to its thrower but whose handle was too short to grasp without burning the hand; the strange parentage of Sleipnir, Odin's eight-legged steed, who could carry his rider over land, sea, or air — are laid bare. This simultaneous effect of wonderment and acceptance, this doubled strength, allows the d'Aulaires to balance their re-creation of the Norse world exactly on its point of greatest intensity: the figure of Loki.

Ally and enemy, genius and failure, delightful and despicable, ridiculous and deadly, beautiful and hideous, hilarious and bitter, clever and foolish, Loki is the God of Nothing in Particular yet unmistakably of the ambiguous World Itself. It was in reading this book that I first felt the power of that ambiguity. Loki never turned up among the lists of Great Literary Heroes (or Villains) of Childhood, and yet he was my favorite character in the book that was for many years my favorite, a book whose subtitle might have been "How Loki Ruined the World and Made It Worth Talking About." Loki was the god of my own mind as a child, with its competing impulses of vandalism and vision, of imagining things and smashing them. And as he cooked up schemes and foiled them, fathered monsters and stymied them, helped forestall the end of things and hastened it, he was god of the endlessly complicating nature of plot, of storytelling itself.

I grew up in a time of mortal gods who knew, like Odin, that the world of marvels they had created was on the verge, through their own faithlessness and might, of Ragnarokk, a time when the best impulses of men and the worst were laid bare in Mississippi and Vietnam, when the suburban Midgard where I grew up was threatened — or so we were told — by frost giants and fire giants sworn to destroy it. And I guess I saw all of that reflected in the d'Aulaires' book. But if those parallels were there, then so was Loki, and not merely in his treachery and his urge to scheme and spoil. Loki was funny — he made the other gods laugh. In his fickleness and his fertile imagination he even brought plea-sure to Odin, who with all his well-sipping and autoasphyxiation knew too much ever to be otherwise amused. This was, in fact, the reason why Odin had taken the great, foredoomed step of making Loki his blood brother — for the pleasure, pure and simple, of his company. Loki was the god of the irresistible gag, the gratuitous punch line, the improvised, half-baked solution — the God of the Eight-Year-Old Boy — and like all great jokers and improvisers, as often the butt and the perpetrator of his greatest stunts.

In the end, it was not the familiar darkness of the universe and of my human heart that bound me forever to this book and the nine worlds it contained. It was the bright thread of silliness, of mockery and self-mockery, of gods forced (repeatedly) to dress as women, and submit to the amorous attentions of stallions, and wrestle old ladies. The d'Aulaires' heterogeneous drawings catch hold pre-cisely of that thread: they are pre-Raphaelite friezes as cartooned by *Popeye*'s creator Elzie Segar, at once grandiose and goofy, in a way that reflected both the Norse universe — which begins, after all, with a cow, a great world-sized heifer, patiently, obsessively licking at a salty patch in the primal stew — and my own.

We all grew up — all of us, from the beginning — in a time of vi-olence and invention, absurdity and Armageddon, prey and wit-ness to the worst and the best in humanity, in a world both ruined and made interesting by Loki. I took comfort, as a kid, in knowing that things had always been as awful and as wonderful as they were now, that the world was always on the edge of total destruction, even if, in Maryland in 1969, as today, it seemed a little more true than usual.

MARK DOTY

Pipistrelle

FROM *Ploughshares*

His music, Charles writes, makes us avoidable.
I write: emissary of evening.
We're writing poems about last night's bat.

Charles has stripped the scene to lyric,
while I'm filling in the tale: how,
 — when we emerged from the inn,

an unassuming place in the countryside
near Hoarwithy, not far from the River Wye,
two twilight mares in a thorn-hedged field

across the road — clotted cream
and raw gray wool, English horses,
self-contained, vaguely above it all —

came a little closer. Though
when we approached they ignored us,
and went on softly tearing up audible mouthfuls,

so we turned in the other direction,
toward Lough Pool, a mudhole scattered with sticks
beneath an ancient conifer's vast trunk.

Then Charles saw the quick ambassador
fret the spaces between boughs
with an inky signature too fast to trace.

We turned our faces upwards,
trying to read the deepening blue
between black limbs. And he said again,

There he is! Though it seemed only
one of us could see the fluttering pipistrelle
at a time — you'd turn your head to where

he'd been, no luck, he'd already joined
a larger dark. There he is! Paul said it,
then Pippa. Then I caught the fleeting contraption

speeding into a bank of leaves,
and heard the high, two-syllabled piping.
But when I said what I'd heard,

no one else had noticed it, and Charles said,
Only some people can hear their frequencies.
Fifty years old and I didn't know

I could hear the tender cry of a bat
— *cry* won't do: a diminutive chime
somewhere between merriment and weeping,

who could ever say? I with no music
to my name save what I can coax
into a line, no sense of pitch,

heard the night's own one-sided conversation.
What to make of the gift? An oddity,
like being double-jointed, or token

of some kinship to the little Victorian handbag
dashing between the dim bulks of trees?
Of course the next day we begin our poems.

Charles considers the pipistrelle's music navigational,
a modest, rational understanding of what
I have decided is my personal visitation.

Is it because I am an American that I think the bat came
especially to address me, who have the particular gift
of hearing him? If he sang to us, but only I

heard him, does that mean he sang to me?
Or does that mean I am a son of Whitman,
while Charles is an heir of Wordsworth,

albeit thankfully a more concise one?
Is this material necessary or helpful to my poem,
even though Charles admires my welter

of detail, my branching questions?
Couldn't I compose a lean,
meditative evocation of what threaded

over our wondering heads,
or do I need to do what I am doing now,
and worry my little aerial friend

with a freight not precisely his?
Does the poem reside in experience
or in self-consciousness

about experience? Shh,
says the evening near the Wye.
Enough, say the hungry horses.

Listen to my poem, says Charles.
A word in your ear, says the night.

BRIAN DOYLE

Eddy

FROM *Portland*

AT ABOUT HALF PAST TWO on the afternoon of Wednesday, January 24, 1945, a young American named Eddy Baranski shuffled into a basement in Mauthausen, Austria. He was twenty-seven years old. He was told to remove his clothing and walk into the next room, where his photograph would be taken. He was told to stand against the wall. Probably he was told to stand as motionless as possible, so as to yield the most exact photograph. As soon as he was lined up properly with the camera he was shot from behind, in the brain, from perhaps three inches away. He died instantly. A Polish prisoner named Wilhem Ornstein then carried Eddy into an adjacent cold storage room, where he was laid until Ornstein had finished mopping the blood from the floor. Ornstein then carried Eddy to the adjacent crematorium, where an Austrian prisoner named Johann Kanduth roasted Eddy and scattered his ashes atop a vast pile of ashes of men and women and children from around the world.

So vanished Army Air Corps Captain Edward Baranski, whom the Nazis considered a cunning spy, whom the Nazis had tortured so thoroughly that he could no longer properly use his arms, whom the Nazis blamed for his role in the Slovakian revolt against the Nazis in 1944. And so vanished Eddy Baranski from the lives of those he left behind in Utah: among them his father, who never spoke his son's name again the rest of his life; and his mother, who prayed for her boy every day the rest of her life; and his young wife, Madeline, who had a vision of him, whole and smiling, in the Utah darkness, at exactly the moment he died in Austria; and his daughter, Kathleen, who was two years old when her daddy flew off to fight

Hitler, and who spent the next fifty years fatherless, without a memory of his voice or face or smell, without even the cold facts of his murder.

In 1993 the University of Portland admitted a young woman to the Class of 1997. Her name was Christina Lund. Intrigued by the university's extensive foreign study opportunities, she applied and was accepted to the university's oldest and largest adventure abroad, in Austria. One annual aspect of the Salzburg Program is a trip to Mauthausen, one of the many lairs of hell operated by the Nazis during World War II, and the one from which legendarily no one ever returned.

Christina's mother, Kathleen, Eddy Baranski's daughter, decides to visit Mauthausen while she and her husband, university regent Allen Lund, are visiting their daughter in Salzburg.

I'd never wanted to go there before, not in fifty years, says Kathleen. But something then made me want to go, and we went, and it was chilling. I walked around. I found the place where he was shot, and I waited for something there, some feeling, some message; but there was nothing.

They went home, Kathleen and Allen, and they went about their lives, but something had changed in Kathleen, some seed opening, some cold place warming; and she began to inquire about her father, and poke her uncle John for information about his beloved brother, and write to the National Archives, and to museums in Europe, and to the United States Army, and slowly, miraculously, Eddy Baranski's story flew toward her, into the world, into the hearts of his children and grandchildren; and that, says Kathleen, was his first gift.

Somehow he began to find me, she says.

Eddy Baranski grew up in Chicago, was an all-city football player for McKinley High, and went on to college at the University of Illinois. There he joined the Army cadet corps, sang in a quartet, led the Catholic student group, and waited tables in the student cafeteria. One day in the cafeteria he gets to talking with a witty, cheerful, sparkling girl named Madeline Cleary, and pretty soon Madeline and Eddy are in love, and they marry, and they have a child, Kathleen, and they move to Utah, and then suddenly the worst war in the history of the world erupts, just as they have another child,

Gerald, and soon Eddy is Lieutenant Edward Victor Baranski of the
Army Air Corps, flying into the very heart of the Nazi juggernaut at
the peak of its savagery.

Because he spoke German and Slovak, legacies from his Slovakian
mama, Eddy was recruited by the mysterious OSS, the Office of
Strategic Services, the most secretive and dangerous of the Allied
intelligence units in the war. He served in North Africa, Algeria, Italy, and England (where he worked with the Czechoslovakian government in exile) before being quietly sent into Slovakia to help
with a rumored partisan uprising there. In August of 1944 the
Slovakian partisans did rebel against the Nazis, who crushed the
rising immediately. Eddy Baranski, by now an Air Corps captain,
slid out of his American identity altogether and into life as a German seller of firewood, living in the villages of Zvolen Slatina and
Piest, trying to find and help partisans, tracking and radioing Nazi
activity to the OSS. On December 9, 1944, the Nazi secret police, the Gestapo, having tortured residents of Zvolen Slatina for
news of Eddy's whereabouts, captured him in a farmhouse in Piest,
and took him eventually to Mauthausen. His friends in Piest kept
Eddy's personal belongings secret for the next half a century: a
Gillette shaver in a silver case, a first-aid kit, a prayer book.

In May of 1945 a German citizen named Werner Muller dictated
an extraordinary document to an Australian lieutenant named
Danny Hunter. Muller, who spoke English, French, and Italian, had
been an interpreter for the Wermacht, the Nazi army under Hein-
rich Himmler. Ordered to Mauthausen in October of 1944, Muller's job was to help with the interrogations of Allied prisoners.
When Mauthausen was liberated, in May of 1945, Danny Hunter
wrote down Muller's account of his months in hell. Muller remembered one prisoner above all: Eddy Baranski.

Eddy and his radioman, Daniel Pavletich, had both been impris-
oned and questioned first in Bratislava, where they told the Nazis
they were American flyers. On arrival in Mauthausen, Pavletich was
interrogated without incident, remembered Muller, but Baranski
was a different story. *Since this fellow seems to be so very clever,* said the
commandant, *he deserves special treatment. This one we will hang.*

"When Baranski saw [Nazi officers] all crowded in the room and the chain over the table," remembered Muller, "he turned to me smiling and said, *I know what they are going to do now.*

"They tied his hands behind his back," remembered Muller, "and attached his wrists to the chain above, which they drew upwards. Although he must have been suffering terrible pain, he kept himself wonderfully. The Kommandant did not seem to like that and said, *I think the fellow still enjoys himself.* They pulled his legs down so his whole weight was hanging on his arms. In the end he couldn't stand it any longer. He cried and begged to be let down, but the Kommandant insisted on keeping him suspended in that dreadful position. My eyes were filled with tears. Baranski started praying and the Kommandant asked me what he was saying, and when I told him he and the other officers laughed. In the end however they let him down . . ."

His prayers, says Eddy's daughter, Kathleen — that's my father's second gift to me. At the very end of his tether, he prayed. To hear the depth and breadth of his faith, to know that now, after not knowing him for fifty years — that is a gift.

"He was completely broken," remembers Muller. "His poor hands looked dreadful. He was offered some water but he had to hold it himself which he was incapable of doing with his hands. It was a terrible sight how he tried at first to sip some water with the bottle held between his arms. This was the most dreadful half hour I have ever been through in my life and I was ashamed to be there."

And Muller remembers one more detail, before Eddy Baranski and ten American men and four British men and one Slovakian woman were executed naked in the basement with the fake camera; that when he offered Baranski a cigarette after his torture, Eddy grinned.

In August of 1999 Kathleen Baranski Lund and thirty of her family and friends were honored guests of the American embassy in Bratislava, where her father had been interrogated by the Nazis. They visited Tri Duby, where the president of Slovakia dedicated a monument to Eddy Baranski and his fellow Allied soldiers who aided the 1944 rebellion against the Nazis. They went to Banska Bystrika, where Eddy Baranski is honored in the National Museum of Slovakia. They went to Piest, where Eddy was captured, and they went to the house where he was captured, and there they met Maria Lakotova, who wept when she remembered Kathleen's father singing lullabies to her at night when she was a toddler in that house. And finally they went to Mauthausen, and prayed at the place where so many thousands of souls fled the earth.

Your father used to sing to me at night, Maria Lakotova told Kathleen. He would hold me on his knee and sing his songs. He was so kind and he had such a lovely voice. But I know he was not singing to me. He was singing to you, to his little girl far away.

His songs, says Kathleen — his songs are his final gift to me. It's like I am finally hearing them after fifty years. I finally found my father. Now I know he never gave up, and he prayed, and he sang, and now he's alive to me like he never was, not for fifty years. No one ever talked about him after he was murdered, so I never had a father at all. But now I do. Now I'll have my dad forever and ever. It's not sad. It's joyous. It's a miracle.

In 2004 the University of Portland admitted a young woman to the class of 2008. Her name is Noel Peterson. She is from Shadow Hills, California. She wants to major in education. She is witty and cheerful and sparkling and lives in Shipstad Hall. Her mother is Natalie Baranski Peterson. Her grandmother is Kathleen Baranski Lund. Her great-grandfather was a most remarkable young man, a devout youth with a lovely voice and a ferocious courage and an irrepressible belief that his brains and energy and creativity and finally his life could be brought to bear to destroy a foul empire that sought to enslave the world. His name was Eddy Baranski, and his story will never die again.

ANTHONY ESOLEN

A Manna for All Seasons

FROM *Touchstone*

TIRIOLO — LITTLE TYRE, a trading fortress founded by the ever-busy Phoenicians twenty-five hundred years ago — would now be no more than a sleepy village, were it not for the herds of goats that crowd its streets in the early morning once a week, and the Italians that crowd them at all other hours. People live well in Tiriolo, by their easy standards: they have good food and clean clothes, and it hardly ever rains. They work, but they don't blow trumpets before them as they go. So it didn't surprise me when my cousins — all of them grown up, with families — decided one fall afternoon, in the middle of the week, not to win bread but to hunt mushrooms.

Do not suppose we had baskets for assiduous gathering. The larger breeds of mushrooms, or *funghi* as the Italians so accurately call them, are shy, hiding under a fall of rotten leaves or in the wet crook of a half-dead oak. I might sit on a rock with a commanding view of the hill, combating a kind of spore-grown heresy with Francesco, *un Testimonio di Gehova,* and not catch a single mushroom battening on the wind.

The poisonous ones, I was told, are small and white, like those we eat in America. The really good ones, never to be purchased but only to be found, are rare behemoths, gaudy yellow and streaky red, sometimes capped like the umbrellas we know, sometimes just slabs of flabby tofu.

"What's that thing?" I asked, warily. But they cried out, *"Antonio, hai fatto bene!"* It was a crimson blotch that might have corrupted the liver of Saint Peter himself. That was the success of the day. For

three hours we shouted and argued and complained about the walk back uphill, and all we had for profit were a half-dozen fungi.

The cousins were sweaty and happy, and I was shaking my head, American that I am, calculating how many hours the three men had taken from work, how much they could have earned, and how many baskets of spores they could have bought with the wages. But cousin Adriana cooked the mushrooms in our supper, and though they tasted like any mushrooms — that is, they savored of warm mold and woody mildew — they were good, no one died of liver failure, and the bank did not come to repossess the furniture.

The Week's Purpose

It wasn't the Sabbath, but it might as well have been. My cousins should have been working, I thought. Man is supposed to work — most of us have little choice in the matter, or loudly protest that we have no choice — except on the Sabbath, when we rest. But is that all there is to the relation between the days? Might there be something about the Sabbath that makes for good work the day before? Can you enjoy the Sabbath rest in the midst of labor on Thursday? What kind of hard Thursday work — or Thursday play — is like Sunday feasting? And what is the Thursday work for, if not ultimately for feasting?

My mind returns to that day in Little Tyre whenever I forget that the end of the week, the purpose of the week, is its return to the feast in the beginning. The Sabbath is a gift for man, says Jesus, and not man the sacrifice for a grim and demanding Sabbath. Profit be damned. When you forget the Sabbath, you mistake the other days, too. When you forget the feast, you forget what your work is for.

Before the Lord cast Adam and Eve out of Eden, where the fruit of the vine hung bountiful and free, he had a few words to say to the man about his labor: "Cursed is the ground for thy sake: in sorrow shalt thou eat of it all the days of thy life: Thorns also and thistles shall it bring forth to thee; and thou shalt eat the herb of the field; In the sweat of thy face shalt thou eat bread, till thou return unto the ground; for out of it wast thou taken: for dust thou art, and unto dust shalt thou return."

Now, one way to fight a curse — our modern way, I think — is to deny that it *is* a curse. If God says we shall eat our bread in the sweat of our brows, then we make an idol of necessity and worship the sweat of our brows. We say, "How hard have we worked to build that granary and stuff it with grain!" We hug ourselves for our intelligence, our diligence, our seizing of the main chance, our scratching a bare meal out of the flinty soil, a meal that in our memory grows ever barer as we grow older and better satisfied with our victorious perseverance.

How did the famous woman, suddenly raised high on the national stage, become a lawyer of such station? "Not by staying home and baking cookies," said she.

Now it is bad enough to have to sweat to please the whims of an imperious master, whether Nature or an Egyptian foreman; but to sweat to please the petty god of one's small profit is a slavery as absurd as it is common. Old, too. No sooner are Adam and Eve driven from the garden than we are told of two workers, one who took care to do what was not worth his while, and one who did not. For the things most worth doing are those worth nothing: as a kiss that can be bought is not a kiss.

When Abel "brought of the firstlings of his flock and of the fat thereof," he had to work to choose which sheep were the fattest and the finest. That was the work of worship, or the robust play of worship; and in one fine gesture of thanksgiving, as the flesh lay roasting on the stone of sacrifice, Abel enjoyed the tossing away of his profit, and so gained the favor of the Lord. His sweat became his blessing.

But as for Cain, the church fathers say that when he "brought of the fruit of the ground an offering unto the Lord," he chose whatever was to hand, heedlessly, and so his offering was rejected. Cain was no indolent man, as the world judges indolence. Wandering over the land of Nod, a restless exile, finding the ground ever harsher and stingier, Cain came to consummate his vagabondage by building a city. He was negligent not in farming but in offering away the fruits of his farming. To put it a different way, Cain never knew the restful sweat of the Sabbath.

Sweating for Bread

I said that Abel had turned a curse into a blessing, but in his grace the Lord does nothing but bless mankind, as he blessed Adam

when he drove him from the garden, setting him free from an immortality of sin and alienation. Here I am not thinking about the
so-called *protevangelion,* the first good news, the prophecy of a Redeemer who would come to crush the serpent's head. Look at the
curse again: "In the sweat of thy face shalt thou eat bread." *Bread* —
the first use of the word in Scripture.

Sweat was bread's greatest ingredient: the grain had to be sown
and tended and reaped; the stalks had to be thrashed and the chaff
winnowed; the kernels had to be ground to powder, and in the days
before mills and grindstones, that meant they had to be pounded
in stone bowls by hand. Then came the kneading and baking — all
for a dark, thick loaf that would easily be consumed by a single
small family in a single meal.

If fruit is plentiful and nourishing, who would ever do something
as laborious as bake bread? But for that very reason I like to think
that, had man not sinned, we would have had bread in Eden, as we
would have had art, and play, and garlands on the trees for days of
worship. There would have been all kinds of generous things not
worth doing, in praise of the God who labored six days over a world
that profited him nothing to make.

Bread would then have been not the staff of life, but a very flag,
gladdening the heart like the wine we would have washed it down
with. Or so I imagine; I cannot pass an Italian house on baking day
without feeling that the Sabbath has joined the grandmother in
the kitchen and is floured with her up to the elbows.

No surprise that a Christian or a Jew should feel so. When the inspired author wrote of that bread to come, he knew there would
fall from heaven a bread which man could never win and for which
he was forbidden to work. For it came to pass that the Israelites, set
free from Egypt through no exertion of their own save the sweat
they shed unloading the Egyptians of their gold, began to murmur
against Moses: "Would to God we had died by the hand of the Lord
in the land of Egypt, where we sat by the flesh pots, and when we
did eat bread to the full; for ye have brought us forth into this wilderness, to kill this whole assembly with hunger."

Holiday Bread

At this point, a god of self-help, an American drudge-ethic god,
would have commanded them to dig irrigation trenches or sow sa-

cred kernels or do something else of the sedulous sort. God is not pleased with the people, true, but he grants them a bread that requires only bending down and gathering.

It is a free, holiday bread, this manna, a funny who-knows-what, to be eaten with the foundling quail: "And when the dew that lay was gone up, behold, upon the face of the wilderness there lay a small round thing, as small as the hoar frost on the ground. And when the children of Israel saw it, they said to one another, It is manna: for they wist not what it was. And Moses said unto them, This is the bread which the Lord hath given you to eat."

Every family is granted a measure of manna to be gathered by the men and the women and the children; enough is provided for everybody, and, on the day before the Sabbath, twice as much as enough. So "they gathered every man according to his eating." But on the Sabbath no manna was to be gathered, nor was it to be saved beyond the Sabbath.

Of course, to do so would be to violate the law requiring Sabbath rest. But more: it is to misunderstand both the manna and the Sabbath. To hoard manna is to regard it as a commodity for which one has labored and upon whose store one reckons, and not as a gift pure and simple. When the manna falls on every day but the Sabbath, it is the gift of the Sabbath that falls, and, regardless of the sore backs everybody must have had by evening, the celebratory "finding" of the little kernels is not like the stooping of a farmer over his stick-plow. Rather, it seasons all the days of the week with Sabbath cheer.

One must not, then, undo the blessing by reducing the Sabbath to sweat. No such work can prosper, as the few manna-grubbers found: "Notwithstanding they hearkened not unto Moses; but some of them left of it until the morning, and it bred worms, and stank." But when the manna was boiled into porridge or baked into flatbread, "the taste of it was like wafers made with honey," as sweet and delicate as the morning of a holiday.

Playing with Gargoyles

On the morning of the day before Thanksgiving, the smells of pumpkin pie a-baking come to me from downstairs. Maybe manna tasted a little like that, who knows, or maybe the pie is manna to me, because for all I have to do with its making, I might as

well have found it hot and steaming under a tree, placed there by
elves.

My wife's cooking makes me think of all kinds of hard work leavened by play. I think of the turned porch posts of the old house we
live in, and wonder that people so much poorer than we, with so
many fewer days to see the sun rise and set, yet spent so much time,
so much cramped muscle and sweat, to turn logs on a lathe and
make them into ringed and scalloped posts, with calculus defying
curves, to look fine on a sunny day.

Why did they do that? Or why are Gothic cathedrals so playful? I
have heard that gargoyles serve at least two practical purposes:
their weight helps nail down the pillars or buttresses they cap, and
they make fine downspouts. But wouldn't a large sluice of scooped
stone have done as well? Some unknown sculptor, no doubt a gan-
gly apprentice named Wat, labored over the comic-book grimaces
and the googling eyes, sweating and (if his chisel missed the mark)
swearing in the service of the Lord.

That is, he labored and earned his handful of pence every day
but the Sabbath day, yet I wager that if something of the Sabbath
did not season his work on those other days, the demon's grimace
would not be quite so taut nor the leer quite so rakish. Neither
does one buy gargoyles from a store.

In *Leisure: The Basis of Culture,* Joseph Pieper said that ours is a society of "total work," with the weekend, that calendrical device for
the maintenance of rested labor, having replaced the Sabbath. The
weekend exists to make our labor on Monday-Tuesday-Wednesday-
Thursday-Friday more productive, which is to say more efficient,
which is to say not at all like the labor of baking pies, chiseling demons, hunting the wild mushroom, culling one's best ram to sacrifice, or seething manna to pat into wafers. If anything, the spirit of
Monday Unlimited has infiltrated the weekend too, as was to be expected given its lordship over those days, so that many of us now
look at the weekend as the time when we can catch up on work.

The sin we commit when we allow work to crowd out celebration,
said Pieper, is the one we are least likely to acknowledge, because
our busyness hides the truth from us so well. It is sloth, that devil of
the noonday sun. For sloth, he points out, is not only quite compatible with a society of total work, it is what such a society inevitably
produces, and produces more efficiently than drywall and fiber-
glass.

Working Sin

Thomas Aquinas says that sloth is the sin against the Sabbath rest, not because it is a perversion of rest, but because it prevents us from enjoying the festivity, the wheat and the oil and the wine. Sloth is spiritual torpor. The body may run like a robot, accomplishing task after task, and deriving no joy from any of it; the soul that drives such a body is in the grip of that dead sin. You may get a lot done. So does a derrick, so does a winch.

And what of that work? What, at last, is the value of productivity, when the work is not shot through with care, with love, with the humility to dally upon the small? Some work, no doubt, has always been backbreaking and necessary. Farmers used to have to clear fields of stumps, from dawn to dusk, the men taking two weeks at the job, using axes and fire and oxen harnessed to pulleys and chains. But is there not at least some savor of hard celebration when two or three are gathered together to root up stumps, and sweat and swear, and set their aching arms and backs against the cold roots?

That work had to be done with care — care for one's family; otherwise, your negligence would be scored on your plowshare soon enough. But work done for the sake of work, or work processed along the chain *only* for the sake of a salary or, worse, for power and prestige, is the work of a slave, the more slavish as it is the more voluntary. It is the manna scrambled up for the manna trough, and it grows wormy. It stinks to heaven.

As the gentle prophet might say, "Why spend your labor for what is not bread?" Why turn your back upon the festive day? The Sabbath, and work undertaken in its refreshing shadow, is too much celebration for our weak nerves, too much labor of heart and mind and soul for our impoverished will; at the same time, it is too humble a surrender to the God who made all creatures great and small. So we retreat from it, retreat from work into work.

I see this torpidity in my profession, literary studies, wherein young professors (I was one) are lashed and whipped into producing, according to our field's own pyramidal templates, article after strawless article that turn the awe or joy of a Shakespeare into a political grind, a ducking and scraping for advancement. But to mesh in that machine is more comfortable than to confront the tremendous mystery of God and man that Shakespeare confronts. And the brand name of that machine — shut down on the weekends only to be oiled and made ready for the days that matter — is sloth.

Parents now hire other people to throw parties for their children. Do they hire other people to laugh, too, when their children prattle? Do they sublet their joy? Ah, so they do, at many dollars a day. We leave the labor of home to grind it out in the desert. Sure, it is a desert without manna, but not to worry: its caravan routes are strewn on both sides with the same old fleshpots everywhere to help you make it through the dead and dry. Sloth sells, sloth pays.

One of the Fools

What do we work for, finally, if not somehow for *life,* and that in abundance? Again my thoughts turn to better people than I have been. My grandmother had terrible circulation in her legs all her born days, but she was too busy to sit down, unless it were to watch *Gunsmoke* with her husband. I see them still, each more a child than I: two Italians cheering a sheriff named Dillon, laughing at the bad guy and holding a perfectly silly and animated conversation with the tube.

Even when cancer had withered her right arm, she would somehow swing her limbs and roll the dough for a great bowl of anise Easter cookies, or, in ordinary time, confect a leaden mixture of raisins, coffee, dough, sugar, and fat — lots of fat — into what my childhood revered as "boiled cake," rich and good for ballast, nor to be tasted again by anyone this side of the grave. By no means was her life all sweet: for many years without complaint she washed and fed her bedridden father, and then, with no intermission, she did the same humble and noisome duties for her half-mad ingrate of a father-in-law. She raised six children through poverty, then tended the grandchildren, of whom there were nineteen, all nearby.

I have never known a woman or a man who worked harder and more heroically than she, nor have I known anyone who tired less. She was no great intellect — I recall with fondness her being always scolded by her memorious husband and partner in pinochle — but when it came to the tricks of this world, she was never trumped, not she. I am persuaded that in her work she was one of the fools to whom great mysteries have been revealed, hidden from us noisemakers.

Angeline was her name, and like an angel she ascended and descended. She was always working at something true, like a loaf of bread; therefore, she was always at rest. She was a laborer at the harvest. She was a lily of the field.

Gathering Manna

Whether those irresponsible cousins of mine, erratic attenders of church on Sunday, had been granted an odd glimpse of the Sabbath that I had long denied myself, I don't know. It wouldn't surprise me. We might say of joy itself, "What is this thing?" — because if we can work for it, it isn't. God's gift to the hungry Israelites was something suddenly there to be found, to send everybody scampering to gather. Manna takes a lot of time to gather, I think; six days, to be precise. Takes that time, and redeems it.

For whenever you sweat to do the generous thing that makes no workaday sense, you gather manna. The flash of the preacher's alb and the straining of the local choir, in praise of a body broken and raised, of a small wafer, of bread that is true bread; the grip of a mischievous hand with a chisel, a woman festooning the house for her child's birthday, the high spirit hallooing down the hillside, the hunt for the small because it is small and not worth the hunt, the hunt for the sheep that is lost because it is lost and is not worth the finding, the making of a world that did not need to be made, a world of flowers and mushrooms; these partake of true labor and true play.

For in the end as in the beginning, ours is a Sunday world. May I not forget it. And may I meet again, at that distant feast, the old lady who tended a gift as small and round as a coriander seed. I want to ask what work *she* did to raise her to so high a station. She never did write down a recipe.

MALCOLM GLADWELL

The Cellular Church

FROM *The New Yorker*

ON THE OCCASION of the twenty-fifth anniversary of Saddleback Church, Rick Warren hired the Anaheim Angels' baseball stadium. He wanted to address his entire congregation at once, and there was no way to fit everyone in at Saddleback, where the crowds are spread across services held over the course of an entire weekend. So Warren booked the stadium and printed large, silver-black-and-white tickets, and, on a sunny Sunday morning last April, the tens of thousands of congregants of one of America's largest churches began to file into the stands. They were wearing shorts and T-shirts and buying Cokes and hamburgers from the concession stands, if they had not already tailgated in the parking lot. On the field, a rock band played loudly and enthusiastically. Just after one o'clock, a voice came over the public-address system — "RIIIICK WARRRREN" — and Warren bounded onto the stage, wearing black slacks, a red linen guayabera shirt, and wraparound NASCAR sunglasses. The congregants leaped to their feet.

"You know," Warren said, grabbing the microphone, "there are two things I've always wanted to do in a stadium." He turned his body sideways, playing an imaginary guitar, and belted out the first few lines of Jimi Hendrix's "Purple Haze." His image was up on the Jumbotrons in right and left fields, just below the Verizon and Pepsi and Budweiser logos. He stopped and grinned. "The other thing is, I want to do a wave!" He pointed to the bleachers, and then to the right-field seats, and around and around the stadium the congregation rose and fell, in four full circuits. "You are the most amazing church in America!" Warren shouted out, when they had finally finished. "AND I LOVE YOU!"

Rick Warren is a large man, with a generous stomach. He has short, spiky hair and a goatee. He looks like an ex-athlete, or someone who might have many tattoos. He is a hugger, enfolding those he meets in his long arms and saying things like "Hey, man." According to Warren, from sixth grade through college there wasn't a day in his life that he wasn't president of something, and that makes sense, because he's always the one at the center of the room talking or laughing, with his head tilted way back, or crying, which he does freely. In the evangelical tradition, preachers are hard or soft. Billy Graham, with his piercing eyes and protruding chin and Bible clenched close to his chest, is hard. So was Martin Luther King, Jr., who overwhelmed his audience with his sonorous, forcefully enunciated cadences. Warren is soft. His sermons are conversational, delivered in a folksy, raspy voice. He talks about how he loves Krispy Kreme doughnuts, drives a four-year-old Ford, and favors loud Hawaiian shirts, even at the pulpit, because, he says, "they do not itch."

In December of 1979, when Warren was twenty-five years old, he and his wife, Kay, took their four-month-old baby and drove in a U-Haul from Texas to Saddleback Valley, in Orange County, because Warren had read that it was one of the fastest-growing counties in the country. He walked into the first real-estate office he found and introduced himself to the first agent he saw, a man named Don Dale. He was looking for somewhere to live, he said.

"Do you have any money to rent a house?" Dale asked.

"Not much, but we can borrow some," Warren replied.

"Do you have a job?"

"No. I don't have a job."

"What do you do for a living?"

"I'm a minister."

"So you have a church?"

"Not yet."

Dale found him an apartment that very day, of course: Warren is one of those people whose lives have an irresistible forward momentum. In the car on the way over, he recruited Dale as the first member of his still nonexistent church, of course. And when he held his first public service, three months later, he stood up in front of two hundred and five people he barely knew in a high-school gymnasium — this shiny-faced preacher fresh out of seminary — and told them that one day soon their new church would number twenty thousand people and occupy a campus of fifty acres. Today, Saddleback Church has twenty thousand members and occupies a campus of a hundred and twenty acres. Once, Warren wanted to increase the number of small groups at Saddleback — the groups of six or seven that meet for prayer and fellowship during the week — by three hundred. He went home and prayed and, as he tells it, God said to him that what he really needed to do was increase the number of small groups by three thousand, which is just what he did. Then, a few years ago, he wrote a book called *The Purpose-Driven Life,* a genre of book that is known in the religious-publishing business as "Christian Living," and that typically sells thirty or forty thousand copies a year. Warren's publishers came to see him at Saddleback, and sat on the long leather couch in his office, and talked about their ideas for the book. "You guys don't understand," Warren told them. "This is a hundred-million-copy book." Warren remembers stunned silence: "Their jaws dropped." But now, nearly three years after its publication, *The Purpose-Driven Life* has sold twenty-three million copies. It is among the best-selling nonfiction hardcover books in American history. Neither the *New York Times,* the *Los Angeles Times,* nor the *Washington Post* has reviewed it. Warren's own publisher didn't see it coming. Only Warren had faith. "The best of the evangelical tradition is that you don't plan your way forward — you prophesy your way forward," the theologian Leonard Sweet says. "Rick's prophesying his way forward."

Not long after the Anaheim service, Warren went back to his office on the Saddleback campus. He put his feet up on the coffee table. On the wall in front of him were framed originals of the sermons of the nineteenth-century preacher Charles Spurgeon, and on the bookshelf next to him was his collection of hot sauces. "I had dinner with Jack Welch last Sunday night," he said. "He came to church, and we had dinner. I've been kind of mentoring him on his spiritual journey. And he said to me, 'Rick, you are the biggest thinker I have ever met in my life. The only other person I know who thinks globally like you is Rupert Murdoch.' And I said, 'That's interesting. I'm Rupert's pastor! Rupert published my book!'" Then he tilted back his head and gave one of those big Rick Warren laughs.

Churches, like any large voluntary organization, have at their core a contradiction. In order to attract newcomers, they must have low barriers to entry. They must be unintimidating, friendly, and compatible with the culture they are a part of. In order to retain their membership, however, they need to have an identity distinct from that culture. They need to give their followers a sense of community — and community, exclusivity, a distinct identity are all, inevitably, casualties of growth. As an economist would say, the bigger an organization becomes, the greater a free-rider problem it has. If I go to a church with five hundred members, in a magnificent cathedral, with spectacular services and music, why should I volunteer or donate any substantial share of my money? What kind of peer pressure is there in a congregation that large? If the barriers to entry become too low — and the ties among members become increasingly tenuous — then a church as it grows bigger becomes weaker.

One solution to the problem is simply not to grow, and, historically, churches have sacrificed size for community. But there is another approach: to create a church out of a network of lots of little church cells — exclusive, tightly knit groups of six or seven who meet in one another's homes during the week to worship and pray. The small group as an instrument of community is initially how Communism spread, and in the postwar years Alcoholics Anonymous and its twelve-step progeny perfected the small-group technique. The small group did not have a designated leader who stood at the front of the room. Members sat in a circle. The focus was on discussion and interaction — not one person teaching and the others listening — and the remarkable thing about these groups was their power. An alcoholic could lose his job and his family, he could be hospitalized, he could be warned by half a dozen doctors — and go on drinking. But put him in a room of his peers once a week — make him share the burdens of others and have his burdens shared by others — and he could do something that once seemed impossible.

When churches — in particular, the megachurches that became the engine of the evangelical movement, in the 1970s and 1980s

— began to adopt the cellular model, they found out the same thing. The small group was an extraordinary vehicle of commitment. It was personal and flexible. It cost nothing. It was convenient, and every worshipper was able to find a small group that precisely matched his or her interests. Today, at least forty million Americans are in a religiously based small group, and the growing ranks of small-group membership have caused a profound shift in the nature of the American religious experience.

"As I see it, one of the most unfortunate misunderstandings of our time has been to think of small intentional communities as groups 'within' the church," the philosopher Dick Westley writes in one of the many books celebrating the rise of small-group power. "When are we going to have the courage to publicly proclaim what everyone with any experience with small groups has known all along: they are not organizations 'within' the church; they are church."

Ram Cnaan, a professor of social work at the University of Pennsylvania, recently estimated the replacement value of the charitable work done by the average American church — that is, the amount of money it would take to equal the time, money, and resources donated to the community by a typical congregation — and found that it came to about a hundred and forty thousand dollars a year. In the city of Philadelphia, for example, that works out to an annual total of two hundred and fifty million dollars' worth of community "good"; on a national scale, the contribution of religious groups to the public welfare is, as Cnaan puts it, "staggering." In the past twenty years, as the enthusiasm for publicly supported welfare has waned, churches have quietly and steadily stepped in to fill the gaps. And who are the churchgoers donating all that time and money? People in small groups. Membership in a small group is a better predictor of whether people volunteer or give money than how often they attend church, whether they pray, whether they've had a deep religious experience, or whether they were raised in a Christian home. Social action is not a consequence of belief, in other words. I don't give because I believe in religious charity. I give because I belong to a social structure that enforces an ethic of giving. "Small groups are networks," the Princeton sociologist Robert Wuthnow, who has studied the phenomenon closely, says. "They create bonds among people. Expose people to needs, provide opportunities for volunteering, and put people in harm's way of being asked to volunteer. That's not to say that being there for worship is not important. But, even in earlier research, I was finding that if people say all the right things about being a believer but aren't involved in some kind of physical social setting that generates interaction, they are just not as likely to volunteer."

Rick Warren came to the Saddleback Valley just as the small-group movement was taking off. He was the son of a preacher — a man who started seven churches in and around northern California and was enough of a carpenter to have built a few dozen more with his own hands — and he wanted to do what his father had done: start a church from scratch.

For the first three months, he went from door to door in the neighborhood around his house, asking people why they didn't attend church. Churches were boring and irrelevant to everyday life, he was told. They were unfriendly to visitors. They were too interested in money. They had inadequate children's programs. So Warren decided that in his new church people would play and sing contemporary music, not hymns. (He could find no one, Warren likes to say, who listened to organ music in the car.) He would wear the casual clothes of his community. The sermons would be practical and funny and plainspoken, and he would use video and drama to illustrate his message. And when an actual church was finally built — Saddleback used seventy-nine different locations in its first thirteen years, from high-school auditoriums to movie theaters and then tents before building a permanent home — the church would not look *churchy*: no pews, or stained glass, or lofty spires. Saddleback looks like a college campus, and the main sanctuary looks like the school gymnasium. Parking is plentiful. The chairs are comfortable. There are loudspeakers and television screens everywhere broadcasting the worship service, and all the doors are open, so anyone can slip in or out, at any time, in the anonymity of the enormous crowds. Saddleback is a church with very low barriers to entry.

But beneath the surface is a network of thousands of committed small groups. "Orange County is virtually a desert in social-capital terms," the Harvard political scientist Robert Putnam, who has taken a close look at the Saddleback success story, says. "The rate of mobility is really high. It has long and anonymous commutes. It's a very friendless place, and this church offers serious heavy friendship. It's a very interesting experience to talk to some of those groups. There were these eight people and they were all mountain bikers — mountain bikers for God. They go biking together, and they are one another's best friends. If one person's wife gets breast cancer, he can go to the others for support. If someone loses a job, the others are there for him. They are deeply best friends, in a larger social context where it is hard to find a best friend."

Putnam goes on, "Warren didn't invent the cellular church. But he's brought it to an amazing level of effectiveness. The real job of running Saddleback is the recruitment and training and retention of the thousands of volunteer leaders for all the small groups it has. That's the surprising thing to me — that they are able to manage that. Those small groups are incredibly vulnerable, and complicated to manage. How to keep all those little dinghies moving in the same direction is, organizationally, a major accomplishment."

At Saddleback, members are expected to tithe, and to volunteer. Sunday-school teachers receive special training and a police background check. Recently, Warren decided that Saddleback would feed every homeless person in Orange County three meals a day for forty days. Ninety-two hundred people volunteered. Two million pounds of food were collected, sorted, and distributed.

It may be easy to start going to Saddleback. But it is not easy to stay at Saddleback. "Last Sunday, we took a special offering called Extend the Vision, for people to give over and above their normal offering," Warren said. "We decided we would not use any financial consultants, no high-powered gimmicks, no thermometer on the wall. It was just 'Folks, you know you need to give.' Sunday's offering was seven million dollars in cash and fifty-three million dollars in commitments. That's one Sunday. The average commitment was fifteen thousand dollars a family. That's in *addition* to their tithe. When people say megachurches are shallow, I say you have no idea. These people are committed."

Warren's great talent is organizational. He's not a theological innovator. When he went from door to door, twenty-five years ago, he wasn't testing variants on the Christian message. As far as he was concerned, the content of his message was nonnegotiable. Theologically, Warren is a straight-down-the-middle evangelical. What he wanted to learn was how to construct an effective religious institution. His interest was sociological. Putnam compares Warren to entrepreneurs like Ray Kroc and Sam Walton, pioneers not in what they sold but in how they sold. The contemporary thinker Warren cites most often in conversation is the management guru Peter Drucker, who has been a close friend of his for years. Before Warren wrote *The Purpose-Driven Life,* he wrote a book called *The Purpose-Driven Church,* which was essentially a how-to guide for church builders. He's run hundreds of training seminars around the world for ministers of small-to-medium-sized churches. At the beginning of the Internet boom, he created a Web site called pastors.com, on which he posted his sermons for sale for four dollars each. There were many pastors in the world, he reasoned, who were part-time. They had a second, nine-to-five job and families of their own, and what little free time they had was spent ministering to their congregation. Why not help them out with Sunday morning? The Web site now gets nearly four hundred thousand hits a day.

"I went to South Africa two years ago," Warren said. "We did the purpose-driven-church training, and we simulcast it to ninety thousand pastors across Africa. After it was over, I said, 'Take me out to a village and show me some churches.'"

In the first village they went to, the local pastor came out, saw Warren, and said, "I know who you are. You're Pastor Rick."

"And I said, 'How do you know who I am?'" Warren recalled. "He said, 'I get your sermons every week.' And I said, 'How? You don't even have electricity here.' And he said, 'We're putting the Internet in every post office in South Africa. Once a week, I walk an hour and a half down to the post office. I download it. Then I teach it. You are the only training I have ever received.'"

A typical evangelist, of course, would tell stories about reaching ordinary people, the unsaved laity. But a typical evangelist is someone who goes from town to town, giving sermons to large crowds, or preaching to a broad audience on television. Warren has never pastored any congregation but Saddleback, and he refuses to preach on television, because that would put him in direct competition with the local pastors he has spent the past twenty years cultivating. In the argot of the New Economy, most evangelists follow a business-to-consumer model: b-to-c. Warren follows a business-to-business model: b-to-b. He reaches the people who reach people. He's a builder of religious networks. "I once heard Drucker say this," Warren said. "'Warren is not building a tent revival ministry, like the old-style evangelists. He's building an army, like the Jesuits.'"

To write *The Purpose-Driven Life,* Warren holed up in an office in a corner of the Saddleback campus, twelve hours a day for seven months. "I would get up at four-thirty, arrive at my special office at five, and I would write from five to five," he said. "I'm a people person, and it about killed me to be alone by myself. By eleven-thirty, my ADD would kick in. I would do anything not to be there. It was like birthing a baby." The book didn't tell any stories. It wasn't based on any groundbreaking new research or theory or theological insight. "I'm just not that good a writer," Warren said. "I'm a pastor. There's nothing new in this book. But sometimes as I was writing it I would break down in tears. I would be weeping, and I would feel like God was using me."

The book begins with an inscription: "This book is dedicated to you. Before you were born, God planned *this moment* in your life. It is no accident that you are holding this book. God *longs* for you to discover the life he created you to live — here on earth, and forever in eternity." Five sections follow, each detailing one of God's purposes in our lives — "You Were Planned for God's Pleasure"; "You Were Formed for God's Family"; "You Were Created to Become Like Christ"; "You Were Shaped for Serving God"; "You Were Made for a Mission" — and each of the sections, in turn, is divided into short chapters ("Understanding Your Shape" or "Using What God Gave You" or "How Real Servants Act"). The writing is simple and unadorned. The scriptural interpretation is literal: "Noah had never seen rain, because prior to the Flood, God irrigated the earth from the ground up." The religious vision is uncomplicated and accepting: "God wants to be your best friend." Warren's Christianity, like his church, has low barriers to entry: "Wherever you are reading this, I invite you to bow your head and quietly whisper the prayer that will change your eternity. *Jesus, I believe in you and I receive you.* Go ahead. If you sincerely meant that prayer, congratulations! Welcome to the family of God! You are now ready to discover and start living God's purpose for your life."

It is tempting to interpret the book's message as a kind of New

Age self-help theology. Warren's God is not awesome or angry and does not stand in judgment of human sin. He's genial and mellow. "Warren's God 'wants to be your best friend,' and this means, in turn, that God's most daunting property, the exercise of eternal judgment, is strategically downsized," the critic Chris Lehmann writes, echoing a common complaint:

> When Warren turns his utility-minded feel-speak upon the symbolic ico-nography of the faith, the results are offensively bathetic: "When Jesus stretched his arms wide on the cross, he was saying, 'I love you this much.'" But God needs to be at a greater remove than a group hug.

The self-help genre, however, is fundamentally inward-focused. M. Scott Peck's *The Road Less Traveled* — the only spiritual work that, in terms of sales, can even come close to *The Purpose-Driven Life* — begins with the sentence "Life is difficult." That's a self-help book: it focuses the reader on his own experience. Warren's first sentence, by contrast, is "It's not about you," which puts it in the spirit of traditional Christian devotional literature, which focuses the reader outward, toward God. In look and feel, in fact, *The Purpose-Driven Life* is less twenty-first-century Orange County than it is the nineteenth century of Warren's hero, the English evangelist Charles Spurgeon. Spurgeon was the Warren of his day: the pastor of a large church in London, and the author of best-selling devotional books. On Sunday, good Christians could go and hear Spurgeon preach at the Metropolitan Tabernacle. But during the week they needed something to replace the preacher, and so Spurgeon, in one of his best-known books, *Morning and Evening*, wrote seven hundred and thirty-two short homilies, to be read in the morning and the evening of each day of the year. The homilies are not complex investigations of theology. They are opportunities for spiritual reflection. (Sample Spurgeonism: "Every child of God is where God has placed him for some purpose, and the practical use of this first point is to lead you to inquire for what practical purpose has God placed each one of you where you now are." Sound familiar?) The *Oxford Times* described one of Spurgeon's books as "a rich store of topics treated daintily, with broad humour, with quaint good sense, yet always with a subdued tone and high moral aim," and that describes *The Purpose-Driven Life* as well. It's a spiritual companion. And, like *Morning and Evening*, it is less a book than a program. It's divided into forty chapters, to be read during "Forty Days of Purpose." The first page of the book is called "My Covenant." It reads, "With God's help, I commit the next 40 days of my life to discovering God's purpose for my life."

Warren departs from Spurgeon, though, in his emphasis on the purpose-driven life as a collective experience. Below the boxed covenant is a space for not one signature but three: "Your name," "Partner's name," and then Rick Warren's signature, already printed, followed by a quotation from Ecclesiastes 4:9:

> Two are better off than one, because together they can work more effectively. If one of them falls down, the other can help him up. . . . Two people can resist an attack that would defeat one person alone. A rope made of three cords is hard to break.

The Purpose-Driven Life is meant to be read in groups. If the vision of faith sometimes seems skimpy, that's because the book is supposed to be supplemented by a layer of discussion and reflection and debate. It is a testament to Warren's intuitive understanding of how small groups work that this is precisely how *The Purpose-Driven Life* has been used. It spread along the network that he has spent his career putting together, not from person to person but from group to group. It presold five hundred thousand copies. It averaged more than half a million copies in sales *a month* in its first two years, which is possible only when a book is being bought in lots of fifty or a hundred or two hundred. Of those who bought the book as individuals, nearly half have bought more than one copy, 16 percent have bought four to six copies, and 7 percent have bought ten or more. Twenty-five thousand churches have now participated in the congregation-wide "40 Days of Purpose" campaign, as have hundreds of small groups within companies and organizations, from the N.B.A. to the United States Postal Service.

"I remember the first time I met Rick," says Scott Bolinder, the head of Zondervan, the Christian publishing division of Harper-Collins and the publisher of *The Purpose-Driven Life*. "He was telling me about pastors.com. This is during the height of the dot-com boom. I was thinking, What's your angle? He had no angle. He said, 'I love pastors. I know what they go through.' I said, 'What do you put on there?' He said, 'I put my sermons with a little disclaimer on there: "You are welcome to preach it any way you can. I only ask one thing — I ask that you do it better than I did.'" So then fast-forward seven years: he's got hundreds of thousands of pastors who come to this Web site. And he goes, 'By the way, my church and I are getting ready to do forty days of purpose. If you want to join us, I'm going to preach through this and put my sermons up. And I've arranged with my publisher that if you do join us with this campaign they will sell the book to you for a low price.' That became the tipping point — being able to launch that book with eleven hundred churches, right from the get-go. They became the evangelists for the book."

The book's high-water mark came earlier this year, when a fugitive named Brian Nichols, who had shot and killed four people in an Atlanta courthouse, accosted a young single mother, Ashley Smith, outside her apartment, and held her captive in her home for seven hours.

"I asked him if I could read," Smith said at the press conference after her ordeal was over, and so she went and got her copy of *The Purpose-Driven Life* and turned to the chapter she was reading that day. It was Chapter 33, "How Real Servants Act." It begins:

> We serve God by serving others.
>
> The world defines greatness in terms of power, possessions, prestige, and position. If you can demand service from others, you've arrived. In our self-serving culture with its *me-first* mentality, acting like a servant is not a popular concept.
>
> Jesus, however, measured greatness in terms of service, not status. God determines your greatness by how many people you serve, not how many people serve you.

Nichols listened and said, "Stop. Will you read it again?"

Smith read it to him again.

They talked throughout the night. She made him pancakes. "I said, 'Do you believe in miracles? Because if you don't believe in miracles — you are here for a reason. You're here in my apartment for some reason.'" She might as well have been quoting from *The Purpose-Driven Life*. She went on, "You don't think you're supposed to be sitting here right in front of me listening to me tell you, you know, your reason for being here?" When morning came, Nichols let her go.

Hollywood could not have scripted a better testimonial for *The*

Purpose-Driven Life. Warren's sales soared further. But the real lesson of that improbable story is that it wasn't improbable at all.
What are the odds that a young Christian — a woman who, it turns
out, sends her daughter to Hebron Church, in Dacula, Georgia —
isn't reading *The Purpose-Driven Life?* And is it surprising that Ashley
Smith would feel compelled to read aloud from the book to her
captor, and that, in the discussion that followed, Nichols would
come to some larger perspective on his situation? She and Nichols
were in a small group, and reading aloud from *The Purpose-Driven
Life* is what small groups do.

Not long ago, the sociologist Christian Smith decided to find out
what American evangelicals mean when they say that they believe
in a "Christian America." The phrase seems to suggest that evangelicals intend to erode the separation of church and state. But when
Smith asked a representative sample of evangelicals to explain the
meaning of the phrase, the most frequent explanation was that
America was founded by people who sought religious liberty and
worked to establish religious freedom. The second most frequent
explanation offered was that a majority of Americans of earlier generations were sincere Christians, which, as Smith points out, is empirically true. Others said what they meant by a Christian nation
was that the basic laws of American government reflected Christian principles — which sounds potentially theocratic, except that
when Smith asked his respondents to specify what they meant by
basic laws they came up with representative government and the
balance of powers.

"In other words," Smith writes, "the belief that America was once
a Christian nation does not necessarily mean a commitment to
making it a 'Christian' nation today, whatever that might mean.
Some evangelicals do make this connection explicitly. But many
discuss America's Christian heritage as a simple fact of history that
they are not particularly interested in or optimistic about reclaim-
ing. Further, some evangelicals think America never was a Christian nation; some think it still is; and others think it should not be a
Christian nation, whether or not it was so in the past or is now."

As Smith explored one issue after another with the evangelicals
— gender equality, education, pluralism, and politics — he found
the same scattershot pattern. The Republican Party may have been

adept at winning the support of evangelical voters, but that affinity appears to be as much cultural as anything; the party has learned to speak the evangelical language. Scratch the surface, and the appearance of homogeneity and ideological consistency disappears. Evangelicals want children to have the right to pray in school, for example, and they vote for conservative Republicans who support that right. But what do they mean by prayer? The New Testament's most left-liberal text, the Lord's Prayer — which, it should be pointed out, begins with a call for utopian social restructuring ("Thy will be done, On earth as it is in Heaven"), then welfare relief ("Give us this day our daily bread"), and then income redistribution ("Forgive us our debts as we also have forgiven our debtors"). The evangelical movement isn't a movement, if you take movements to be characterized by a coherent philosophy, and that's hardly surprising when you think of the role that small groups have come to play in the evangelical religious experience. The answers that Smith got to his questions are the kind of answers you would expect from people who think most deeply about their faith and its implications on Tuesday night, or Wednesday, with five or six of their closest friends, and not Sunday morning, in the controlling hands of a pastor.

"Small groups cultivate spirituality, but it is a *particular kind* of spirituality," Robert Wuthnow writes. "They cannot be expected to nurture faith in the same way that years of theological study, meditation, and reflection might." He says, "They provide ways of putting faith in practice. For the most part, their focus is on practical applications, not on abstract knowledge, or even on ideas for the sake of ideas themselves."

We are so accustomed to judging a social movement by its ideological coherence that the vagueness at the heart of evangelicalism sounds like a shortcoming. Peter Drucker calls Warren's network an army, like the Jesuits. But the Jesuits marched in lockstep and held to an all-encompassing and centrally controlled creed. The members of Warren's network don't all dress the same, and they march to the tune only of their own small group, and they agree, fundamentally, only on who the enemy is. It's not an army. It's an insurgency.

In the wake of the extraordinary success of *The Purpose-Driven Life*, Warren says, he underwent a period of soul-searching. He had suddenly been given enormous wealth and influence and he did not know what he was supposed to do with it. "God led me to Psalm 72, which is Solomon's prayer for more influence," Warren says. "It sounds pretty selfish. Solomon is already the wisest and wealthiest man in the world. He's the King of Israel at the apex of its glory. And in that psalm he says, 'God, I want you to make me more powerful and influential.' It looks selfish until he says, 'So that the King may support the widow and orphan, care for the poor, defend the defenseless, speak up for the immigrant, the foreigner, be a friend to those in prison.' Out of that psalm, God said to me that the purpose of influence is to speak up for those who have no influence. That changed my life. I had to repent. I said, I'm sorry, widows and orphans have not been on my radar. I live in Orange County. I live in the Saddleback Valley, which is all gated communities. There aren't any homeless people around. They are thirteen miles away, in Santa Ana, not here." He gestured toward the rolling green hills outside. "I started reading through Scripture. I said, How did I miss the two thousand verses on the poor in the Bible? So I said, I will use whatever affluence and influence that you give me to help those who are marginalized."

He and his wife, Kay, decided to reverse tithe, giving away 90 percent of the tens of millions of dollars they earned from *The Purpose-Driven Life*. They sat down with gay community leaders to talk about fighting AIDS. Warren has made repeated trips to Africa. He has sent out volunteers to forty-seven countries around the world, test-piloting experiments in microfinance and HIV prevention and medical education. He decided to take the same networks he had built to train pastors and spread the purpose-driven life and put them to work on social problems.

"There is only one thing big enough to handle the world's problems, and that is the millions and millions of churches spread out around the world," he says. "I can take you to thousands of villages where they don't have a school. They don't have a grocery store, don't have a fire department. But they have a church. They have a pastor. They have volunteers. The problem today is distribution. In the tsunami, millions of dollars of foodstuffs piled up on the shores and people couldn't get it into the places that needed it, because they didn't have a network. Well, the biggest distribution network in the world is local churches. There are millions of them, far more than all the franchises in the world. Put together, they could be a force for good."

That is, in one sense, a typical Warren pronouncement — bold to the point of audacity, like telling his publisher that his book will sell a hundred million copies. In another sense, it is profoundly modest. When Warren's nineteenth-century evangelical predecessors took on the fight against slavery, they brought to bear every legal, political, and economic lever they could get their hands on. But that was a different time, and that was a different church. Today's evangelicalism is a network, and networks, for better or worse, are informal and personal.

At the Anaheim stadium service, Warren laid out his plan for attacking poverty and disease. He didn't talk about governments, though, or the United Nations, or structures, or laws. He talked about the pastors he had met in his travels around the world. He brought out the president of Rwanda, who stood up at the microphone — a short, slender man in an immaculate black suit — and spoke in halting English about how Warren was helping him rebuild his country. When he was finished, the crowd erupted in applause, and Rick Warren walked across the stage and enfolded him in his long arms.

MARY GORDON

Moral Fiction

FROM *The Atlantic Monthly*

A MONTH OR SO AGO I read an account of an event that took place in Atlanta earlier this year. During his trial for rape a man overpowered one of the courtroom guards, stole her gun, and killed three people. Escaping, he ended up in the home of a twenty-six-year-old woman, and took her hostage. While she was his prisoner, the woman read to him from the inspirational book *The Purpose-Driven Life,* by Rick Warren. The accused rapist saw the error of his ways and surrendered to the police. When this event became public, the book shot to number one on the *New York Times* best-seller list. Ask yourself: can you imagine this happening if she had read to him from one of the great classics of moral fiction — from *Middlemarch,* or *Jude the Obscure,* or *Moby-Dick,* or *War and Peace?*

Another story: a group of scholars, anthropologists, and art historians were assessing the likelihood of a cross-cultural aesthetic standard. The scholars gathered a group of African mask makers, spread a collection of masks before them, and asked them to decide which was the best. The mask makers immediately turned the masks over and looked at the backs. They all agreed on which one was best. When they were asked how they knew, they said they could see which of the masks was most worn on the inside. The most-worn mask was the best because the masks were used for ritual, and the one most often used intrinsically had the most power. It was therefore the best. If the best and most powerful mask maker is the one whose product is used most often, does this mean by analogy that Danielle Steel is a better, more powerful writer than William Trevor?

I have told these stories in order to make clear my understanding that those of us who care about serious fiction are drastically marginal in the culture in which we live. When we talk about the moral aspect of fiction — that is, its concern with questions of right and wrong — we should be very modest indeed about assuming that such an aspect has a connection to behavior. The most successful literary novel would be considered a crashing failure if the number of copies sold was calculated by the producers of *Fear Factor* or *American Idol*. This may be nothing new. Some people like blaming the postmodernists, or even the modernists, on the grounds that the death of narrative marked the death of fiction as a moral force. I tend to blame technology. But what is the use of all this blame? We are where we are. On the margins.

Far greater minds than mine have considered the relationship between art and morality. Sir Philip Sidney and Percy Bysshe Shelley come immediately to mind. In our own day John Gardner, a distinguished novelist, a learned and serious man, wrote a book called *On Moral Fiction*. It was published in 1978, which happens to be the year I published my first novel, *Final Payments*. So to return to Gardner's book is to return to my youth as a writer — a time that seems younger, more buoyant, more innocent, than the present.

I think Gardner is both too hopeful about the nature of fiction writers, about their instinct for the truth, and too dire in his belief that bad art creates bad natures. He says, "Show the artist a Nazi Frankenstein monster and his reaction is simple — 'Get it out!'" This is, unfortunately, not true. Consider Celine and Ezra Pound, to name only two writers who had no trouble with fascism. And I think Gardner is too confident in his belief that artists are more moved than others by ethical considerations. He writes, "What . . . artists care about — what they rave or mourn or bitterly joke about — is the forms of truth: justice, fairness, accuracy." The terms are too *large*, the range of people who could be defined as artists too great, to deserve such a generalization.

I believe that if your primary motivation in life is to be moral, you don't become an artist. You do good works. Perhaps, like Chekhov, you divide your time among healing the sick, bearing witness to appalling prison conditions, and writing masterpieces. But if Chekhov had turned from a bleeding patient — had let up the pressure on the tourniquet — to put the finishing touches on *The Cherry Orchard,* this would not have been a moral act. And insofar as we

would rather he let a peasant die than fail to create the play that
has given us such joy, insofar as we mourn a stolen Vermeer more
than a kidnapped Iraqi child, we have to understand that we are in
the grip of something (and it may be something wonderful, something without which life isn't worth living) that, whatever it is, isn't
moral. We are able to endure the idea of suffering in the flesh
more easily than the destruction of the uniquely well-wrought urn.
We choose beauty over goodness. That is who we are. This is not admirable. But we should try not to forget that rejecting the idea of
beauty for the idea of the common good has a very bad record.

Isak Dinesen brilliantly limns this conflict in her story "Babette's
Feast." Babette, master chef and communard, has been taken in by
two pious Scandinavian spinsters after being forced to leave France
because of her radical political activity. Years later she wins a lottery
and spends all the money to make a memorable feast for the sisters who have sheltered her. Afterward they ask if she will return
to France. She says that she cannot, because the world in which
her art could be appreciated was destroyed by the communards.
A friend asks if she regrets her part in its annihilation. Oh, no,
Babette says — it was a very bad world. But yet I mourn it, for only
the people in that world could understand my art.

You see the problem — and its flip side. I don't agree with Gardner that bad art creates bad morals. Some of the most heroic people I know have decorated their walls with paintings on velvet and
think Louis L'Amour was a genius. If good fiction created good
morals, English departments would be utopian oases. In my experience they are sometimes dreadful and sometimes wonderful. Just
like the rest of the world.

For Gardner, the enemies of moral fiction, by which he means
"hard-won, defiant affirmations," are writers who dishonor the seriousness of their calling, writers who are more concerned with technique than with content, writers who think of their work as a species of play. "Motion, glitter — texture for its own sake — has come
to be the central value in the arts," he writes.

Although I would certainly have taken that position in 1978,
the events of the past twenty-seven years have sapped my energy
for such a fight. In 1978 Jimmy Carter was in the White House,
only a few experts had heard of a *fatwa*, and the catalogs of main-

stream publishers didn't include the category "Christian fiction." Moreover, the realities of the marketplace have ensured that the experimentalists Gardner vilifies probably can't even get published anymore. As a feminist coming of literary age in the seventies, I spent a lot of time pointing out the ubiquity of horrible images of women perpetrated by revered male writers like Ernest Hemingway and John Updike. Nothing has changed; I still don't want to read those guys. But feeling as I do that we are all rowing in a boat that is being swamped, I have less will to attack my fellow oarsmen. And I am leery of using the label "immoral" or "amoral" when what I really mean is people who do something different from what I do. If you take Gardner's position, that fiction more concerned with the play of language than with human behavior is "false," then what do you do with a book like *Finnegans Wake*? I would like to think that anything that gives joy because of its mastery of language must be on the side of the angels. Or at least it is not on the side of the devil — should he exist and should he be taking sides.

And so, for all its passionate energy, Gardner's book seems sometimes to be skating dangerously near the thin ice of special pleading. He juxtaposes trivial or frivolous or false art against true art, which "clarifies life, establishes models of human action, casts nets toward the future, carefully judges our right and wrong directions, celebrates and mourns."

> It does not rant. It does not sneer or giggle in the face of death, it invents prayers and weapons. It designs visions worth trying to make fact. It does not whimper or cower or throw up its hands and bat its lashes. It does not make hope contingent on acceptance of some religious theory. It strikes like lightning, or *is* lightning.

To question this eloquent ideal of Gardner's would seem churlish, and yet I do question it. I would certainly concur that true art celebrates, mourns, and does not rant or sneer or giggle in the face of death. But what would be the nature of the prayers it might invent? And what the weapons? And does true art really establish models of human action? Or, if it does, is that what it does better than any other medium? I have had fiction at the center of my imagination for as long as I have had a memory of a self, and yet my models of right action — the ones who have really helped me in the struggle to be good — are not fictional characters. I may have wanted to be as cool and witty as Elizabeth Bennet, as ferociously passionate as Jane Eyre, as endlessly maternal as Mrs. Ramsay, as ethically indefatigable as Dorothea Brooke, but in moments of moral crisis I have not said to myself, "What would Dorothea Brooke do in this situation?" Not once. When I have modeled myself on my heroines, I have done so in order to make myself more desirable, not more ethical. I made a bad first marriage, thinking I was Clarissa Dalloway marrying Richard "for solitude." In moments of moral crisis I have sometimes invoked models from history: Joan of Arc, Nelson Mandela. But my moral exemplars have tended to be people I know, such as my uncle Joe, who probably never heard of Melville, though the name Moby-Dick might have rung a bell.

So when we put together the words "moral" and "fiction," we must be careful to remember that we mean something very special and very limited. Fiction that aspires to the condition of art must work in a way exactly opposite to the way pornography works. Pornography offers images to elicit a very direct and very predictable response: sexual stimulation resulting in orgasm. The pornographer knows his market, and knows to what use his product will be put. Fiction writers have no such luxury. We never know what we're doing — not really. I learned this to my sorrow once when traveling in the Caribbean with my children and a friend. We stopped to get lemonade at a beach stand. Two Labrador retriever puppies were playing in the sand. I asked the woman behind the counter if my children could play with them. "No," she said. "I don't like them to be friendly to too many people, because I have to keep them away from the coloreds." I ran with my children down the beach. Later, when the power gave out at our house, we were forced to go to this same woman for food. As she served us hamburgers, she said, "The thing that insulted me most as an American voter was Geraldine Ferraro. The idea that I might even think of voting for a woman as vice president of the United States!" When she heard my friend using my name, she asked if I was the writer. "Oh, my God," she said, "*Final Payments* changed my life."

In 2005 what would be at stake in naming some kinds of fiction as moral — with the concomitant understanding that some would then have to be named immoral? What is lost if we give up the category? What is gained if we invoke it? Why should we use these terms for black marks on a white page that perform the trick of making us believe that people who have never existed are as real as our best friends? As a species we seem to have a relationship to story that is very deep indeed. We want to sit around the fire and hear what happens next. But why? Why isn't life enough for us? Why do we need these alternative lives — neither ours nor those of anyone we might have known? Are we after a predictability that life in the body doesn't offer? And if part of our pleasure is moral — if we want the hero to triumph and the villain to be punished — is that proof of the inherently moral nature of our consciousness? But what about Becky Sharp and Amelia Sedley in *Vanity Fair*? No one in her right mind likes Amelia better; no one in her right mind would say that Becky was morally superior. Consider the vexing question of charm, and the colorlessness of life without it. Is this a moral issue? Should color and charm be redefined as virtues, along with honesty, fortitude, generosity, a sense of justice, and filial love?

Not all virtues are equal to all people at all times. At certain historical moments some virtues may be more important than others. At the time of the writing of the *Iliad*, Greek culture could be kept alive only by a warrior class; courage in battle was of primary importance. What virtues are most needed now? Most readers of serious fiction would probably have a list different from those of most Muslim fundamentalists and evangelical Christians. The latter might have a lively sense of the sin that reading certain books could lead to — a sense that would seem quite foreign to the former.

I am no stranger to what I would like to call literary protectionism; in the Catholic Church of my childhood certain books were forbidden to me under pain of mortal sin. The range of the interdiction was wide; it traveled from Voltaire to Erskine Caldwell. (I would like to say this is a thing of the past in Catholicism, but recent actions taken by the Vatican lead me to believe that that is too hopeful a position.) The Church fathers would have said they were protecting me from the temptation to leave the comforting bosom of Mother Church, sparing me the blandishments of atheistic freethinking and the seductions of free love. Broadly speaking, then, impiety and unchastity were the sins they feared most, the ones feared by fundamentalists of all stripes.

For most readers of serious fiction in 2005 these words are archaic and irrelevant. We serious readers, even if we call ourselves religious, are more concerned with oppressive religious and civil structures than with the dangers of a life unsheltered by them. As readers of novels we stake our claim in the territory of the individual — for the novel, in its form and its history, is a celebration of the honorable task of creating an individual self through reflection and experimentation in the stress of a lived life. Some novels treat the relationship of the individual to the community — but this is the exception rather than the rule. Fundamentalists believe that individualism has gone too far — that the notion of personal good has trumped a sense of responsibility to the larger group. Most often, though, this idea is called up in regard to sexual issues; when the issue is whether to pay more taxes so that wealth can be spread to the group, the sacredness of the individual is brought to the fore. What some of us call compassion, others call naiveté. Those of us who are accused of being naive point to the fact that the desire to repress freedom results in deaths that can be laid directly at its feet, whereas the dangers of unchastity or impiety, whatever they may be, have no direct connection to firing squads or torture chambers.

In a country where pornography is ubiquitous and twelve-year-olds on school buses are performing oral sex, I can understand the longing for a return to a world in which the idea of chastity is once more in the conversation. I can understand a revulsion against unbridled individualism, a longing for community in a world where families are fragmented and loneliness can eat into the soul. I can see that strict rules — even, or perhaps especially, tied to punishment — might seem the only way to stem the chaos in which we feel we are drowning. We in the West must come to grips with the fact that we are vulnerable to people we are used to thinking of as our inferiors; that gender roles are confusing and vexed; that the economy seems to be spiraling out of control, with no one to understand it.

But the novel has never been very good at shaping people up in predictable and orderly ways. Sometimes, as in the case of Tolstoy (I once knew someone whose father gave up a fortune after visiting Tolstoy on his estate), a novel can help eat into the cancer of greed. The novel is uniquely qualified to provide some virtues: the virtues of compassion, openness, and attentiveness. Serious fiction is uniquely qualified to combat the sound bite. It says to us that the truth of human beings is often more complicated than we think. What we might like to call the truth is often made up of several truths, including the first thing we thought, its opposite, and something in between. Some things cannot be known without careful pondering; horror can sometimes be averted only if we take our time to look and think and look and think and look and think again.

In her book *Reading Lolita in Tehran,* about a group of women reading novels during the reign of Ayatollah Khomeini's successors, Azar Nafisi tells a story about a student's homage to her former literature professor.

> One day she had been watching the trial of a secret-police agent on television when a familiar voice, Dr. A's, attracted her attention. He had come to testify in favor of his former student . . . who had been enrolled in the university's night classes . . . a prison guard who had apparently been charged with beating and torturing political prisoners . . . [Dr. A believed the guard] to be a compassionate individual, a man who often helped out his less fortunate classmates. Dr. A told the Revolutionary Court: "I believe it is my duty as a human being to acquaint you with this aspect of the accused's personality." Such an action, during those initial black-and-white days of the revolution, was unheard of and very dangerous . . . It was said that mainly because of Dr. A's testimony in his favor, [the guard] got off easy.

The student concludes that "Dr. A's action was a manifestation of the principles he had taught in his literature classes."

> Such an act . . . can only be accomplished by someone who is engrossed in literature, has learned that every individual has different dimensions to his personality . . . Those who judge must take all aspects of an individual's personality into account. It is only through literature that one can put oneself in someone else's shoes and understand the other's different and contradictory sides and refrain from becoming too ruthless. Outside the sphere of literature only one aspect of individuals is revealed. But if you understand their different dimensions you cannot easily murder them.

The moral complexity of this story makes it attractive to the kind of mind that is drawn to serious fiction. Should the guard have gotten off easy? What about justice for those he tortured? These intriguing and unanswerable questions are the territory of great fiction — a territory we would be a far poorer commonwealth without.

If the moral good of fiction stems mainly from a habit of mind it inculcates in the reader, styles are neither good nor bad, and to describe some fictional enterprises as false is pointless. García Márquez's magic realism sheds a light on tyranny that is no less illuminating for its kaleidoscopic nature; Toni Morrison's opulent, curvaceous sentences give us a taste of the poison of racism, as do J. M. Coetzee's angularities. Gogol's ironies breathe air into a stifling room; Trollope's tenderly comic tales of a vicarage paint a portrait of everyday heroism; Proust's evocation of Bergotte, the writer holding up as an artistic ideal Vermeer's perfectly painting a little patch of yellow, gives us a model of selfless devotion to work. All these, in all their different ways, point to something we find difficult to name and yet know as our treasure.

Pope John XXIII once said, "An old world disappears, another one is being formed, and within this I am trying to conceal some good seed or other that will have its springtime, even if it is somewhat delayed." When those of us who read and write fiction invoke the category of the moral, I think we need to look to Pope John's modesty of tone. The precious seeds of complicated thought and large awareness may lead to something, or they may not. They are seeds only; and when they mature they will have been absorbed into a growth (leaf, flower), invisible or transformed beyond our recognizing. But what is there without these seeds, these vessels of possibility, and what they promise? Without them we would be locked into fear of the other, rigid adherence to inhuman rules, delusion about the true nature of the world. We would find ourselves entrapped in the corral of the familiar. And we would be confronted with the terrible conviction that when we ask the questions that alarm and chill us, we cannot hope for conversation, for someone to whisper across the ages and the miles, "I was thinking of that too. It is what you thought. But listen to me: it may be less frightening than what you imagine. Follow me through this wood. It winds, and it is dark. But you are not alone."

ROCHELLE GURSTEIN

The Tragic Fate of John Ruskin

FROM *Salmagundi*

ON JANUARY 1, 1871, John Ruskin published the first monthly installment of *Fors Clavigera: Letters to the Workmen and Laborers of Great Britain.* The title was meant to evoke the terrifying image of the Roman goddess Fortuna, bearing a club, whose purpose it was to nail down every man's appointed fate and his audience he envisaged as anyone left in the world who still engaged in or sought "honest" labor. "Friends," this first pamphlet opens, "We begin today another group of ten years, not in happy circumstances." England was deeply unsettled by the calamities that had befallen Europe with the Franco-Prussian War, and even though "many ingenious persons say we are better off now than we were ever before," Ruskin pointed to his own desk "full of begging letters, eloquently written by distressed or dishonest people." He then announced in a manner so personal and direct that it shocked his first readers just as it continues to shock readers today: "For my part, I will put up with this state of things, passively, not an hour longer." It was not only Ruskin's well-known hatred of injustice that forced him to act — during the 1860s, his attacks on laissez-faire economics, *Unto This Last* and *Munera Pulveris,* were so scandalous that their serial publication was halted to appease outraged readers. But also, in what is surely one of the most unsparing confessions in all the writings of people of good social conscience, Ruskin declared:

I am not an unselfish person, nor an Evangelical one; I have no particular pleasure in doing good; neither do I dislike doing it so much as expect to be rewarded for it in another world. But I simply cannot paint,

nor read, nor look at minerals, nor do anything else that I like, and the
very light of the morning sky, where there is any — which is seldom,
now-a-days, near London — has become hateful to me, because of the
misery that I know of, and see signs of, where I know it not, which no
imagination can interpret too bitterly.

Ruskin's awareness that he was no longer able to live the life he
was made for became all the more unbearable with his appoint-
ment in 1869 as first Slade Professor of fine art at Oxford in recognition for his unrivaled influence in that long-neglected domain.
In the astonishingly vivid word-paintings that even today sing out
from the books that made his reputation — *Modern Painters, The
Seven Lamps of Architecture,* and *The Stones of Venice* — Ruskin gave an
entire generation the eyes to see what they had never before perceived: glorious beauty in art, architecture, and nature, the kind of
ecstatic engagement with the world that his own quickening social
conscience was making impossible for him to feel. Yet, the very labor of composing those unwieldy volumes — *Stones of Venice* swell-
ing to three, *Modern Painters* to five — sharpened his preternatu-
rally sensitive vision, so that the apostle of beauty had no choice but
to become an interpreter of what Thomas Carlyle (whom Ruskin
revered as his "master") called the "signs of the time." Ruskin's vision was now so penetrating that he saw works of art and architecture as tangible, physical manifestations of the moral and spiritual
condition of the individual and of the nation. Beauty was a sign of
joy in labor; ugliness a sign of degradation. With each volume of art
history and appreciation, his writing became more urgent. The decline of Venice, in particular, stood as a cautionary tale for modern, industrial England, consumed as it was with avarice and greed:
the fine arts, Ruskin had come to see, could flourish only in a reverent and virtuous age; without faith, justice, and good order, they
would inevitably and irrevocably decay.
    And so Ruskin, tormented by the fearful signs of moral and spiri-
tual corruption that he saw in the blighted nature, broken men,
and squalor of his time, set out to show by his own example how to
live an honest life. *Fors Clavigera* would be his organ of truth, but he
always believed this publication would be a passing occupation, "a
byework, to quiet my conscience, that I might be happy in what
I supposed to be my own proper life of Art-teaching at Oxford

and elsewhere; and through my own happiness, rightly help others." Beginning this venture, he could never have foreseen how fully consumed he would become by the cruelties and ugliness all around him; nor could he have imagined the herculean exertions he would endure so that he could return, with a clear conscience, to his true life of reading, drawing, teaching, traveling, and collecting watercolors, paintings, engravings, marbles, illuminated manuscripts, books, gemstones, meteors, minerals, dried flowers, stuffed birds (and giving his collections away to friends and museums). In truth, he would never regain that peace of mind, even though he would spend more than a decade pulling six hundred fifty thousand words — ninety-six pamphlets — out of his anguished soul. His task would turn out to be so all-encompassing that an index, sixty-seven pages, double-column, can only begin to suggest what is contained in *Fors Clavigera:* wild, satirical assaults on modern machinery, industrialism, trade, usury, pollution, and war; startling insights into painting, sculpture, poetry, novels, religion, mythology, education, landscapes, gardening, and everyday life; tranquil meditations on the vanishing world of his childhood but also intensely personal soliloquies and confessions, at times bordering on delirium. Newspaper clippings, letters from friends and strangers, snippets of conversations overheard on trains, excerpts from critics' attacks on *Fors,* financial accounts of his many reform projects, a recipe for Yorkshire pie all appear on the same pages, often in the same sentence, with images and allusions from Ruskin's deep and constant reading in the Bible, Shakespeare, Sir Walter Scott, and Dante.

There is a vertiginous feel to Ruskin's quest to picture all the world on a page, and not only his friends, who knew too well the toll it was exacting from him, but also his more sensitive readers who could only guess, began to fear that Ruskin would go mad. In Letter 48, "The Advent Collect" (December 1874), Ruskin, in a gesture of extraordinary personal candor that was a common feature of *Fors,* prints a few lines from a concerned reader: "'Does it never occur to me,' (thus the letter went on) 'that I may be mad myself?'" To which he replies with a sincerity as poignant as it is startling, "Well, I am so alone in my thoughts and ways, that if I am not mad, I should soon become so, from mere solitude, but for my *work*" (his emphasis) — specifically, the work of his hands, drawing.

Reading this astonishing Christmas letter, which, like all *Fors* pamphlets, jumps from one impression, one subject, and one tone to another, straining, in its enormous variety and energy, almost to the breaking point, one is thrust directly into Ruskin's ravaged consciousness — an experience that, like poetry or prophecy, can only be deformed by paraphrase. And because Ruskin never makes a sustained, rational argument — not just in *Fors,* but in any of his writing — the only way to be faithful to his vision is to follow its meanderings in a single letter.

Letter 48 opens gently enough with a self-mocking report on the progress of St. George's Company, Ruskin's plan to establish a community dedicated to making some small part of English soil beautiful, peaceful, and fertile again by the honest labor of its members' hands. Ruskin had donated a generous portion of his inheritance to this enterprise and, in *Fors,* he repeatedly appealed to readers to give a tenth of their income. He begins by admitting that the number of subscriptions might have disappointed him, had he not been happy to amuse himself with his stones and pictures — that is, with his proper work in the "wholesome seclusion" of his study at Oxford. He then launches into a whimsical account of some "experiments" he has made with his own money in hopes of winning his readers' confidence with theirs, only to warn that "the results, for the present, are not altogether encouraging." His land at his home at Conistan in the Lake District has a pretty kitchen garden, "which will probably, every third year, when the weather is not wet, supply me with a dish of strawberries." He had tried to purify the polluted source of a stream near his mother's childhood home in Croydon as a memorial to her (she had recently died), but it was sullied again by the "carelessness" of the parish, who "insist on letting all the roadwashings run into it." On the banks of the spring, Ruskin erected a memorial tablet that read, "In obedience to the Giver of Life, of the brooks and fruits that feed it, of the peace that ends it, may this Well be kept sacred for the service of men, flocks, and flowers, and be by kindness called MARGARET'S WELL." But the flowers he planted were trampled, the stream again polluted by the action of the local authorities, and the tablet taken down. He had hoped to keep a street clean in a slum district in London to demonstrate that such a thing could be done, but the young man he hired to head the sweeping crew turned out to be a "rogue," so he was forced to abandon the project. He also set up a teashop in a poor neighborhood in London so that pure tea in small quantities would be available, only to find that he could not compete either with the false claims of neighboring tradesmen or with the people's preference for spirits. To which he adds that his own indecision about a sign — whether it should be "of a Chinese character, black upon gold; or of a Japanese, blue upon white; or of pleasant English, rose color on green" — was perhaps the real culprit for the shop's languishing. His sheepish conclusion that he was "defeated" only because he had "too many things on hand" would be funny if this bit of understatement did not say so much about the nature of his enforced work of reforming the world, but also of his proper work as lover of beauty.

These jocular confessions are what come directly before Ruskin's deadly earnest confession that he would go mad if it were not for his drawing. But it was not just his own sanity that was in peril; Ruskin believed that "we are in hard times, now, for all men's wits." And he could hear the common wisdom meant to rebut any doubts about modern progress ringing in his ears: "The men of his generation [according to W.E.H. Lecky] are the wisest that ever were born — giants of intellect, according to Lord Macaulay, compared to the pigmies of Bacon's time, and the minor pigmies of Christ's time, and minutest of all, the microscopic pigmies of Solomon's time, and finally, the vermicular and infusorial pigmies — twenty three million to the cube inch — of Mr. Darwin's time, whatever that may be." The sheer impudence of such thinking throws Ruskin into one of the maddening rages that makes reading *Fors* such a harrowing experience:

> But for us of the old race, few of us now left, children who reverence our fathers, and are ashamed of ourselves, comfortless in that shame, and yearning for one word or glance from the graves of old, yet knowing ourselves to be of the same blood, and recognizing in our hearts the same passions, with the ancient masters of humanity; — we, who feel as men, and not as carnivorous worms; we, who are every day recognizing some inaccessible height of thought and power, and are miserable in our shortcomings, — the few of us now standing here and there, alone, in the midst of this yelping, carnivorous crowd, mad for money and lust, tearing each other to pieces, and starving each other to death, and leaving heaps of their dung and ponds of their spittle on every palace floor

and altar stone, — it is impossible for us, except in the labour of our hands, not to go mad.

The bittersweet invocation of the world that is lost by one who knows the terrible meaning of that loss; the recognition of the desolate few who still retain the glimmering of something more noble; the visceral image of the bestial crowd soiling all that should be held sacred — in one, single cascading sentence, Ruskin brands the reader with his searing vision of the shamelessness of the modern world, forcing us to feel in all its horror what it is like to be a person of his excruciating sensitivity.

One moment, Ruskin — and the reader with him — is caught up in a sublime rage, and the very next, in an absurdist comedy about the contentment of a "Bewickian little pig in the roundest and conceitedest burst of pig-blossom," as Ruskin takes a swipe at the critic Leslie Stephen for having joked in a review of *Fors* that it was better to have a thick skin and a good digestion. It is juxtapositions of scale such as these that make the reader wonder if the whole thing will fall apart, whether Ruskin will actually go mad on the page before us. Mercifully, he breaks off the letter, as if to calm himself, and returns at a later date with a quieter, though still piercing, reading of the signs of the time, in this case, the breakfast tray served to him at the Hotel Meurice in Paris. At first glance, everything appears in order: the linen, china, and silver, the bread and butter, the coffee and milk — "all of the old regime." But then he sees what would have fallen below the notice of most people at the time and surely everyone today: there are no sugar-tongs, the sugar is made of beet root, and worse yet, it is in "methodically similar cakes." To those who know how to read the signs, every detail, no matter how seemingly small or trivial, could have enormous significance: "Because people are now always in a hurry to catch the train, they haven't time to use sugar-tongs, or look for a little piece among differently sized lumps, and therefore they use their fingers." But it is not just the diminished quality of everyday life that Ruskin gleans; the very flourishing of nature is in danger when farmers care more for profit than for taste and beauty. And so the sentence enlarges, indeed reverberates, in visual and moral intensity: "[they] have bad sugar instead of good, and waste the ground that would grow blessed cherry trees, currant bushes, or wheat, in growing a miserable root as a substitute for sugar cane, which God has appointed to grow where cherries and wheat won't, and to give juice which will freeze into sweet snow as pure as hoarfrost."

The image of God's blessed land returns Ruskin to thoughts of St. George's Company and to readers' continual complaints that he has not told them enough of his plan of life. But he insists that he has; that it will be "agricultural life, with as much refinement as I can enforce in it" — one of Ruskin's most concise descriptions of his model community, which, by contrast, would show the bitterness of modern industrial life. On the poorest farm of St. George's Company, Ruskin proclaims, there will be pure, unadulterated sugar or there will be none. From earliest childhood, "decent behaviour at table" will be practiced, among the most essential decencies, "the neat, patient, and scrupulous use of sugar-tongs instead of fingers." And because St. George's Company will exemplify Ruskin's craftsman ideal of joy in labor and self-sufficiency, "the boys of the house shall be challenged to cut, and fit together, the prettiest and handiest" sugar-tongs they can imagine.

Then, in the same pleasant mood, Ruskin moves from the Meurice Hotel and his disquisition on sugar to his study at his childhood home at Herne Hill in London, where the sound of the cuckoo clock striking seven prompts him to confess, in a desultory paragraph, how little he knows of the workings of household machines, which again puts him in mind of St. George's Company, where there will not be "a single thing in the house which the boys don't know how to make, nor a single dish on the table which the girls will not know how to cook." A tone of irritation begins to be felt when Ruskin suddenly chastises readers who have been sending him puzzled letters about the recipe for Yorkshire pie he gave them the year before: "Do not my readers yet at all understand that the whole gist of this book is to make people build their own houses, provide and cook their own dinners, and enjoy both?" And, above all else, that they be "content with them both." The evocation of the joys of the simple life, however, only irritates Ruskin's own raw sorrows, flaring into a warning meant as much for himself as for the reader: "If you are discontented, your life will be poisoned." At which point he again conjures the contented little pig and the comfort he took in seeing him and, his temperature rising, the comfort he took at the thought of Mr. Leslie Stephen who is "wholly content to be Mr. Leslie Stephen." Ruskin, in contrast to all this cheery complacency, declares that he is "miserable" because he is "always wanting to be something else than I am." In an astonishing yet characteristic flight of fancy and self-mockery, he impresses upon the reader the boundlessness of his imagination and power:

> I want to be Turner; I want to be Gainsborough; I want to be Samuel Prout; I want to be Doge of Venice; I want to be Pope; I want to be Lord of the Sun and Moon. The other day, when I read that story in the papers about the dogfight, I wanted to be able to fight a bulldog.

The newspaper story, Ruskin mentions in a footnote, concerns a fight alleged to have taken place between a dwarf and a bulldog, both chained to stakes as in Roman days. He has heard "everybody screaming out how horrible it was," but he wants to know, "What's horrible in it?" Ruskin, of course, grants that "it is in bad taste, and the sign of a declining era of national honour — as all brutal gladiatorial exhibitions are." He is even willing to grant that "there might be something loathsome, or something ominous, in such a story, to the old Greeks of the School of Heracles; who used to fight with the Nemean lion, or with Cerberus, when it was needful only, and not for money." And he will go so far as to acknowledge that "there might be something loathsome in it, or ominous, to an Englishman of the school of Shakespeare or Scott; who would fight with men only, and loved his hound." But the notion that his own brutish contemporaries would have enough shame to find a fight between a dwarf and bulldog loathsome or ominous makes Ruskin boil with indignation, driving him to one of the fiercest satires in all of *Fors*.

> But for you — you carnivorous cheats — what, in dog's or devil's name, is there horrible in it for *you?* Do you suppose it isn't more manly and virtuous to fight a bulldog, than to poison a child, or cheat a fellow who trusts you, or leave a girl to go wild in the streets? And don't you live, and profess to live — and even insolently proclaim there's no other way of living than — by poisoning and cheating? And isn't every woman of fashion's dress, in Europe, now set the pattern to by prostitutes?

In a telling piece of autobiography in the preface to *Sesame and Lilies* (1871 edition), Ruskin confided to his readers that in his "constant natural temper and thoughts of things and people," he had "sympathy" with Marmontel (the great eighteenth-century memoirist of the peaceful, peasant way of life in old France), but that in his "enforced and accidental temper and thoughts of things and people," he was closer to Jonathan Swift. Ruskin's awe and reverence before the glories of Turner and Giotto and Tintoretto and the Rouen Cathedral and the Swiss Alps once inspired the ecstatic word-paintings of his earlier writings, which were in harmony with his "constant natural temper." But in frenzied speeches like the one above, we see the alarming consequences of his "enforced and accidental temper": it plunges him into the center of everything his tender nature and exquisite sensitivity cannot bear. And so Ruskin's indignation at the shamelessness of the modern world elicits in him a kind of equivalent brazenness that threatens to eat him up alive if he cannot give form to it. At moments such as these, when Ruskin just manages to educate his rage through the medium of satire, he is able to preserve his sanity. As for his writing, the power of his earlier stunning word-paintings of the beauty and metaphysical grandeur of art and nature that he was forced to abandon because of his anguished conscience, is transmuted into equally stunning prose-pictures, but now of the ugliness and moral terror of modern life.

Ruskin, however, is not yet through with the popular uproar over the dogfight, demanding, for a third time, "What's horrible in it?" To which he answers, "I hate, myself, seeing a bulldog ill-treated, for they are the kindest and faithfullest of living creatures if you use them well." And so Ruskin shifts perspective, mercifully leaving behind his inflamed vision of modern perversities for an unexpectedly delightful moment of calm — a picture of the happy life seen through the eyes of his own bulldog: "If he found he could please me by holding on with his teeth to an inch-thick stick, and being swung round in the air as fast as I could turn, that was his own idea of entirely felicitous existence." But this disarmingly personal and tender reminiscence of his own dog only serves to remind him of a recent event that was even "more horrible, in the deep elements of it" than the dogfight. A young friend, the son of an English clergyman, who had come to visit Ruskin at his country home in Brantwood, enthusiastically told him of having watched his coachman throw a stone at a big squirrel, nearly hitting it. The typical, glib response to such childish antics, "thoughtlessness — only thoughtlessness," presses Ruskin to reflect,

Well, perhaps not much worse than that. But how *could* it be much worse? Thoughtlessness is precisely the chief public calamity of our day; and when it comes to the pitch, in a clergyman's child, of not thinking that a stone hurts what it hits of living things, and not caring for the daintiest, dextrousest, innocentest living thing in the northern forests of God's earth, except as a brown excrescence to be knocked off their branches, — nay, good pastor of Christ's lambs, believe me, your boy had better have been employed in thoughtfully and resolutely stoning St. Stephen — if any St. Stephen is to be found in these days, when men not only can't see heaven opened, but don't so much as care to see it, shut.

Here Ruskin was alluding to Saint Stephen's vision of the heavens opening up, revealing Christ at God's right hand, at the very moment he was stoned to death for calling people back to righteousness. The reason it would be better if his young friend were among their company, Ruskin explains with bitter irony, is that "they, at least, meant neither to give pain nor death without cause," for the hardhearted mob held Saint Stephen guilty of blasphemy, a crime punishable by death. And so what begins as sheer vacancy of thought in a boy — the stoning of a guiltless squirrel — can ultimately give rise to what Ruskin describes elsewhere as "a dreadful callousness, which, in extremity, becomes capable of every sort of bestial habit and crime, without fear, without pleasure, without horror, without pity." The stoning of a saint is the final fulfillment of this dreadful callousness, but so, too, as Ruskin makes apparent in all his writing, is the poisoning of the earth's soil, streams, and skies through carelessness or commercial exploitation; the ruin of the world's art treasures through neglect or aggressive restoration; the degradation of men's spirit through the division of labor; the devastation of lives and cities through ceaseless wars. And so a recently built warship aptly named *Devastation* serves as the occasion for the concluding section of Ruskin's Christmas letter — a sermon on the need to gird oneself not with the armory of war, but with the armory of truth, justice, peace, and faith.

In this breath-taking installment of *Fors Clavigera*, the reader is made to feel the force of Ruskin's dizzying vision, which, because it strains to make visible so many hideous, indeed, deranging, dimensions of modern life previously indistinct to the ordinary eye, threatens to dissolve into anarchy, yet always manages, at precisely that treacherous instant, to fall back into an unexpected order —

an order ruled not only by Ruskin's idiosyncratic train of thought (what would later become, in modernist fiction, stream of consciousness), but even more frequently by a habit of mind engrained in him in earliest childhood by daily reading of the Bible, where seemingly trivial events foreshadow future ones of enormous significance. Thus the reader is forced to experience the full measure of Ruskin's insight and anguish — the one relentlessly following upon the other — and like Ruskin himself, is constantly on the verge of being overwhelmed.

With every successive monthly installment of *Fors,* Ruskin's sense of the desperateness of his mission of purifying the world intensifies, and with it, the calamity of his isolation. Nowhere is this more apparent than in Letter 58, "The Catholic Prayer" (October 1875), in which Ruskin sets out the governance of St. George's Company. Explaining why he alone is entitled to be its single master, Ruskin mercilessly turns himself inside out, making us feel not only his shame at having been forced to go against his gentle nature and assume the role of angry prophet, but also the solitude that comes from seeing deeper than anyone else and that was now so extreme as to be unendurable:

> And what am I, myself then, infirm and old, who take, or claim, leadership even of these lords? God forbid that I should claim it; it is thrust and compelled on me — utterly against my will, utterly to my distress, utterly, in many things, to my shame. But I have found no other man in England, none in Europe, ready to receive it, — or even desiring to make himself capable of receiving it. Such as I am, to my own amazement, I stand — so far as I can discern — alone in conviction, in hope, and in resolution, in the wilderness of this modern world. Bred in luxury, which I perceive to be unjust to others, and destructive to myself; vacillating, foolish, and miserably failing in all my own conduct in life — and blown about hopelessly by storms of passion — I, a man clothed in soft raiment — I, a reed shaken with the wind, have yet this Message to all men again entrusted to me. "Behold, the axe is laid to the root of the trees. Whatsoever tree bringeth not forth good fruit, shall be hewn down and cast into the fire." (The quoted words are the warning of John, the Baptist, of the need for immediate repentance [Matthew 3: 10].)

Ruskin also had good reasons of a more personal nature for these feelings of desolation. Only a few months before, the young woman he hoped to marry, Rose LaTouche, had died, bringing to

sad conclusion a story of unrequited, or imperfectly requited, love
that for years had kept him in a state of emotional agitation. Ruskin
had been the girl's drawing teacher when she was nine years old
and he thirty-nine, and when she turned sixteen, he proposed marriage to her. Her parents, pious evangelicals who were disturbed by
Ruskin's falling away from the faith, disapproved and Rose's own
religious fervor put distance between them. With so many obsta-
cles, Rose asked Ruskin to wait for her answer until she was older.
Six years later, as Ruskin anxiously watched her become increasingly deranged by religious mania, she finally refused him. Then,
after Ruskin endured another excruciating three-year period of
alternate hopefulness and disappointment, Rose, only twenty-
seven years old, died insane — a shock from which Ruskin never
properly recovered. This troubled young woman is a constant, if
oblique, presence in *Fors,* and her illness is mentioned in passing,
but the depth of the anguish she caused Ruskin would not be publicly known until he spoke directly of her in his beautiful memoir,
Praeterita; and then after his death in 1900, with the first wave of bi-
ographies and publications of his letters, more of the unhappy
story was given to the public.

Shattered by the death of the young woman he had loved for so
long, Ruskin could deliver only one series of lectures at Oxford
that year and was excused from his duties for two years. Somehow
he managed to travel and to work, publishing a guide, *Mornings in
Florence* (1875–1877), and a new history of Venice, *St. Mark's Rest*
(1877–1884), along with the first parts of a number of charming,
deeply humanized studies (never to be completed) of birds, *Love's
Meinie* (1873–1881), flowers, *Proserpina* (1875–1886), and minerals, *Deucalion* (1875–1883), all the while pouring out his indignation at the world and his personal sorrow in monthly installments
of *Fors.* All his life Ruskin had been saved by what Victorians called
the "gospel of labor" and during this dark period, he labored incessantly. "I'm perfectly overwhelmed," he wrote a friend in the autumn of 1877, "under the quantity of things which must be kept in
mind, now, going like a juggler's balls in the air — a touch first
to one, then another." At the beginning of 1878, he began yet
another project — a catalog for an exhibition of his Turner drawings to be held at the Fine Art Society in London early in March.
Ruskin's first book, *Modern Painters,* began as a vindication of

Turner's late work, which, at the time, had been thoughtlessly dismissed by critics, and Turner remained Ruskin's lifelong passion. According to Ruskin's disciple, friend, and biographer E. T. Cook, Turner's work was "to him a microcosm; it represented to his imagination all the beauty, all the sadness, all the mystery and the suffering of the world." The strain was finally too much. After a month of feverish work and feverish dreams, Ruskin collapsed into a state of delirium that terrified all those around him.

During the month of the Turner exhibition, bulletins from Brantwood announcing Ruskin's condition were released daily and read by visitors to the gallery. These same bulletins were reported by newspapers as far away as western towns in America. In Italy, prayers were said for his recovery. After two months of care by anxious family and friends at Brantwood, Ruskin seemingly returned to himself. Early in 1879, he resigned from Oxford, giving the Whistler decision as the reason. (In *Fors* no. 79, Ruskin contemptuously dismissed Whistler's paintings in half a paragraph; Whistler famously brought a libel suit against him, and in November 1878, won, only to recover a single farthing in damages.) But the real reason for Ruskin's resignation was his weakened state.

Throughout his life — whether writing on art, architecture, nature, political economy, morals, religion, education, society, everyday life — Ruskin had become used to hearing his highly unorthodox, frequently shocking, views dismissed as mad. But now that he had actually been overcome by a fit of madness, this familiar rebuke acquired new sting. So, when he found the strength to take up *Fors* two years later, the first thing he spoke of was his illness (Letter 88, "The Convents of St. Quentin," February 1880). Ruskin desperately wanted his readers to know that there was a difference between madness and inspiration, even if it was so subtle that his physicians and most other people failed to perceive it. And so he was at great pains to distinguish between "a state of morbid inflammation of brain," which, during his illness, gave rise to "false visions (whether in sleep, or trance, or waking, in broad daylight, with perfect knowledge of the real things in the room, while yet I saw others that were not there)" on the one hand, and on the other, "the not morbid, however dangerous, states of more or less excited temper, and too much quickened thought, which gradually led up to the illness." This second state, Ruskin insists, was "entirely healthy . . . just as the natural inflammation about a healing wound in flesh is sane, up to the transitional edge where it may pass at a crisis into morbific [sic], or even mortified, substance." Indeed, before it reached that crisis point, Ruskin believed this mental power — call it insight or genius (though he did not name it) — actually intensified his vision. He thought it could be traced in *Fors,* almost from the beginning — "that manner of mental ignition or irritation being . . . a great additional force, enabling me to discern more clearly, and say more vividly, what for long years it had been in my heart to say."

For Ruskin, then, madness and insight were kindred experiences, alike in intensity but different in kind. Both mental states dramatically heightened the senses, but where madness gave rise to feverish hallucinations, insight (or genius) gave rise to visions, as true as they were sane. But Ruskin could not let the matter rest there; he also insisted on pondering the more personal side of madness, speaking frankly of his own "wounded nature." His doctors, he complained, saw in his collapse only morbid brain inflammation and thus lost hope of his recovery, but he knew that its source lay also in his "mental wounds," which, given enough time, could be healed. Ruskin regretted that the doctors' one-sided explanation caused his friends unnecessary anxiety and pain, but he regretted even more, his old tone of gentle irony reappearing, that "it makes them more doubtful than they used to be (which, for some is saying a good deal) of the 'truth and soberness' of itself." (The quoted words allude to Paul's defense of himself against the charge of madness [Acts 26: 25].)

To silence his doubters, Ruskin launched into a passionate declaration of the "one consistent purpose" of *Fors,* culminating with a sincere avowal of a creed devastating in its simplicity: "Whether there be one God or three, — no God, or ten thousand, — children should have enough to eat and their skins should be washed clean." To which he immediately adds, "It is not *I* who say that. Every mother's heart under the sun says that, if she has one." In another paragraph in the same vein, he again insists that it is not he who is speaking, thereby repudiating the popular Victorian figure of the eccentric, romantic genius — be it inspired seer or raving lunatic — and puts in its place an unimpeachable, ideal medium through which universal experience speaks: "Whatever is dictated in *Fors* is dictated thus by common sense, common equity, common humanity, and common sunshine — not by me."

But Ruskin's ruthless candor about himself was such that he could not resist touching upon one last element of *Fors,* the one that had most puzzled his readers and most troubled those closest to him — what he calls its "trivial and desultory talk by the way." He acknowledges that there is "much casual expression of my own personal feelings and faith, together with bits of autobiography," and that he allowed such things because he thought they might be "useful," but he also admits that he had been "imprudent," "even incontinent," for the simple reason that "I could not at the moment hold my tongue about what vexed or interested me, or returned soothingly to my memory." So Ruskin cautions his readers to "carefully sift" the "personal fragments" from the rest of the book, and then, with excruciating detail, provides some extremely obscure keys to some extremely idiosyncratic, personal references in *Fors* — an exercise that, unfortunately, was just as likely to convince skeptics, and even friends, that he was still in the throes of madness. By the end of this exposition, even Ruskin seems exasperated, but recovers himself enough to conclude, with his old prophetic sharpness, that if his "scientific friends . . . can see nothing in Heaven above the chimney tops, nor conceive of anything in spirit greater than themselves, it is not because they have more knowledge than I, but because they have less sense." To which he adds, most emphatically, "Less *common* sense, — observe: less practical insight into the things which are of instant and constant need to man."

Here Ruskin was trying to refute the familiar charge against his many reform projects, especially St. George's Company, that they were impractical, utopian. No judgment stung him more deeply, since his most fervent desire to regain a life of beauty without guilt, depended, above all else, on the efficacy of his projects — that his efforts actually succeeded in diminishing the misery and ugliness all around him. Yet, no matter how much he might protest to the contrary, Ruskin could not, in good conscience, still the sound of this devastating reproach in his own ears. Thus in one of the most stunning moments of all of *Fors,* he confesses the true cause of his madness: "I went mad because nothing came of my work. . . . Nobody believed a word of them." Ruskin further confided that the futility of his work brought him "humiliation," which could only be "resisted by a dangerous and lonely pride." Ruskin's pride ultimately blinded him to the obdurate nature of evil and made him overreach; yet, the fact that Ruskin's passion for justice finally plunged him into the abyss of madness is an indictment of the modern world even more damning than any that ever flowed from his pen, for it makes apparent that a man of Ruskin's sensitivity simply could not live in the modern age.

No matter how useless Ruskin thought his writing, the gospel of labor did save him a little longer, for he managed, under increasingly trying circumstances, to keep working. He revised, rearranged, and reissued the earlier books that had made his name; published pamphlets and lectures on art, architecture, fiction, and natural history; traveled, after another attack of brain fever in 1882, to work at French churches and again in the Alps; resumed the Slade professorship at Oxford; and intermittently brought out *Fors Clavigera* until 1884, when at last he abandoned that intensely personal communication that for so long had allowed him to pour out his thoughts and feelings on every conceivable subject. And in abandoning *Fors,* he also finally let go of his self-torturing dream of changing the world. Not that conditions had improved. Indeed, Ruskin, who for more than fifty years had recorded sunsets and storms in his diaries and had drawn and painted these phenomena in loving detail, was becoming increasingly aware of disturbances in the climate itself — "plague clouds," "strange, bitter, blighting winds," a sun that was "blanched" rather than "reddened."

The same year that he was struggling to publish the final installments of *Fors,* he gave one of his last public lectures to a London audience about this impending man-made apocalypse, "The Storm-Cloud of the Nineteenth Century" (1884). If the storm cloud was not a judgment from heaven, Ruskin warned, it was a fearful sign, at least for "the men of old time," of the corruption of a nation that had "blasphemed the name of God deliberately and openly; and had done iniquity by proclamation, every man doing as much injustice to his brother as it was in his power to do." In a footnote, Ruskin defined blasphemy as "'harmful speaking' — not against God only, but against man, and against all the good works and purposes of Nature." He also pointed out that "the universal instinct of blasphemy in the modern scientific mind" was manifested in "its love of what is ugly, and natural enthrallment by the abominable." At the same time, Ruskin was fighting another battle against modern science at Oxford — the establishment of a physiological laboratory that would practice vivisection. "To endow vivisection," according to Ruskin's apostle, friend, and first biographer, W. G. Collingwood, "to him meant not only cruelty to animals, but a complete misunderstanding of the purpose of science, and defiance of the moral law." Ruskin resigned from Oxford a second and final time when the laboratory was approved. His sense of futility was complete. He felt, in Collingwood's words, "that all his work had been in vain, that he was completely out of touch with the age, and that he had best give up the unequal fight."

And so Ruskin returned to his home at Brantwood to live out the time remaining to him in peaceful retirement. His powers were beginning to wane, yet he found the strength to resume, at last without guilt, his proper life of beauty when, in fleeting lucid intervals, he composed *Praeterita* (1885–1889), his hauntingly beautiful, unfinished memoir. "The Storm-Cloud" and *Praeterita,* both in their different ways, were dedicated to capturing the past that was on the verge of being lost forever not only because Europe's accumulated art treasures — the very things he had devoted so much of his life to glorifying and preserving — were going to ruin either through commercial rapaciousness or insensitive restoration; not only because the azure skies, clear streams, and majestic mountain ranges — the natural paradise of Ruskin's youth and the source of inspiration of the greatest artists — were being poisoned by modern industry; and not only because the sweet, pure way of life embodied in farming and handicrafts — which Ruskin tried to sustain through St. George's Company — was being made extinct by the factory system; but also because the memory of all that was noble in the nineteenth century was also falling into ruin as Ruskin suffered repeated lapses into madness. By the final decade of his life, Ruskin was at last widely revered as "the prophet of Brantwood," but the tender spirit who had sacrificed his love of beauty, his personal fortune, his time, and finally his health, trying to awaken people's consciences was so tragically broken that he would live that final decade in virtual silence.

It has been a long time since anyone went mad because the evils of the world were too much with him. Today, social critics are more likely to end up as successful professors or celebrity pundits than as shattered souls. Even poets and artists rarely lose their minds these days and if they do, it is more likely to be thought the result of personal demons that can be managed by medication than the result of the misery and ugliness of the world that cannot be repaired by any single individual. To speak this way, of course, is to open oneself to the charge of romanticism, as if there were something inherently ridiculous in the idea that a sensitive soul could be driven mad by the modern world or that a social critic might actually be a visionary. Without the example, experience, memory, or hope of another, better world, it is no wonder that people's imaginations and sympathies have so shriveled that they see romanticism where they ought to see possibility. Such cynicism is as much a consequence of the dramatic collapse of communism as it is of the bloating of the ineffectual welfare state, but it also has deeper roots in the terrible fact that grand political doctrines, in perverted form, gave rise to the modern murderous regimes of imperialism, fascism, and totalitarianism.

Yet, without grand ideas — the only contemporary exception being religious fundamentalisms — we are left on the one hand with Bush's hollow American triumphalism and on the other with tired resignation. Given the poverty of these alternatives, it is worth asking whether we can continue to do without visionaries and, more to the point, whether, after so many years of political "realism," we in the West would even recognize a visionary if a figure like Ruskin or Carlyle or our own Emerson or King should appear in our company. Frederic Harrison, the great popularizer of Comte who was also Ruskin's friend and biographer, spoke for Ruskin's admirers when he wrote to Ruskin in 1876 that he had a faculty of "seeing what we, the rest, are blind to." This faculty Harrison called "genius" and he believed it allowed Ruskin to "teach rightly — above other men in our age, the life, the tenderness, the truth of art, the loveliness of what we see around us, or might see, the faculty of insight of the great poets, and much as to the vileness of modern plutonomy and industry, and the dignity and beauty of true work." Students who had heard Ruskin's lectures at Oxford spoke of him in more reverential tones. One recalled being "overwhelmed with the thrilling consciousness of being in the immediate presence, and listening to the spontaneous exercise of creative genius" and another recalled being "overwhelmed with solemn awe." He reported that when Ruskin concluded his lectures, the audience sat "absolutely silent. We no more thought of the usual thunder of applause than we should have thought of clapping an angel's song that makes the heavens be mute."

Such appreciations could easily be multiplied, but what is important is that Ruskin was revered, above all, for his visionary powers. Yet, it is just Ruskin's revelatory mode of expression — whether in the stinging idiom of satire or the plain style and simple moral language of the sermon — that has disappeared from public discourse today. The best of our social critics speak the language of reason founded in sober recitations of facts — there are more young black men in prison than in college; more money is spent on building prisons than on building low-cost housing; the top 1 percent of Americans control 38 percent of the nation's wealth, while the bottom 80 percent have amassed only a paltry 17 percent — but so far at least, the dry facts, dreadful as they are, have apparently awakened few consciences. In contrast, Ruskin's hellish vision of the "yelping, carnivorous crowd, mad for money and lust, tearing each other to pieces, and starving each other to death," like his sincere avowal of the primitive Christian creed, "children should have enough to eat and their skins should be washed clean," makes us feel viscerally how the world appears from the standpoint of common decency. Unfortunately, in our tone-deaf, pseudosensitive times, ridiculing the "yelping, carnivorous crowd" is more likely to be regarded as feeling superior to such people, as "elitism," than as the necessary unmasking of the society that has turned individuals into a thoughtless, bestial crowd. Satire, by caustic exaggerations such as these, attempts to shame people into recognizing that there is something better than what merely happens to exist, just as Ruskin's declarations of simple truths dictated by "common sense, common equity, common humanity, and common sunshine" accomplish the same thing. Their absence in our public discourse is a sign of the terrible impoverishment not only of our moral and political imaginations, but also of our capacity for shame.

Ruskin was one of our last visionary social critics and even though he believed that no one listened to him and went mad for the futility of his life, he was wrong; his extraordinary word-pictures did touch the lives of many people. *Modern Painters, The Seven Lamps of Architecture,* and *The Stones of Venice* did nothing less than shape a new aesthetic sensibility. For the first time ever, early Italian "primitives," Gothic architecture, and mountain vistas were held to be proper objects of aesthetic contemplation. Leslie Stephen spoke for his generation when he told of the power of *Modern Painters:* "People who shared the indifference to art of those dark ages (I can answer for one) were suddenly fascinated, and found to their amazement that they knew a book about pictures almost by heart." After Ruskin, Stephen declared, "a comfortable indifference to artistic matters, instead of being normal and respectable, [was] pitiable and almost criminal." Ruskin's beautiful descriptions of Gothic cathedrals inspired William Morris (who revered Ruskin as his "master") to found the Society for the Preservation of Ancient Buildings in order to stop their further destruction by restorers. Ruskin Societies, dedicated to the study of his work, flourished in Britain and in America throughout the early twentieth century, and his writings became the foundation for arts and crafts movements as well as for modernist design and architecture. What is more, Ruskin's exquisite, serpentine sentences deeply touched Marcel Proust, who not only translated a number of his books, but knew extended passages by heart.

His cries in the wilderness of modernity also did not go unheard. Tolstoy wrote, "He was one of those rare men, who think with their hearts, and so he thought and said not only what he himself had seen and felt, but what everyone will think and say in the future." After his death, Ruskin's blistering attacks on laissez-faire economics were adopted by the Left (an ironic outcome, since Ruskin called himself "a violent Tory of the old school — Walter Scott's school . . . and Homer's"). George Bernard Shaw was a disciple, and a survey of the first Parliament in which the British Labor Party gained seats showed that Ruskin's *Unto This Last* had a greater influence on them than *Das Kapital. Unto This Last* also "marked the turning point" in the life of Mahatma Gandhi. He translated it in 1908 and declared that "it captured me and made me transform my life." Gandhi discovered some of his "deepest convictions in this great book of Ruskin's" not least because of its aesthetic resonance. "A poet," he affirmed, "is one who can call forth the good latent in the human breast."

SAM HAMILL

Arguing with Milosz in Vilnius

FROM *Ploughshares*

You are recently dead, old man,
    with your thunderous brows
and voice like a vast sea
    hinting at a dangerous undertow —
you are gone, your generation
    of testimony, of witness,
gone, gone among the ancient rites
    of passage, gone,
taking with you the innumerable
    names of the lost.

And yet I am here, walking
    the broad, freshly bricked avenue
of a democratic Vilnius,
    the Mother Sun
pouring amber on a world
    you would barely recognize,
where women are the ones
    dressed to kill, and the world
does what it will to be reborn.
    The poet is reborn
on each new old street,
    born in the process of the song.
You gave me Anna Swir.

Do you remember how we argued
    in Berkeley

when you told me, "I dislike nature,"
    and said it again
in comments on your beloved Jeffers —
    "a huge museum of inherited images" —
and how could I not remember that
    as I rode in a van to Druskininkai?
How I loved the slender birches
    among the red pine,
the forest floor a bed of moss
    and a hundred kinds of mushrooms.
Bury a trout in mushrooms,
    cream and wine,
and bake it, and hear me sigh.

And you were with me again
    in "Scoundrel Square"
(I renamed it) where the sculptures
    of the Soviet regime
provide inherited imagery
    of another kind, museum
of our agonies and tragedies where
    I knew once again
that your world
    could not be mine —
and yet I am here, the bland faces
    and stern faces — Russian, Lithuanian —
of ordinary men who sold
    their countrymen for a song
are carved into my mind.

Tyranny is so banal.
    Jackdaws clack and squabble.
Sparrows flock to the square.
    Lenin Boulevard is gone.
I cross the square at the cathedral
    and turn up a narrow cobbled street,
Old Town, tiled roofs
    and freshly painted shutters,
where a hundred vendors will,
    in an hour or so,

present their wares to tourists.
   Four hundred thousand people
disappeared. Each had a name,
   a life filled with passion
and despair and all those
   ordinary irritations
too small and too many
   to enumerate —
It's more than one mind's heart can bear.

And yet the same brown river flows
   quietly between the same banks
as it did a thousand years ago.
   Here, it turns north.
Where is Bakszta Street? Where
   is Antokol? I sat
in the courtyard of the old monastery
   you so long ago admired,
the bench a little askew, grass overgrown,
   but a sanctuary from
the relentless noise of the city,
   as my friend Mindaugas explained
how you sought refuge here
   long before the war.
Was there a certain guilt
   from having merely survived?
Is it criminal to be lucky?

You were right, of course.
   "The struggle for poetry in the world
cannot take place in a museum."
   And the fact that you reject,
out of hand, my "eastern wisdom"
   also does not offend.
As little as I knew you, I knew
   you well enough to learn.
Our friend Rexroth introduced us
   on the streets of that great city
you came to call "nearly a home."
   You were a totem, an icon, a teacher.

Nevertheless, I say the world's a museum,
   the poem a record of survival
and betrayal, of human longing —
   vision and commitment —
and if I smell the bear or the wolf
   that once haunted the woods near here,
I say the wolf is alive
   in the eyes of men, alive
in the hearts of all who survive.

You were a great exile of the war;
   I was merely an orphan.
You were a child of Vilnius,
   of Europe; I was a child
of the wilderness of the west
   and know the track of the wolf,
the terrible odor of bear. Nevertheless,
   you civilized me some.
You were a great modernist,
   full of conviction,
sometimes a little short on patience.
   I could not fully grasp your history
or your god. And yet I am here.
   Vive la difference!
I bow to your presence
   as I stand among the ancients.

JESSIE HARRIMAN

This Soul Has Six Wings

FROM *Portland*

THE WAY I SEE IT, a mystic takes a peek at God and then does her best to show the rest of us what she saw. She'll use image-language, not discourse. Giving an image is the giving of gold, the biggest thing she's got. Mysticism suggests direct union, divine revelation, taking a stab at the Unknown with images, cryptic or plain, sensible or sensory. A mystic casts out for an image in whatever is at her disposal and within reach, like a practiced cook who can concoct a stew from the remaining carrots and a bruised potato, or like a musician improvising with buckets and wooden spoons. She does not circumvent; she hammers a line drive. A mystic is a kid finding kingdom in ash heap.

The thirteenth-century Beguine mystics were women with their eyelids licked open by God, like those of monkey-faced puppies. These women seemed slipped into history, or in between histories. Though their only options were marriage or the cloister, they carved out a new option by forming quirky spiritual communities, out from under the rule of men or monastic structure. They spanned about a hundred years and covered some ground circulating a few manuscripts before they were married off or shuffled into approved orders. The lay women's movement spread like a brushfire over northern Europe. Women grouped into Beguinages, small cities within cities. Some of the larger ones, like the Beguinage of Ghent hosting a thousand women, had a church, cemetery, hospital, streets. They cropped up on the outskirts of cities in the Netherlands, Belgium, Germany. The women took no conventional vows. They were free to leave the community to marry; some brought along their children. They retained private property; they didn't beg; they did manual work for pay. They had no founder, no common rule that dictated community life. And no signing or changing your name.

Wars of the thirteenth century left a surplus of solitary women, and they also made way for a pop religion upsurge: meetings dotted the hillsides like Baptist tent revivals. Women made up the majority of the penitent, and many sought a full-time religious life, flocking to the doors of Cistercian Orders, but denied access. This huge batch of proselytes was sniffing out a Way beyond a doctrine. In 1175 Lambert le Bègue, a sympathetic priest of Liège in Belgium, encouraged a group of lay women to form an independent religious community. Their main tenets were voluntary poverty and freedom. They held fast to the Eucharist and the humanity of Jesus; they were chaste and charitable and unpopular with most parish priests. They came to be known as the Beguines.

The surviving texts of the Beguine mystics deliver image-language in the form of allegory and dialogue and lyric. A Beguine named Margaret Porette wrote the controversial text *The Mirror of Simple Souls* in the French vernacular, personifying Love, the Soul, and Reason. She claimed that a human soul can be joined at the hip with God through love: This Soul, says Love, has six wings, just as the Seraphim. She no longer wishes for anything which comes by an intermediary, for that is the proper state of being of the Seraphim; there is no intermediary between their love and God's love. She taught the soul's annihilation: that the soul, in Holy Church the Greater, might have no will of her own, that it serve only as a mirror for God's image and will. Porette's book was burned publicly by the Bishop of Cambrai, but she made no concessions. In fact, she added seventeen more chapters, moved her allegory forward, spruced up her characters. She was burned at the stake in 1310.

Another main text came out of Germany: *Flowing Light of the Godhead,* by Mechthild of Magdeburg. Her first manuscript is in the low-German dialect and draws on images from courtly love, a secular tradition. Mechthild admits: I do not know how to write nor can I, unless I see with the eyes of my soul and hear with the ears of my eternal spirit and feel in all the parts of my body the power of the Holy Spirit. And, to convey the Spirit, she uses what's available, what she sees out her window, touches to her lips, knows in her body.

A mystic is unapologetic for a lack of theological education, a scholar's explanations. (Porette: You must let Love and Faith together be your guides to climb where Reason cannot come.) The Beguines' writings play out scenes in common tropes of spiritual literature: a bride, a desert, a bed of pain. These images trigger something in me. What if I cast about for my own, for things that have caught my attention the way a fence barb does a loose shirt? What if that's all you have? Just the images? Perhaps images leave room or make room for mystery. Image as a felt truth for the weak who need more than doctrine. You struggle for an image; it wriggles into life and is born.

Is there a place for the contemporary mystic? Can someone try again to crawl into the big shell of mystical tradition and holler and hear her small voice echo back? Can she reclaim it in some way?

The way I see it, a mystic simply believes that God visits.

A mystic stays with what's striking: out the windshield, in between the intermittent wipers, a shadow, a flash of light, color, a face. She sees something, she sees and then she runs to show and tell, or at least she practices speeches in her head. She mulls over her images, arranges her sermon in a picture book — it's like a touch-and-feel kids book, furry cloth for monkey feet, a bit of rubber ball for bear nose. She wants her images vivid.

The Beguines had two main takes on the image of the desert. Some references pointed to the wilderness where the Old Testament children of Israel wandered for forty years, in exile, in desperation, trying to make it to the Promised Land of Milk and Honey. Life is exile, according to these writings, life is the trial to be endured, the soul's desolate journey home to God. The other manifestation of the desert image is an encounter: the desert isn't the thing to be endured for the goal; it is the goal; it is the landscape of union. It is, from the Book of Hosea, the place where God will allure her, bring her into the wilderness, and speak comfort to her. It's where you learn how to love.

*

A burned-down trailer is a desert of ash, silt, secrets. It is exposure, down to the ground, to wind to sun to rain. Brought to nothing. A melted photograph here, a charred unfastened locket there. A blackened mirror.

A fencerow, attended by walnut and hickory trees and under-brush, separated my house from Christy Gribbles's trailer. Before the trailer burned, Christy and I made a break in the fence so she could come to my side and I could go to hers.

A grease fire on the stove started the fire. It was in late fall. My brother Luke and I were just returning from a walk. We'd seen a deer close-up, licking water from the streambed. We had been si-lent with it and after it quenched its thirst, it picked its way through the underbrush into the cloak of the pines. We were heading back when we saw the huge piles of black smoke stacking on top of the bare trees. The trailer seemed to burn clear to the ground in minutes. Nobody was caught inside, and they even got some of the clothes out. But Christy and her younger brother G.W. were standing outside, close to the fence, with smoky blank faces. They seemed exposed there to the wind and the bits of ash flaking down like dirty snow. From my front porch, I stood watching her home become nothing.

What happens, Christy, when you lose everything? I picture that charred trailer-desert in my head now, remembering how they stayed for a time up at Nolan Wilson's old place and how we gave bags of clothes and a Glow Worm that lit up when you pressed him, trying to fill their new Nothing. In the beginning, there was a home with rooms and maybe not plenty but at least something, and then there was wasteland, No-place, No-home.

What happens when you lose everything? When you slip out, down the chainlink fire escape ladder and leave all evidence of self behind in the rubbish? I think sometimes: I could throw my day, my lifework out a window. And try to learn emptiness, a trailer-desert, a sigh in the soul.

Why speak in images? In trailer fire? What's the point when they leave you winded? Well, you don't know what else to say or how else to say it, like holding the hand of someone who's lost everything. It is an inexplicable being-with, a fleshing, a new Way.

Is a mystic anyone who realizes a truth and flashes it like a strong poker hand? She is the checkout lady at the Dollar General, talking on the phone to her husband who's trying to get the title for the truck but can't, and she has to go, there are customers. And she realizes and she says, This is all too much. On her face you see clearly where her weeping goes. You remember exactly what she looks like.

A neighbor calls in early evening about the double rainbow in the sky. Another and another calls, Judy, my aunt Kathy from town. From the porch, we can see the full arc of one, the marvelous ghost of the other. We have not lost this need to tell, to show, to point.

Sometimes you see nothing in the sky, no promises or mark of Jesus's feet, no sign that he's coming back to bring you home — so you write down the Nothing and the No-place, too.

Beguines weren't recluses. Uncloistered, they grouped their small cabins together into their Beguinages on the outskirts of cities where they worked making lace or gardens, teaching or nursing, managing shelters for urban women and kids who worked in textiles. Their cabins made a half-circle; one could see the other's light from her stoop, could string together two tin cans, window to window. Out from this half-circle shelter, Beguine mystics attracted the urban faithful, with their penchant for heresy and the use of the vernacular, the tongue of fire making sense. They gathered in the exiled and wandering. They had a context for dealing with suffering.

I gather with a group of women in Philadelphia, all of us assembling around Jesus, perked for evangel like girls hovering around a radio. But as you hover in a circle, you brush arms with each other. Liz Lopez was a woman among us whose husband was incarcerated, and she had three boys and a tiny frame; she looked like she could blow away. And still, she beautifully braced herself under her heavy beam of a dadless series of days that bore down with the weight of her boys' birthdays, street hockey games, piss-the-bed nights. Nobody skirted around her; we entered in as best we could, catching her insides as she spilled out, ready, at any moment, to spill ourselves.

We met in Susan's house in Hunting Park. We ate and then sang a few choruses and discussed sermons. One night the sermon was on James's epistle in the New Testament: Count it all joy, he says, when you fall into various trials, knowing that the testing of your faith produces patience. We cried onto our plates of Spanish rice and chicken that Blanca had brought, because the trials were various: Wendy's husband left her and the kids, another husband had cancer, Celeste and her girls lost their row house.

Often a woman takes tentative steps toward another, shy about the magnetic pull of this other's wounds. A raw, undisguised wound pulls you out of your own general okayness: your safe bed, your comfort. There is something about her uncontained and spilling-out life, a doll losing its fiber-fill, the dazed hungry look of one knocked off course. You want to zip up the back of her dresses, paint your lips with Bonnie Bell Cranberry or Smolder, and borrow her wakefulness that came the moment she was left. You feel that you've been drawn away from your life till you missed it with a fresh homesickness, so you can see it and take off its walls and shiver, alive again, as though you've taken a dip in icy cold water.

But is it a longing for laceration? That extreme mystical asceticism or mortification of flesh and the wakefulness it affords? Or is it maudlin, sentimental, like a rhyming couplet in a sympathy card?

I don't think so. I don't think that's what it was for most of the Beguines. It's just the fact of suffering, the dealing with it, making meaning out of it, and if there is no meaning, just to share it.

Here's my image: a gathering on a porch stoop, maybe some of the women smoking, maybe some just watching the door to the neighboring convenience store, but a group surely bound to each other. The image goes as follows: a girl alone, hugging her knees on the stoop — she's missed a period, or she's lost her baby, or her husband's left, or she simply couldn't get out of bed till two in the afternoon — the fire hydrant shooting out streams in the July heat and kids galloping this way and that, and she suffers, and the others come around, from other porches. They bring Spanish rice and chicken, boiled milk for coffee. And the gathered women stay there, through the early fall, into November. They are entering winter together out there, pointing, Look: how gentle the snow.

I wonder if mystical life is really about visions, or if it's about looking again at the pieces you've already got: of a rocky marriage, a job at Dollar General, a double rainbow. And if you see the kingdom of God there if you stare long enough. I wonder if it's about holding yourself still as a mirror. Or just about making a big old scene, waving your arms wildly.

What's dangerous about a mystic?

Held suspect from the beginning for their disregard for ecclesiastical hierarchy, the unschooled Beguines fell out of favor with the clerics. The women fueled the Church's disapproval by reading biblical texts to everyday folks in their native tongue. In 1274 the Council of Lyons banned any new spiritual orders from forming; new groups had to operate within an existing, approved order. There were rumors of prostitution, sexual license. The Inquisition wasn't kind. In 1312 the Council of Vienne officially declared the Beguines heretical, accusing them of association with antinomian adherents of the Free Spirit. Their property was confiscated; many women had to marry. Many were forced to sign up with a convent.

But what's dangerous about a mystic? Hurling and wielding the best stuff she can imagine, insisting on an unmediated Way of Wakefulness. A mild heretic with dyed pink hair and a threadbare T-shirt with the slogan *Take me seriously.*

Today I don't suppose she fears the Inquisition and its fire — just dullness, just missing it. She fears dismissal. She wrestles, she squints the eyes of her soul. Perhaps she doesn't ditch tradition as much as take it for its word and peer inside its cavernous shell. There must still be something worth saying, worth pointing to.

EDWARD HOAGLAND

The Glue Is Gone

FROM *The American Scholar*

THERE'S A FLUTTER TO SOCIETY NOW, a tremulousness: young people studying yoga therapy after college instead of essaying graduate school, and their parents taking cooking very seriously, with Hummers in the suburbs but debt a major household topic, and several grandmothers I know unexpectedly becoming "primary caregivers" because of a divorce. The presidency seems to have gone quite slapstick, with another Texan mocking the two seaboards with an ill-considered, long-term foreign war. Yet our brains' functional areas, our pharmaceutical needs and desires, in fact our genome itself, all seem to have been mapped. We look scientifically as well as affectionately at children, we think we know so much about their stages of development (about our need for them, as well). From daycare to an eventual hospice, their every twitch has been accounted for.

Yet we don't know why we are widely hated so, when America was created to be imitated and loved. Now we sometimes have to force people to love us — send in the SEALS. Our democracy, at the moment, requires other countries not to be democracies to service us with Saudi Arabian or Nigerian oil, sweatshop textiles, and electronic parts. We want authoritarian governments to preside over our suppliers, although incongruously we feel astonished at the phenomenon of "asymmetric warfare" by "those who hate our way of life." I once met a SEAL whose mother used to spit on the floor and make him lick it up, when he was small. Thus he became enthusiastic in his twenties about a career of going in for regime change. My graduating college students don't do that, but face a tougher vocational start than my own class did half a century ago. At our recent reunion, almost everyone who had functioned in a profession was glad to have practiced it when he did, not just because we were now grumpy old men but because the linkages have been dissolving in law, medicine, accounting, and so on, the ethics that, however imperfectly, have served as glue.

But death is easier, verging on the casual when we "go," with less of a mysterious or religious fulcrum to launch us up or down. It pinches when another friend departs, but his pain factor was well controlled and we don't think of him arraigned at St. Peter's Gate for a summation, and have a starkly shrinking assemblage of relatives that we acknowledge ourselves as kin to. More stratified by age and class, we're tethered to our beepers and screened e-mail instead. One hears a man with a cell phone talk first to his mistress, fobbing her off for another night, then to his wife, while fingering a loose pill from his breast pocket and swallowing it dry, screwing up his face at the bad taste. People had mistresses before, but didn't want such intimacies overheard: whereas, in this jam-packed, jittery world, who will you run into again?

We learn to skitter underneath the radar nearly everywhere, in evading rush-hour highway jams or airport security shakedowns, tax audits, or a siege of downsizing or insurance cancellations. Being alert to the conveniences of anonymity, we want the camera's eye to sweep over us without pausing, and the computer, if we're juggling plastic. We want our numbers to be in order — Social Security, passport, Zip and PIN, area code, driver's license, E-ZPass. Our divorce or retirement papers may be in a safe-deposit box, but otherwise most people trust in a backup hard drive somewhere to record their bank balance, etc., knowing hunger is for other continents. God's imprimatur has been upon us. Yet we do sense that seismic changes will be necessary to address the jumbled emergencies arising unpredictably, from watering the city of Phoenix to salvaging Africa. We can map every yard of the earth from space, telephone from moving cars, melt the shelves of Antarctica, sock a cancer radiologically, and get a hard-on from a pill. But it's all pell-mell, novelty as an addiction. Normality implies a permanence that people doubt, although their unease may be subterranean and perhaps they find the Lord on Sundays and tidy up.

How long does it last? What happens next? People of retirement age may be relieved to be able to indulge a taste not only for laziness, but also for moral clarity. Now that they are spectators, they feel like themselves. I have a friend, a financial analyst who was on the seventy-something floor of the South Tower of the World Trade Center when it was struck on 9/11, and he survived simply by descending the stairs relentlessly, regardless of smoke, heat, debris, counterinstructions, and cries for help — hundreds of cries for help. As a black person, he found the experience not so different from the rest of his life. Having scrambled to that level of prosperity from the ghetto he'd grown up in, he had been ignoring cries for help from many directions for many, many years.

Hardball versus team play, agility versus duty, these contrasts jerk in constant tension in entrepreneurialism. But we feel even less ambiguity about our self-interest now that we are so mobile. We wonder what on earth to do. Conscience doesn't register, especially, but what *is* in our self-interest? Our democracy has overripened to the point where politicians poll us before they speak their minds, which creates no leaps of inspiration, but instead a circle of confusion. Agility isn't buoyancy, doesn't make us happy. This reliance on the common wisdom puts the cart before the horse because of course the theory was not that the people might somehow formulate enlightened national policies — rather that collectively, intuitively, they could best fathom who ought to be entrusted to do so.

Our responses are turning generic, too. When I see a bicyclist on the road, I'll swing a bit wider than I need to for safety's sake, not knowing who the person is but because I'm sympathetic in general to bicyclists, don't want them to feel bullied by the traffic. *In general* is how we tend to operate, in other words: in the plural, less and less in the presence of each other as flesh and blood because so much of our gabbing is done by keyboard or conversations bounced up to a satellite and back. This means we don't judge people by the honesty of their handshake or their visage anymore (Orwell's yardstick was that anybody at age fifty had earned the face he wore), or even a lifetime's reputation for integrity or its opposite, since we rarely shake hands or deal repeatedly for years with the same people now. We are zoned for housing, schooling, occupation, and so on, in hordes of interest groups, with friendship like a magic-lantern show — this one, that one hopscotching to another job on the geographic checkerboard. Nor is body language the lingua franca that it used to be. Like facial expressions, such subtleties may become vestigial, because of e-mail and what not, and go the way of the dodo bird. Nature doesn't squander energy on superfluous methods of communication.

During this transition toward more wooden faces, however, our cities' streets are sometimes incongruously transformed by domestic theater, with frowns of empathy or loverly exasperation — intimate, openhearted expressions — walking toward us on the sidewalk, not brusque at all, but inward, the feet of the person slowing as if in the kitchen or a bedroom, while he or she confides with a delicate succession of smiles into the cell phone. People are still used to the privacy of wired telephoning, and perhaps a world where you speak mostly face-to-face, still free to touch and kiss or poke and glare, and the voice, not deracinated by talking into ubiquitous answering machines, reverberates with a nuance of emotion the way that the eyes do. Will our voices, as well, shed spontaneity: the huskiness that betrays the tears on a friend's face across a thousand miles of phone lines and makes you automatically begin to mime your distress?

We're circling our wagons in private as well as public life — unilateralist in our gym regimens and quirky diets, in choosing pets as close companions, or soft pornography and bulky cars. Yet such a circle may add up to a zero, so that although church attendance is down, people shop around for a credo to believe in: not just Adam Smith's atavism or New Age narcissism, but an idealism marbled with faith and logic, and a limber minister to explain the details. Although I don't regard myself as dilettantish or unusually disoriented, within the past year I have received a Christmas communion wafer from Milan's cardinal in his duomo and held hands in a circle of Quakers in a library basement in Vermont. I've knelt in Methodist, Episcopal, and Pentecostal churches in America and watched Mother Teresa beatified by the pope on the steps of St. Peter's in Rome. Other visitors in these houses of worship, nibbling politely at the catechism and maneuvering in and out of half-remembered pews, also seemed to be sliding emotionally between aloofness and immersion in the happiness of being able to believe. Most of us have enough common sense to know there is some kind of God because joy wells in us perhaps analogously to photosynthesis in plants. The question is His location: inside, outdoors, in human guise, or every moist, synaptic charge? The serenity of devotion (and we do want to find that) seesaws with the allure of rebellious skepticism, plus our recent habit of surfing a surfeit of channels, abruptly moving on.

I liked the architecture of the pope's basilicas, the rationality of the Quakers, and getting hugged by the Pentecostals, with whom you could at least share a good, unshamefaced cry. But jubilation, like cynicism, can be a slippery slope, and when we switch from a fillip of reality TV or Oprah to smashmouth hockey or a soap opera or three shouting heads, our own tempo slides toward a more digital than biological mode. Professional football, for example, is edited to resemble animation, fast-forwarding the natural capacities of the body, to be replayed in further stylizations until it parallels the abbreviated summary of a fashion shoot or how speeches of potential import are diced into sound bites that aren't of a piece with real-time life. Thus, will we grow so addicted to speedy denouements and deadpan reactions that we appear like mutants to backward people who still blush on occasion or tentatively venture half a smile to express uncertainty, and part or tighten their lips in readable moods? Airport machines will scan our retinas for identification, and camera phones attempt to approximate the pungency of friendship. But will we see the picked-at nails, the pudge or scrawn, the tinge of jaundice, physical and spiritual, in the eyes that a betrayal may have left?

Advertisers, paying by the second to grab a handle on us, keep goosing the technology to crowd more images into our attention span, snapping us into and out of focus faster, as automation, on the other hand, makes us pause a dozen times a day for rote procedures that allow us clearance into our previously recorded thoughts and assets, as if we too have become decimalized. We are not digits, however, and have fuses that may blow if a disarticulation sets in. Cities have always worked because behind the imperturbability on the thoroughfares were expletives, kickbacks, impromptu generosity, and improvisation. If you had a fender bender or locked yourself out of your apartment at one A.M., a friend was going to pick up the telephone and take you in. It wasn't turned off for voicemail screening. People cut and pasted a life out of the parade of freebies on the street. Experience wasn't virtualized from a memory bank of eclipsed realities, voyeuristic patinas, electronic simulations (although it's true that in the past half-century movies became more memorable for many people than their own humdrum lives). Information is fun, but this is a matter of distortion instead, while in the meantime our secularism powers our recent obsession with longevity, hypochondria, and the like. If there is no afterlife, by all means go for the Prozac, Viagra, Botox.

The instantaneous transmission of churned-up data may burst our eardrums for the natural to-and-fro of emphasis: what should or ought not to be in italics. Not just warfare has become asymmetric. Hired therapists lend an ear to our lamentations in place of friends, and domesticated animals are factory-farmed as squeeze toys, lovebugs. Chaos had been a frequent theme for artists since the buildup to the last world conflagration, but when the dizzy spiral turns centrifugal, it's not Chaplinesque or Dada anymore. It's not Salvador Dalí, Andy Warhol — we don't laugh or dither with Woody Allen and Federico Fellini, or wait with Samuel Beckett, because the social breakdown no longer seems to resemble the random sort of self-correcting physics of Brownian motion, a metaphor that democracy has depended on, by which deceits and incompetencies are nullified and made up for. During the 1960s three charismatic American leaders were shot and killed, yet even so, because we assumed the Kennedy and King assassinations were an outgrowth of evil, not chaos, they were bearable as tragedies, indeed bore some political fruit. The nuts and bolts of the system obliged us in that way, as, subsequently, when both Lyndon Johnson and Richard Nixon voluntarily withdrew from public life after hashing up their presidencies.

But we are seasick now. So many loyalties are being atomized, would a call for idealism permeate far through the anthill of Web sites? We are careening as a nation as if on tires that have lost their tread, bald tires that get no traction in a skid. What we have assumed about ourselves — what is ethical, perennial, versus the spam-jam sort of greedfest we are fearfully anticipating — is thrown into question. After bootstrapping an amalgam of immigrants from nearly everywhere into a superpower, we have incubated within ourselves an astonishingly dismissive attitude toward other cultures, other countries. Besides that, there's the blind faith that our melting pot will continue to cast up, whenever necessary, a leader of the stripe of Washington, Lincoln, Franklin D. Roosevelt during any grave emergency. With the primal genius of the ballot box, popular wisdom, like some artesian force of rectitude, will well up and, balancing the alternatives, shove aside the run-of-the-Hill blowhards, choosing the single individual who can coalesce a Constitution, gel a Union, or institute New Deal reforms that diffuse a meltdown. You wouldn't have a Harding in the White House during the Cuban missile crisis, for instance, and George Marshall will be around, with the support of Harry Truman, if Europe ever needs to be rebuilt.

The trouble is we're not so sure right now. Democracy and dogfight capitalism, billed as free-market economics, have not been panning out for many countries, from Russia to Latin America. Remembering the galas of decolonization in Africa, the gaiety in various Soviet possessions as dictatorship fell, it's hard to square such hopes with crestfallen reality. We're not awash in AIDS orphans here; we're tinkering with boutique genetics, fertility drugs, and fretting about childhood obesity. But the constant question people ask in greeting one another — "How're you doin'?" — has acquired a provocative edge, as if any more equivocal reply than "Good!" might undermine the entire edifice of grinding commutes, multitasking laptops, exercise machinery that substitutes for being outdoors, and TV film loops winding extraneously through one's head. With sex becoming apoplectic, will we have room for global warming? Beyond that, as the king of beasts, don't we need the rest of them for scaffolding? Aren't we kneecapping ourselves, cutting our legs out from under us, by killing off everything else? What will our apishness do without grasslands and trees: spin like a monkey in a cage too small for it? Do we cradle house cats, loot coral reefs for tropical fish, and grow quaint rodents like gerbils because our family lives are splintering, or nature is shattering?

At what point — to take it to a tangent — will the churchgoer cease to regard human life as a diamond chip off of the divinity, on a planet not half as green? Will we be so lonesome we finally grieve, when leafing through the tens of thousands of images of extinguished creatures, in their galaxies of shape and ritual and color — that magic roster of the dead? People will come back to the photo archives, marveling, and what will monotheism say? A society being transformed at warp speed is bound to become warped, with many of us withdrawing into a jumpy mode of privacy but the blowback of the new technologies piercing that privacy with unpredicted surveillance techniques. Existentialism, fifty years and more ago, was kind of fun, when hedonism and pessimism still boasted of their novelty, plus the cachet of antifascism because the Nazis had just been unstrung. It was deemed intriguing, not frightening, that God was dead, by a movement less playful but more intellectual than Dada, after World War I, had been. Nor was the planet speckled with hunger and civil hate like ringworm, as it is today. Decolonization was to be a straightforward process, and atheism perhaps a bit comparably liberating — whereas we would regard some peppy new idea that we are alone in the world now as adding to the delirium. With our twelve-step programs and church hopping, we're like characters in search of an Author (although meanwhile converting our trees into paper). Turn in the direction of your skid is the instruction for driving on ice. And so that would mean more greed, more sex and scatterbrained flapping about, and everspeedier transmission of data, until we slide to a halt — unless we discover that, by eviscerating nature, we have changed the rules unwittingly.

I do find at most of the houses of worship I've dropped in on an old-fashioned spirit of communing with the other parishioners that is comforting, nevertheless: of God as a current that radiates impartially through everybody, even those who try to block it off, and through the rest of life. But the days of walking to church, not driving, used to add cloudscapes, birds' songs, the weather's bite, or wildflowers, and a milk snake rustling, all the panoply of green curvaceous terrain, with the grass springing up, the leaves doubling in size on the same May Day when the toads, as well, begin to sing. Nature is spontaneous in that, although we know approximately what's going to happen, not when — whereas we're growing accustomed to an alternative universe of coy and spooling graphics, automated geometries, cute-ified beasties, and a prismatic palette. If we are city folk we hear backfires rather than Hart Crane's "choiring" bridge strings, but even a farmer's tractor-altered ears may have quit distinguishing a doe's bark from a vixen's yap, when each is warning her young, or change-of-weather susurrations, running water burbling, blue jays hollering enviously at a box turtle beaking a slug. These may be the decades of unintended consequences, as when one drops a pair of eyeglasses in a field and the lenses bend the sunlight to ignite a wildfire. The droughts, floods, and hurricanes of global warming may amount to that, but as if to counterbalance our inattention to outdoor nature, the itch of indoor sex seems to have magnified into a kind of cultural epilepsy, not so much endocrinal as autistic and peevish. At the Solid Rock Gospel Church, middle-aged worshippers weep as inconsolably as if they had been virgins last night, submitting to a first Fall.

It used to be that if the town's professed freethinker happened to live next door to a local potentate of the Knights of Columbus, their families would share essentially the same ethics. But with such flux, and marriages in both camps turning squishy or ad hoc, freethinking produces, for example, a retired IBM executive I know who preaches under a hard-shell revival tent that the pernicious theory of evolution, if accepted, will cause rape to be legalized as conducive to "the survival of the fittest." All bets are off as to what your next-door neighbor may believe. Indeed, it's hard to guess who might in the longer run be fittest. Ideology, technology, and political entitlement groups have combined to create a blur. Nor would I want it otherwise; master races don't do well. And yet egalitarianism can foster myopia also, and dissolve our previous benchmarks of normalcy, integrity, without suggesting what should replace them. Will our grandchildren be able to look up on Google a tabulation of whether we lived honorably? Will it even remain a matter of pride that a given person died "an honest man"? Hometown opinion, when we had hometowns, though not infallible, assisted summings-up, which are startlingly less common now, as we mill about in search of an Author. Chaos isn't Groucho Marx or Sartre — it's scarier; and the masked anxiety inscribed on so many faces testifies to nerves being stretched past customary limits.

It's the velocity, however, that's worrisome, not some novel kink human nature has descended to. The cruelties of the ordinary schoolyard are simply broadcast worldwide as professional wrestling, while helicopter gunships give every Goliath a slingshot. Our moorings may have been rather diaphanous to begin with: the epicene Christ Child perched in the Madonna's lap; or the presumption that Jews were somehow singled out by God to be His own; or that there can be no other deity except Allah. But almost any canon might verge upon the suicidal now. The prophets who invented them lived in a tactile, fortuitous world under the rain

and sun, with behemoths in the rivers, lions in the swales, and lep-
rosy a commonplace along the donkey tracks. They used the stars
for navigation, not just a minute's diversion, and grew or killed
their food or bartered for it with those who did, and lived envel-
oped in the wind, the stony footing, the temperature's fluctuations,
with kinship more important than a career. A matrix of mysteries
underpinned so much of religion then — groundwater bubbling
from a hot spring hieroglyphed with lichen, or sundogs, dust dev-
ils, a banshee gale, particular comets, the dentition of flames de-
vouring a bush, a white peak concealed in the moon-drenched
clouds, hallucinatory fumes seeping from the earth's geological na-
vel, as at Delphi — that it must have seemed more approachable.
People lived alongside sheep and goats, like an undertow from
the prelapsarian currents of life, while watching massive flocks of
birds, such as we can't conceive of, migrate overhead as the seasons
changed. The manner of one's death hinged on more decisions
than how much cholesterol one might have chosen to eat or what
health insurance to pay for.

We don't quite know ourselves lately: whether in a pinch we
would be brave or cowardly, kind beyond the routine courtesies
or perhaps a quisling. People here don't die for a belief or even
resign from their jobs on principle anymore, and social workers
and the police are paid to assume some of the tasks a bystander's
conscience or self-respect would once have accomplished. Their in-
terventions oil our way so smoothly that I've seldom seen big-city
faces look so brutal, or the crucifixes dangling in young women's
cleavages appear more like a dollar sign. Our rancid politics,
flotsam mores, the festival of covetousness being hawked by our
pacesetters, our bathroom cabinets full of pills — none of these
please us. But how to break through to each other? Go door-to-
door like a Jehovah's Witness, telephone like a fundraiser, inau-
gurate a blog? When the world was created, we weren't intended
to be left alone with ourselves, according to both common sense
and Noah. I was puzzled at first by the photographs of the Abu
Ghraib atrocities because they reminded me of something, but
I couldn't think what. Then I stumbled on a bout of TV wrestling
— that staple of cable sports — and realized its pretend tortures
were a burlesque of what American MPs had been inflicting
on their Iraqi prisoners, which might have seemed natural to any
Jesse Ventura fan. Will our loneliness, in other words, undo us?

Who will we turn upon after we have finished hacking nature into slivers?

I believe in revelation and reformation — the tick of altruism versus the tock of avarice — and therefore that we can stabilize the biology of the planet once we have sickened of augering it, if our attention span and reverence for reality have not been virtualized. Too glib a pessimism would ignore how well Mozart is being performed — much better, infinitely more often, than he could possibly have dreamed. Ignore also the undiminished revulsion we continue to feel for suffering inflicted upon other people across the world; or the possibility that some gawky scientist may stumble sideways, twist his ankle, and, in falling, attain a plane of consciousness sufficiently out of kilter with the rest of us that he will plumb the question of our Author. (Or that the plants, when we have deciphered their methods of communication, will indirectly inform us of the same.) In the lasciviousness of a gun shop, men lean over the counter, thumbing their clips of fifty-dollar bills, and handle every barrel. Yet we focus more and more upon our children, as if to patch the fissuring forces. In politics we still do cherish the notion of a Jeffersonian continuum that says, "If this guy isn't doing any good, the next one will," though we wish now for a prenuptial agreement. The sheen is off war lovers and junk-stock entrepreneurs for the moment, and our celebrities have become so mercenary or chameleon that some are fading as folk heroes. The brimming, slithering ads in TV simulcolor continue to advocate a hall-of-mirrors redoubling of lifestyle choices, but the thrust seems a bit more claustrophobic.

Nature is fiber, moistened, interlaced, as sounds are, too, in the woods. Mammals can catch a warning of a hunter's stalk from the birds, or the reverse, and the whisk broom of the wind may instigate a thousand pollinations while making a few boughs sough. Yet we don't go in much nowadays for unaugmented sound, being accustomed to the modulations of engineers who titillate our ears with juiced acoustics that imply in their ubiquity, at least to me, the mush of chaos underneath. How long can fossil fuels sustain the buzz? And — engineering aside — are we really wired for it? Like painted apples in a supermarket bin, how red can we get? Will we gradually flatten, like the taste of corn and salmon, as our genes are trifled with? Or, like that car with tires with no tread, will we flip?

MILES HOFFMAN

Music's Missing Magic

FROM *The Wilson Quarterly*

In 1817, Franz Schubert set these words of the poet Franz von Schober to music in his song "An die Musik":

> O gracious Art, in how many gray hours
> When life's fierce orbit encompassed me,
> Hast thou kindled my heart to warm love,
> Hast charmed me into a better world.
> Oft has a sigh, issuing from thy harp,
> A sweet, blest chord of thine,
> Thrown open the heaven of better times;
> O gracious Art, for that I thank thee!

Schubert's song may well be the most beautiful thank-you note anyone has ever written, but it's also something else. It's a credo, a statement of faith in the wondrous powers of music, and by its very nature an affirmation of those powers. We may view it as a statement of expectations as well. The poet thanks Music for what it has done for him, but there is nothing in his words that would make us think that Music's powers are exhausted, and indeed the noble, exalted character of Schubert's music would lead us to believe that Music's powers are, if anything, eternal, and eternally dependable.

But just how does our gracious Art exercise these powers? How does it comfort us, charm us, kindle our hearts? We might start our search for answers by positing two fundamentals: a fundamental pain and a fundamental quest. A fundamental pain of our human condition is loneliness. No surprise here: we're born alone, we're alone in our consciousness, we die alone, and, when loved ones die, we're left alone. And pain itself, including physical pain, isolates us and makes us feel still more alone, completing a vicious circle. Our fundamental quest — by no means unrelated to our aloneness and our loneliness — is the quest for meaning, the quest to make sense of our time on earth, to make sense of time itself.

Where does music come in? Music is both a balm for loneliness and a powerful, renewable source of meaning — meaning *in* time and meaning *for* time. The first thing music does is banish silence. Silence is at once a metaphor for loneliness and the thing itself: it's a loneliness of the senses. Music overcomes silence, replaces it. It provides us with a companion by occupying our senses — and, through our senses, our minds, our thoughts. It has, quite literally, a presence. We know that sound and touch are the only sensual stimuli that literally move us, that make parts of us move: sound waves make the tiny hairs in our inner ears vibrate, and, if sound waves are strong enough, they can make our whole bodies vibrate. We might even say, therefore, that sound is a *form* of touch, and that in its own way music is able to reach out and put an arm around us.

One way we are comforted when we're lonely is to feel that at least someone understands us, knows what we're going through. When we feel the sympathy of others, and especially when we feel *empathy*, we experience companionship — we no longer feel entirely alone. And strangely enough, music can provide empathy. The structure of music, its essential nature — with many simultaneous, complex, overlapping, and interweaving elements, events, components, associations, references to the past, intimations of the future — is an exact mirror of the psyche, of the complex and interwoven structure of our emotions. This makes it a perfect template onto which we can project our personal complexes of emotions. And when we make that projection, we hear in music our own emotions — or images and memories of our emotions — reflected back. And because the reflection is so accurate, we feel understood. We recognize, and we feel recognized. It's a kind of illusion, but it's a beautiful one, and very comforting. And, in fact, it's not entirely an illusion, because even though the specifics may differ, we all share the same *kinds* of emotions. We all know love and loss and longing, and in different measure we all know joy and despair. We're linked with the composer of the music by our common humanity. And if a composer has found a compelling way to express his or her own emotions, then to a certain extent that composer can't really avoid expressing, and touching, ours as well.

Not to be forgotten among these psychological considerations is what Joseph Conrad called "the inexhaustible joy that lives in beauty." The sheer beauty of music lifts us up and gives us hope, reminding us in our darkest moments, in our "gray hours," that life itself can still hold wonders and beauties. Furthermore, the very "movement" of music, its rhythmic movement through time, carries inevitable associations with life, with positive forces and feelings. Life is movement and movement is life, and joyous music can literally get us moving again when we've been stunned or stilled by sadness.

Did I say "movement through time"? Ah, time. It passes in music. But not without purpose, not without reasons, not without . . . meaning. And that's just the point: music gives meaning to time. If all those overlapping and interweaving elements and events in a piece of music indeed mean something, if they remind, reflect, comfort, inspire, or excite — then by definition the time it takes for them to do all that means something too. When I played in the National Symphony Orchestra in Washington, D.C., years ago, I used to have a regular little joke. Before we began a lengthy symphony, I'd turn to my colleague onstage and say, "See you in forty-five minutes." A piece of music *must* take a certain amount of time; there's no way around it. And though it may be just a self-contained fragment of time, a little world of its own, within that fragment time is used, arranged, and manipulated so that the passage of time makes sense.

I have a friend who's fond of saying that it took a thousand years to invent the C major chord. The system of writing music in clearly defined major and minor keys is called *tonality,* or "tonal harmony," and music written in that system is called "tonal music." We can only guess at how the music of the ancients sounded (and my friend exaggerates), but we know that from the beginnings of Gregorian chant, somewhere around A.D. 600, it did indeed take about a thousand years for tonality to evolve, and to find general acceptance. By 1700, it had reached a position of unchallenged primacy in Western music.

What does it mean for a piece to be "in a key"? Well, when a piece of music is in the key of C major, for example, it means that the harmony of C major functions as the home base, the harmonic center of gravity of the piece. A piece in C major will establish the C major harmony at the beginning (using the notes of a C major chord) and return to it in no uncertain terms at the end. In technical terms the home harmony is called the "tonic," and the gravitational force of the tonic — built into the system and cleverly exploited by the composer even if we're not always aware of it — is inexorable. Between its beginning and end, however, a piece will inevitably traverse any number of other harmonies, major and minor. The various harmonies don't follow each other randomly: they're ordered in progressions, one harmony leading to the next, sometimes in predictable ways, sometimes in unusual or surprising ways. And the most important aspect of these progressions — indeed, the defining aspect of all tonal music — is that *dissonant* chords, chords that contain jarring or unsettling sounds, always eventually lead to *consonant* chords, chords that "please the ear."

Let me emphasize immediately that the pleasing qualities of consonant chords and intervals, and the power of tonal relationships in general, are not arbitrary constructs. They were determined empirically, over the course of centuries. And they are firmly rooted in the laws of acoustical physics, with frequency ratios and a natural phenomenon called the harmonic series (or *overtone* series) playing vital roles. This is why Leonard Bernstein, in his 1973 Norton Lectures at Harvard University (published in book form as *The Unanswered Question*), devoted considerable time to a discussion of the harmonic series, and why he said, "I believe that from . . . Earth emerges a musical poetry, which is by the nature of its sources tonal." Or to put it another way, the origins of tonality lie not in a set of inventions and decisions but in the fundamental nature of sound.

To be clear: tonal music contains *lots* of dissonance. If you were to string together all the dissonant chords in a piece by Bach (or Schubert or Tchaikovsky or any other composer of tonal music) with no other chords between, the effect would loosen your fillings. But the dissonances in tonal music are never strung together that way, because the specific function of dissonance in tonal music is to provide tension, and that tension, in whatever degree it is established, is always resolved by a return to consonance. Indeed, the true genius of the tonal system is that in any given piece it enables a composer to combine the power and momentum of harmonic progressions with the simultaneous manipulation of melodic material, in ways that create the impression of a *narrative,* a dramatic structure complete with characters, rhetoric, direction, conflict, tension, uncertainty, and ultimate resolution.

So, pleasing sounds, striking contrasts, coherent dramatic structures based on expressive musical elements that form clear (if sometimes complex) relationships and patterns — for more than two hundred years this remarkable system served as the unquestioned foundation of Western music, the foundation on which the works of the Baroque, Classical, and Romantic periods were all built. From Vivaldi to Mahler, Bach to Verdi, Mozart to Mussorgsky, Beethoven to Fauré, countless composers of every conceivable individual and national style shared the basic framework of tonality; they spoke what was essentially a common musical language. Is the enduring popularity of these composers' works unrelated to that musical language? Is the still-central role of these works in our musical life an accident, a matter of chance or good public relations? No, and no. Is it fair to say that the powerful and perennial emotional appeal of tonal music reflects its extraordinary capacity to meet our oh-so-human musical expectations, to satisfy our longings for beauty, comfort, and meaning? Yes, indeed.

Add two centuries and a little bit to 1700, and you arrive somewhere in the early twentieth century. The basic framework of tonality was still in place, but by this point its boundaries had been shifting and expanding for some time, helped along by the brilliant harmonic innovations of such composers as Richard Wagner and Claude Debussy, and by the massive expansion of forms and forces in the works of composers like Anton Bruckner, Gustav Mahler, and Richard Strauss. As the new century began, this reshaping and expansion of tonality's limits was so extensive that, despite an ever-accumulating repertory of great works, some thought that the potential of Western music's traditional tonal resources was nearing exhaustion. The foundation, according to a particular theory of music history that's still current, was crumbling fast.

But was it? The composers I mentioned in the two paragraphs above worked from the late seventeenth century to the early twentieth. But in listing those whose music either sits comfortably in a conventional tonal framework or makes sense only within a context of tonal elements and expectations, I could include any number of extraordinary composers whose careers extended well into the twentieth century — and, in some cases, well beyond the century's midpoint. I might start with Jean Sibelius and Sergei Rachmaninoff and continue with Igor Stravinsky, Maurice Ravel, George Gershwin, Paul Hindemith, Béla Bartók, Ernest Bloch, Leos Janáček, Sergei Prokofiev, Darius Milhaud, Francis Poulenc, Aaron Copland, Samuel Barber, Benjamin Britten, William Walton, Bohuslav Martinů, Alberto Ginastera, Heitor Villa-Lobos, Dmitri Shostakovich, and Leonard Bernstein. Not a bad list, and by no means a complete one. These composers are among the greatest, most revered musical figures of the twentieth century, and they simply don't fit the theory. If tonality was on its last legs, somebody must have forgotten to tell them.

Another composer made quite an impact in the early part of the twentieth century, however, and his name was Arnold Schönberg. Born in Vienna in 1874, Schönberg was at first an exponent of the expansionist, superheated style of late-nineteenth-century Romanticism. (His string sextet of 1899, *Verklaerte Nacht*, "Transfigured Night," remains a brilliant and much-loved example of that style.) But by the end of the first decade of the twentieth century, he was on his way to a dramatic renunciation of tonality — a renunciation that included a rejection of the importance of consonant harmonies and a happy embrace of dissonance. And by the early 1920s, he had introduced a novel method of composition that came to be known as the "twelve-tone" method. In twelve-tone music, the composer orders the twelve tones of the chromatic scale (the scale that on the piano includes all the keys, black and white, in any one octave) in a series of his choosing called a "tone row," and that row — in place of traditional scales, harmonies, and harmonic progressions — functions in complex ways as the basis for all the musical elements of the piece. Twelve-tone music (also called "serial" music) is by definition "atonal": it's not in a key, and it doesn't depend on consonant harmonies to provide stability or resolve tension. In theory, the point in twelve-tone music is not that dissonance is good and consonance is bad, but rather that they're both irrelevant. In practice, however, Schönberg's twelve-tone works, especially his early ones, were strikingly dissonant.

Schönberg claimed to have "liberated" dissonance — liberated it, that is, from its status as a way station for consonance, from being tonality's tool. And his strict avoidance of consonance in his early twelve-tone works was a means of avoiding even the slightest whiff of tonality. This was necessary, he felt, in order to establish the twelve-tone system on its own solid footing. There are some, however, who would say that, far from leading to a "liberation" of dissonance — a liberation whose necessity was by no means generally acknowledged, I hasten to add — Schönberg's system led, rather, to a tyranny of dissonance.

Not that it led there right away, or that Schönberg himself even did the leading. In his later years, in fact, he actually retreated, moving back toward tonality. To strip certain complicated lines of development down to the bare bones, however, it's accurate to say that the serial music of Schönberg became enormously influential, to an extent way beyond anything having to do with its general acceptance or popularity. This influence came about through Schönberg's own tireless efforts as a teacher and musical zealot, through the proselytizing and philosophizing efforts of various musicians, writers, and critics, and through a strange and complicated confluence of aesthetic and political influences, especially after World War II. The works themselves were controversial from the beginning, to put it mildly. They were often critically reviled, and to this day they have never found more than a very narrow public. But Schönberg's serialism led directly, especially through his student Anton Webern, to a postwar European avant-garde or "modernist" movement spearheaded by such composers as Pierre Boulez, Karlheinz Stockhausen, and György Ligeti. It led to a simultaneous modernist movement in the United States whose seminal figure was John Cage and whose later exponents included such composers as Milton Babbitt, Elliott Carter, Charles Wuorinen, and many of their students and imitators. And it led ultimately to a fifty-year modernist reign in the world of Western classical music, a reign in which to have any hope of being taken seriously by the critical and academic communities, composers were obligated, regardless of their specific styles and techniques, to avoid traditional tonal procedures and the comforts of consonance and to accept that dissonance was king.

Now, it's true that we often add salt and hot spices to our food to enhance its flavor and heighten contrasts, and it's important to remember that some people like their food much hotter and spicier than others. I should emphasize here — and I can't emphasize strongly enough — that there are many contemporary composers, along with a host of not-so-contemporary composers, who have in varying degrees made use of twelve-tone techniques and atonal procedures to write richly expressive and, indeed, powerfully moving and beautiful works. The extraordinary Alban Berg, an early Schönberg disciple, comes immediately to mind, as do some of the names on my earlier list of primarily tonal — but occasionally atonal! — twentieth-century composers.

It's true as well that harsh elements can be a tool of great visual art, and that much great literature makes use of disturbing images or harrowing episodes, or both. But is there a chef on the planet who suggests swallowing a tablespoon of salt for an appetizer and following it with a bowl of Tabasco for an entrée before washing it all down with a cup of vinegar? We know from listening to tonal music that dissonance can be wonderfully useful when it's employed imaginatively. It can enhance and even create meaning. But in and of itself, dissonance is something that people fundamentally *don't like* — that's its very definition. When composers nonetheless demand that their listeners endure dissonance at great length and without letup, it's hard not to see that demand as something spiteful, as evidence of a musical philosophy that is stubbornly aggressive, even hostile. And it's easy to understand why that philosophy has never proved terribly popular with the concert-going public.

The primary proposition in defense of avant-garde music of the relentlessly dissonant and persistently unpopular variety has always been that, through exposure and familiarity, we often come to appreciate, and even love, things that initially confuse or displease us. Here what we might call "the Beethoven Myth" comes into play. "Beethoven was misunderstood in his time," the argument goes, "but now the whole world recognizes his genius. I am misunderstood in my time, therefore I am like Beethoven." This reasoning, unfortunately, has been the refuge of countless second- and third-rate talents. Beethoven ate fish, too. If you eat fish, are you like Beethoven? But there's a much graver flaw in the argument: Beethoven was *not* misunderstood in his time. Beethoven was without doubt the most famous composer in the world in his time, and the most admired. And if there were those who didn't "get" his late string quartets, for example, there were plenty of others who did, and who rapidly accepted the quartets as masterpieces. In fact, the notion that great geniuses in the history of music went unrecognized during their lifetimes is almost entirely false. It's difficult to find an example of a piece we now consider a masterpiece that was not appreciated as such either while its composer was alive or within a relatively short period after his death. "But there was a riot at the premiere of Stravinsky's *Rite of Spring*!" Yes, that was at the premiere, in Paris in May 1913. But the *Rite* was performed again almost immediately, without riots, in Paris and London, and quickly acquired its stature as perhaps the most celebrated and influential piece of the twentieth century. It has since been performed and recorded more times than anyone could possibly count.

Still, tastes do evolve, and we're reminded that people who as children eat and drink only Velveeta and soda pop often later develop a taste for Camembert and cognac. That's fine, even if it may be a little on the generous side to use "Camembert and cognac" as analogues for unpleasant sounds. But I'm afraid the "lesson" has usually been taken considerably further, and reinforced with large doses of intellectual condescension and intimidation. While much of the public would be perfectly willing to acknowledge that Camembert and cognac can be wonderful elements of a diet, what we've heard from the avant-garde establishment for years has been something like this: "Yes, we know from centuries of experience that most people find a steady diet of nothing but Camembert and cognac unappealing, and there is no reason to believe that that will ever change. Nonetheless, starting now we are going to feed you . . . a steady diet of nothing but Camembert and cognac. We don't *care* that you find it unappealing, because we've decided that this dietary change is necessary; it represents Progress. And if you can't accept this Progress, it's only because you're not knowledgeable or sophisticated enough to understand and appreciate it."

If the joys and comforts of beautiful sounds were all we sought in music, the dominance of dissonance would be the only problem of avant-garde music that we'd need to consider. But we're also burdened by our fundamental quest for meaning, our need for music to make sense.

"Before we can process and store the input our senses receive," writes psychiatrist Anthony Reading in his book *Hope and Despair,* "we first have to be able to perceive the *information* that it contains, to distinguish meaningful *signals* from meaningless *noise.* Information detection involves perceiving recurrent patterns in data, deviations from apparent randomness." Reading emphasizes that "information is contained in the way objects are arranged within a system, not in the objects themselves," and just as Bach and Beethoven would wholeheartedly agree, so would Schönberg and his musical descendants. The musical objects — notes, chords, rhythms — in the works of many modernist composers (Babbitt and Carter are excellent examples) are in fact arranged with extraordinary care, and sometimes with dazzling intellectual complexity. The catch is that for the arrangements to convey "information," to be meaningful, they have to be perceivable: unrecognizable or imperceptible patterns are the same as no patterns at all. And without patterns — familiar ones or newly established ones — we lose our bearings. We're not sure where we are or where we've been, and therefore we have little interest in wherever it is we may be going. This is where Schönberg himself so often failed, and where Babbitt and Carter et al. have most grievously failed. They have either grossly overestimated or willfully ignored the limits of the auditory perceptual abilities of most human beings, and somewhere along the way they have either forgotten or willfully ignored the reasons most people listen to music in the first place. They, or their boosters, may write detailed, not to say impenetrably turgid, analyses of the structural underpinnings of their works and the strict mathematical relationships inherent therein, but to the extent that those relationships remain completely unapparent to the human ear — as they so often do — they're meaningless, and what we actually hear is . . . noise.

Or we could just call it bad music. Why not? Molière said, "Anyone can be an honorable man, and yet write verse badly." No one would dispute that there have been many honorable, sincere, dedicated, and very nice men and women writing music over the past eighty years. But if there are such things as "good music" or "good pieces" or "great pieces," then there must also be such things as bad pieces. There must be pieces that don't work very well or don't work at all, pieces that to most ears don't make sense, and that therefore cannot do what honorable, sincere, and open-minded music lovers look for music to do. Do we agree that Bach and Handel were the greatest composers of the Baroque era? Then the other Baroque composers were . . . less great. And some were not very good at all. What's interesting is that we have little difficulty in agreeing on many of these distinctions when the people in question are long dead. Why not make distinctions while people are still alive, when making these distinctions might actually be useful? Despite what we've been told so often to think, why not go by what we hear? Why not say this: if a piece has had thirty or fifty — or eighty — years to be "understood" by the public but still isn't, the chances are extremely good that it's not ever going to be. And that's far more likely the fault of the piece, and the composer, than of audiences. Why not come out and say, without fear and without apology for our supposed shortcomings, that the emperor has been naked, and that too much of the music written over the past five decades has been just plain bad?

Am I being too harsh? Have I exaggerated the intensity of the distaste that so much modernist music has aroused? No, sad to say, not if we keep certain factors in mind. One is the strength of the needs, the intensity of the desires, that we fulfill with music. Our expectations of music — expectations of the type nurtured, reinforced, and *satisfied* for generation upon generation — are enormous, and enormously important to us, and when those expectations are disappointed, we take it very badly indeed. Music is a loved one, after all, a family member. It should be no surprise that we're troubled much more by its bad behavior than by that of strangers. Another crucial factor is time. One of the more obvious reasons we appreciate music's giving meaning to time is that our supply of time is so limited. But this is also why we so strongly resent having our time wasted! If you see a painting hanging on the wall and don't like it, you simply turn your gaze elsewhere, and hardly any time has been squandered. But if you go to a concert and the program includes music you find ugly or unpleasant, precious minutes of your life tick away, lost. You could have done something else with that little part of your life, *anything* else, but you're stuck four seats from the aisle, and time is passing. From resentment to hatred is but a small step.

And, of course, not many people enjoy being insulted, either, or falsely accused. In a 1964 speech at the Colorado campus of the Aspen Institute, the English composer Benjamin Britten said, "It

is insulting to address anyone in a language which they do not understand." And if what's said — or played — seems so often to be
couched intentionally in a language that virtually *nobody* could understand, and yet one finds oneself blamed over and over again for
not understanding. . . .

Let me repeat: people have written, and are still writing, very good
and very moving pieces in styles that have little or nothing to do
with tonality. Good composers find a way to write good music, and
it's just as great a mistake to equate "atonal" with "ugly" as to assume that "tonal" always means "beautiful." heaven knows the history of music is littered with mediocre tonal compositions! But
while tonal music benefits, as we've seen, from a built-in logic established by centuries of development, any primarily atonal idiom
requires the composer to create his or her own logic, and that can
be very difficult. When it's done well, the logic makes itself understood, even on first hearing. Notes, harmonies, and rhythms follow
one another in patterns that make sense, and the musical language, though perhaps unfamiliar, unusual, or highly spiced with
dissonance, is comprehensible and convincing. Narrative, drama,
and emotional impact are all possible.

Inevitably, however, we return to the fact that there's something
basic to human nature in the perception of "pleasing sounds," and
in the strength of the tonal structures that begin and end with
those sounds. Blue has remained blue to us over the centuries, and
yellow yellow, and salt has never started tasting like sugar. With or
without physics, consonances are consonances because to most
people they sound good, and we abandon them at great risk. History will say — history says now — that the twelve-tone movement
was ultimately a dead end, and that the long modernist movement
that followed it was a failure. Deeply flawed at their musical and
philosophical roots, unloving and oblivious to human limits and
human needs, these movements left us with far too many works
that are at best unloved, at worst detested. They led modern classical music to crisis, confusion, and, in many quarters, despair, to a
sense that we've wasted decades, and to a conviction that our only
hope for whatever lies ahead starts with first making sure we abandon the path we've been on.

*

From a distance of centuries, knowledgeable observers can usually discern when specific cultural developments within societies or civilizations reached their peaks. Egyptian painting, Etruscan pottery, Greek tragedy? The experts may argue over precise dates and details, but the existence of the peaks themselves is rarely in question. In the case of Western music, we don't have to wait centuries for a verdict: we can say with confidence that the system of tonal harmony that flowered from the 1600s to the mid-1900s represents the summit, the broad summit, of human accomplishment. Of our subsequent attempts to find successors or substitutes for that system, some have been more noble than others and some have even led to extremely compelling individual works. But from a historical perspective they have been efforts along a downhill slope.

What lies ahead? Nobody can say, of course. But with the peak behind us, there's no clear cause for optimism — no rational cause, anyway, to believe that another Beethoven (or Berlioz or Brahms or Bartók) is on the way. And even if he *were* on the way, in what musical language would he write when he got here? The present is totally free but totally uncertain, the immediate past offers little, and the more distant past is . . . past. And yet, irrational creatures that we are, we keep hoping for the best, and it's right that we do. We owe it to Music. The good news is that there are many composers today who, despite the uncertain footing, are striving valiantly, and successfully, to write works that are worthy of our admiration and affection. They write in a variety of styles, but the ones who are most successful are those who are finding ways — often by assimilating ethnic idioms and national popular traditions — to invest their music with both rhythmic vitality and lyricism. They're finding ways to reconnect music to its eternal roots in dance and song.

They're also rediscovering, in many cases, the potential of tonal harmonies, and this seems like a positive step. Still, I can't help wondering: will anybody ever find ways, *new* ways, that are so striking, so wonderful, that our entire musical landscape will be transformed as if by magic? Well, magic itself may actually turn out to be our only hope for such a transformation. The mathematician Mark Kac, in attempting to describe the extraordinary genius of physicist Richard Feynman, came up with the following formulation: "There are two kinds of geniuses, the 'ordinary' and the 'magicians.' An ordinary genius is a fellow that you and I would be just as good as, if we were only many times better. There is no mystery as to how his mind works. . . . It is different with the magicians . . . the working of their minds is for all intents and purposes incomprehensible." If we're very lucky, a musical magician may come along one day who will perform miracles in ways that are completely unforeseeable to us now. Others will learn from his or her work and contribute new riches. The term "modern music" will take on a wonderfully positive ring, and the heaven of better times will be thrown open to us.

O gracious Art, let's hope we get lucky.

LINDA HOGAN

Waking

FROM *Parabola*

LAST NIGHT thunder and lightning opened the world. Hail beat down on earth, drumming the roof. I watched the round layers of ice bounce off the ground. This morning I wake early to the sound of the young horse running, to the voices of magpies teaching their young to fly, the wings fluttering as they jump only from branch to branch, the parents hovering, urging, flying away, calling the young ones to them. A woodpecker hammers at a hole in the dead tree.

From the swaddling comfort of bed, I look out to watch such joy. It is a new morning and beautiful and I rise with the beauty to a morning knowing more of my past has slipped away and that this night of storms, this morning of beauty may also disappear, so I write it down.

Time. I have lost it, and I think of my ancestors who tied knots in ropes to keep track of it, or other tribes who painted events and each year revealed them, telling the stories.

Daily something is lost from me. It began with an accident I don't remember, an impact to my head, a woman finding my body in the road. I do remember hearing once, as if in a very far distance, the sound of sirens, entrancing like the ones in the *Odyssey* calling me to an island and I surrendered and went to that island where I still live, never going back home, never returning to the same journey and at night there is the unraveling of memory that takes place and parts of my past disappear. Yet I am happy. I think, I have forgotten last month and it should matter, but it doesn't.

I remain on that island without intending it, but I am conscious.

I can recall many things: what I read, that I bought pillowcases. But not what someone said or a movie I saw. We laugh. I can see reruns and think they are new. And the shadows of words sometimes only float past. I try to recall them. I say, It is the thing with a handle. It is the thing that cleans the floor.

But I know there are rooms of jade. From the hospital bed there was a great traveling and I was awake in other worlds. Not dreams, nothing even similar to dreams, but a new kind of waking. I traveled. I described to my daughter and friend in great detail the jade carvings in China. I saw the carved jade and silk embroideries of another world. There were pale animals, beautifully polished, a horse, great detail in the carvings of a wall made of jade, entire vignettes of life carved by some artist of the past, a woman sitting and playing an instrument, trees trimmed to some notion of perfection. Jade, the stone of heaven, once carried from the White Jade River by camels. There were also the fabrics, silks and brocades with embroidery, some with gold stitches. I traveled maps with no roads, no towns, no named waters. The world was China, I suppose, and I was a child digging through earth to the other side and succeeding, through soil, stone, magma, through the darkness of unconsciousness to another kind of waking and seeing.

At the same time, others traveled toward me, passing through the walls. In the room with me were ancestors I hadn't seen, far ones, from before the Trail of Tears of Chickasaws to Oklahoma, a woman dressed in lavender and wearing a turban as our women did in the past. I wonder if she was my own blood. I remember my father's own recent awakening in bed before his death to the old ones, our people. He said the names of the grandmothers, some I'd never heard, as he looked up at them smiling, and then he introduced me, placing me in my line at the bottom of our world, the present, in my own place as a woman, a grandmother.

But for me, I was going to live, and live with memory loss. Important events vanished from my memory. Some didn't. It was random. I forgot neighbors' faces. I remembered some small detail of a poem. Rumi: *Break the wine glass and go toward the glassblower's breath.* The names of the wildflowers in bloom around my house would be gone. What I told someone I told again and again. What I asked, I repeated. Words were gone. I searched for them, coming up with things similar until someone guessed.

No one has ever seen an atom yet they believe it is there. No one has ever understood how the brain works. Who could think that love might be electrical, or that consciousness could be chemical? The brain is an organ. The mind is a transient. But the body, I find, is not the husk for the soul. It is knowing. It is consciousness. For a time I was a divine traveler through no will of my own, far beyond my world and its limits. It was a virginal state. While I slept, a restless spirit woke to travel another reality, another realm or layer of existence. But my body, even without words, knows this world, every morning the first morning. I watch the light move, lengthen. Daily there is beauty. The wildflowers still exist, even nameless. They know their own names and those are beyond human knowing. Ask me the name of the month and I could say October when it is June, but there is bread and butter. Pleasure. I listen to the thunder, look at the dew in the flowers. There is joy even in such vulnerability, such fragility. There is even happiness.

Awakening isn't always to a state of enlightenment. It isn't always a sudden change in consciousness. I can't say I know what it is. I can't say I understand the boundary, the skin, between the worlds we may journey or where I now live. Stirrings there I feel, but don't know.

Unconscious, a richness was there. Perhaps it is because I was missing. This is what is said about the self. That when you are given up, a whole cosmos opens. I remember Lakota Wallace Black Elk once saying about the space program, that we have always traveled through the universe.

I was a sleeper for three weeks and sometimes still. And yet something grows in it, something wakes. Something else owns this mind, this awakening, and it is a mystery, as if the soul lives larger than the human knows or thinks. Morning after morning has been my world, the sunrise always beautiful, everything newly seen. I am afraid to miss any of it.

It is an infant life, too soon to tell what it will become but I trust it is a sacred beginning like all beginnings. Sometimes you drink from an empty bowl thinking it is full and it is. Sometimes you open your empty palm and receive. The world is always fresh. Sometimes there is morning with birds and the sound of a running horse and you are awake.

CHARLOTTE INNES

Reading Ruskin in Los Angeles

FROM *The Hudson Review*

For my grandfather, Bernhard Einzig (1874–1945), who died in a German
concentration camp at Theresienstadt. His books, a three-volume set of the
1902 edition of *The Stones of Venice* by John Ruskin, are my only tangible
inheritance.

The sun at its low winter zenith
lights up the crosshatched pane,
the white curving fern, fossil-like,
that might be an angry boy's knife etching,
or painter's clumsy scratching at the spills
and splashings of a makeshift paint job.

Beyond the pane, a duller gleaming,
drooping green acanthus leaves,
symbol once, in Christian art, of heaven,
before that, classic curlicue of Greek
and Roman art and architecture. Inside,
a patch of sun pools on taut silk,

old table lamp, red shade
faded to brown, long uneven drift
of fringes also edged with light,
cocked slightly, like a languorous
woman with an age-old question,
at dusk, a jaded invitation.

Lamp, windowpane, and tree,
made things, all, by God or man,

or woman, pulled together by the sun,
my eye, my place. This accidental harmony
of mismatched elements, what story's
told here? "There is no subject

of thought more melancholy,
more wonderful than the way in which
God permits so often His best gifts
to be trodden under foot of men, His
richest treasures to be wasted by the moth."
So John Ruskin said. "The fruit struck

to the earth before its ripeness." Oxford don,
who in the 1800s walked the streets
of Venice, read its stones as if they lived,
pondered natural beauty in translation — how
to tell an Englishman who's never seen an olive tree
of tracing "line by line" its "gnarled writhing" —

who held that art's a universal tongue,
hated human cruelty, ugliness, and saw
the truth of poor Italian peasants
lounging jobless in old Venetian squares,
John, you'd understand the awful beauty,
the despair, of windows, lamps, trees.

ALAN JACOBS

Into the Wonder

FROM *Christianity Today*

IN MARCH OF 1949, C. S. Lewis invited a friend named Roger
Lancelyn Green to dinner at Magdalen College of Oxford University, where Lewis was a tutor. Green had attended Lewis's lectures a
decade earlier, and their friendship had grown over the years. It
must have been especially refreshing for Lewis to contemplate an
evening of food, wine, and conversation, for his life was miserable
at that moment.

He lived with his brother and an elderly woman named Mrs.
Moore, whom he often referred to as his mother — though she was
not. Both of them were unwell and dependent upon him. Just a few
days before his dinner with Green, Lewis had written to an American friend that he was "tied to an invalid," which is what Mrs.
Moore had become, confined to bed by arthritis and varicose veins.
For her part, Mrs. Moore proclaimed that Lewis was "as good as an
extra maid in the house," and she certainly used him as a maid. She
seems also to have become obsessive and quarrelsome in her latter
years, worried always about her dog and constantly at odds with the
domestic help.

Lewis hired two maids to help with cleaning and nursing when
he had to be at Magdalen, where he maintained a grueling sched-
ule of lectures, tutorials, and correspondence. But for a time, one
of the maids became mentally unstable, and he occasionally had to
return home to sort out conflicts the women had with each other
and with Mrs. Moore. In 1947, he had been asked by the Marquess
of Salisbury to participate in meetings, along with the archbish-
ops of Canterbury and York, to discuss the future of the Church of
England (of which Lewis was a member). He had declined: "My

mother is old and infirm . . . and I never know when I can, even for a day, get away from my duties as a nurse and a domestic servant.(There are psychological as well as material difficulties in my house.)"

In the intervening two years, the miseries had if anything intensified. There are dark hints in some of his writings that the suffering shook Lewis's Christian faith to the core. Though he had written of the joys of heaven, in the year of the Marquess's letter, he found himself consumed by a "horror of nonentity, of annihilation" — that is, of finding that the God in whom he had trusted had no eternal life to offer.

Lewis was a famous man who would in a few months find himself on the cover of *Time* magazine and who was besieged by a blizzard of daily letters. He was determined to answer every correspondent, and his brother Warnie normally assisted him, primarily by typing dictated or drafted letters and keeping the files organized. But at the beginning of March 1949, Warnie was in Oxford's Acland Hospital, having drunk himself into insensibility. After his release, Warnie wrote in his diary that his brother's "kindness remains unabated," but C. S. Lewis's resources were failing. In early April, he wrote to a friend who had reproached him for not replying promptly to a letter, "Dog's stools and human vomit have made my day today: one of those days when you feel at 11 A.M. that it really must be 3 P.M." Two months later, he collapsed at his home and had to be taken to the hospital. He was diagnosed with strep throat, but his deeper complaint was simply exhaustion.

The Perfect Distraction

Such was C. S. Lewis's world the evening he had Roger Lancelyn Green to dinner. It's unlikely that Green had any idea how miserable his friend had been. Lewis was a charming host, and, as Green wrote in his diary, they had "wonderful talk until midnight: He read me two chapters of a book for children he is writing — very good, indeed, though a trifle self-conscious." The book would become *The Lion, the Witch and the Wardrobe,* the first story about a world called Narnia.

What is remarkable is that in the midst of all his miseries, Lewis turned to the writing of a story for children. He was already famous, but his fame was chiefly that of a polemical contender for

Christianity. Certainly that was the thrust of *Time*'s cover story on Lewis, which emphasized his then-forthcoming book arguing for the validity of belief in miracles. He was also a highly accomplished scholar, perhaps already (in his mid-forties) the most proficient among Oxford's English faculty. He had written fiction, too, but of a highly intellectual character. The bachelor with no children of his own, and with relatively few friends whose children he knew, did not seem a likely author of a children's book.

In the year before his death, Lewis told a correspondent, "My knowledge of children's literature is really very limited. . . . My own range is about exhausted by MacDonald, Tolkien, E. Nesbit, and Kenneth Grahame." He hadn't even read *The Wind in the Willows* or Nesbit's stories until he was in his twenties. Yet he never outgrew his love of the children's stories he did know. Once he discovered *The Wind in the Willows,* it was forever precious to him. (He told a friend that he always read Grahame's masterpiece when he was in bed with the flu.)

Moreover, Lewis served almost as a midwife to many children's stories of his friends. In 1932, Tolkien took the chance of reading aloud to Lewis a story he had written. Lewis badgered Tolkien into seeking to have it published, which eventually he did in 1938: the story was called *The Hobbit.* So those who knew Lewis best weren't surprised when he produced drafts of *The Lion, the Witch and the Wardrobe* or when he published it in 1950. Perhaps they would have been surprised had they known that the story, and the six Narnia books that followed it, would bring him greater fame and influence than all his other books combined, making his name known around the world. The *Chronicles of Narnia* have been translated into more than thirty languages and, worldwide, have sold more than eighty-five million copies.

Though Lewis was a man who valued friendship above almost all else, such fame made him deeply uncomfortable. He had been a solitary child and always loved being alone. "I am a product," he wrote, "of long corridors, empty sunlit rooms, upstairs indoor silences, attics explored in solitude, distant noises of gurgling cisterns and pipes, and the noise of wind under the tiles. Also, of endless books."

In the books that peopled his solitude, Lewis discovered a range of interests ("nonsense, poetry, theology, metaphysics") that, nurtured and matured, nearly all found their way into his career as a writer. The books by Lewis that Macmillan published in 1943 and 1944 alone (some had been written several years earlier) included two science fiction novels, a theological treatise about suffering, a satire in the form of letters from a devil, and two brief works in explanation and defense of the Christian faith. Looking at such variety, we can understand why Owen Barfield once wrote an essay about his famous friend called "The Five C. S. Lewises."

Yet the chief point of Barfield's essay is that what's remarkable about Lewis is not the diversity of his writing, but the unity: the sense that something ties them all together. What is this unity? Barfield's attempt to explain it is intriguing:

"There was something in the whole quality and structure of his thinking, something for which the best label I can find is 'presence of mind.' . . . Somehow what he thought about everything was secretly present in what he said about anything."

So, what, specifically, was present to his mind?

Pictures in His Head

I want to suggest that Lewis's willingness to be enchanted held together the various strands of his life: his delight in laughter, his willingness to accept a world made by a good and loving God, and his willingness to submit to the charms of a wonderful story. What is "secretly present in what he said about anything" is an openness to delight, to the sense that there's more to the world than meets the jaundiced eye, to the possibility that anything could happen to someone who's ready to meet anything.

For someone with eyes to see and the courage to explore, even an old wardrobe full of musty coats could become the doorway to another world.

After all the Narnia books were done, Lewis wrote an essay in which he explained that the stories began when he started "seeing pictures in [his] head" — or rather, when he started paying attention to pictures he had been seeing all along, since the "picture of a Faun carrying an umbrella and parcels in a snowy wood," which we find near the beginning of *The Lion, the Witch and the Wardrobe,* first entered his head when he was sixteen years old. It was only when he was about forty that he said to himself, "Let's try to make a story about it."

As we have seen, it was a particularly trying time in his life when he wrote the first Narnia tale. Yet something — some instinctively strong response to the offer of enchantment, perhaps made all the more strong because of his difficult circumstances — made him start writing, even though he "had very little idea how the story would go."

What made him write this way, and why it is such a good thing that he did — these are hard topics to talk about without seeming sentimental. Yet they are necessary topics. In most children, but in relatively few adults, we see a willingness to be delighted to the point of self-abandonment. This free and full gift of oneself to a story is what produces the state of enchantment. Why do we lose the ability to give ourselves in this way? Perhaps adolescence introduces the fear of being deceived, the fear of being caught believing in what others have ceased to believe. To be naive, to be gullible — these are the great humiliations of adolescence.

Lewis never seems to have been fully possessed by this fear, though he felt it at times. "When I was ten, I read fairy stories in secret and would have been ashamed if I had been found doing so. Now that I am fifty, I read them openly. When I became a man, I put away childish things, including the fear of childishness and the desire to be very grown up."

It was Richard Wagner's vast landscapes of heroic myth that captured Lewis above all, and the gentler "faerie" world of the English imagination, from Spenser to Tennyson, William Morris, and George MacDonald. He once wrote that stories which sounded "the horns of Elfland" constituted "that kind of literature to which my allegiance was given the moment I could choose books for myself." It was perhaps inevitable that he would become a scholar of medieval and Renaissance literature, and that his first work of fiction would be an elaborate allegory based on Bunyan's *Pilgrim's Progress*. He consumed works of fantasy and then science fiction (in which genre he would write his first novels). It was not likely that such an open mind would remain an atheist long, though Lewis did hold out as an unbeliever until nearly thirty.

Wide Open to Glory

Lewis remained, in this particular sense, childlike, that is, able to receive pleasure from the kinds of stories that tend to give pleasure to children. Ruth Pitter, a poet and close friend of Lewis's, wrote, "His whole life was oriented and motivated by an almost uniquely persisting child's sense of glory and of nightmare. The adult events were received into a medium as pliable as wax, wide open to the glory and equally vulnerable, with a man's strength to feel it all, and a great scholar's and writer's skills to express and interpret."

Surely Lewis would have said that when we can no longer be "wide open to the glory," we have lost not just our childlikeness, but also something near the core of our humanity. Those who will never be fooled can never be delighted, because without self-forgetfulness there can be no delight, and this is a great and grievous loss.

Often, when we talk about receptiveness to stories, we contrast an imaginative mindset to one governed by reason. We talk about freeing ourselves from the shackles of the rational mind. But no belief was more central to Lewis than the conviction that it is eminently and fully rational to be responsive to the enchanting power of stories. Lewis passionately believed that education is not about providing information so much as it is about cultivating habits of the heart — producing "men with chests," as he puts it, people who not only think as they should, but also respond as they should, instinctively and emotionally, to the challenges and blessings the world offers them.

Lewis noted in the dedication of his book *A Preface to Paradise Lost* that "when the old poets made some virtue their theme, they were not teaching but adoring, and that what we take for the didactic is often the enchanted." It is the merger of the moral and the imaginative — the vision of virtue itself as adorable, even ravishing — that makes Lewis so distinctive.

He achieves this merger most perfectly in his children's books. He was quite aware of the restraints imposed on a person writing for children: "Writing 'juveniles' certainly modified my habits of composition. Thus: (a) It imposed a strict limit on vocabulary. (b) Excluded erotic love. (c) Cut down reflective and analytical passages. (d) Led me to produce chapters of nearly equal length for convenience in reading aloud." But "all these restrictions did me great good — like writing in a strict meter."

Writing for children also forced Lewis to concentrate on what was most essential — in the story, yes, but also in his own experience. In writing these tales for children, he found the bedrock of his own imagination and belief.

In 1954, Lewis responded to an invitation of the Milton Society of America to honor him for his contribution to the study of John Milton's poetry. They asked him to "make a statement" about his published works, and he insisted that through them all "there is a guiding thread."

> The imaginative man in me is older, more continuously operative, and in that sense more basic than either the religious writer or the critic. It was he who made me first attempt (with little success) to be a poet. It was he who, in response to the poetry of others, made me a critic, and in defense of that response, sometimes a critical controversialist. It was he who, after my conversion, led me to embody my religious belief in symbolic or mythopoetic forms ranging from Screwtape to a kind of theologized science fiction. And it was, of course, he who has brought me, in the last few years, to write the series of Narnian stories for children; not asking what children want and then endeavoring to adapt myself (this was not needed), but because the fairytale was the genre best fitted for what I wanted to say.

Lewis was honored by the approval of the Miltonists, but he had to admit that he wasn't really one of them. He was not one for whom scholarship was an end in itself. At the heart of his impulse to write — even to write scholarly works of literary criticism — was his warm and passionate response to literature as an "imaginative man."

Lewis could make Narnia because the essential traits of Narnia were in his mind long before he wrote the first words of the *Chronicles*. He was a Narnian long before he knew what name to give the country. It was his true homeland, the native ground to which he hoped, one day, to return.

At the darkest moment in the first Narnia tale, when Aslan's tortured and humiliated body lies dead on the Stone Table, Lewis writes: "I hope no one who reads this book has been quite as miserable as Susan and Lucy were that night, but if you have been — if you've been up all night and cried till you have no more tears left in you — you will know that there comes in the end a sort of quietness. You feel as if nothing was ever going to happen again."

Only one whose misery had taken him to such devastated "quietness" could write these sentences. Lewis had known misery as a child; he knew it again as a middle-aged man. Yet it was out of this misery that a story for children came — at first a bumbling story, flat and uninspired, but one that Lewis couldn't ignore.

As he wrote after all the Narnia stories were done, it was only when the great lion Aslan "came bounding into it" that he stopped bumbling and the story began to move in its proper course: "He pulled the whole story together, and soon he pulled the six other Narnian stories in after him."

Into Narnia he also pulled Lewis, and then us.

CORBY KUMMER

The Kosher Conversion

FROM *The Atlantic Monthly*

PASSOVER is when Jewish eating habits seem the most distinct from those in the rest of the world — the most restrictive, the most inexplicable. Keeping Passover means adhering to rules and tradi- tions on top of the standard rules of kashrut, or keeping kosher, which include not eating shellfish or pork and separating anything containing milk from anything containing meat. At Passover bread and all other leavened foods are banned, and the questions of what is and isn't allowed only start there. Corn or no corn? Rice or no rice? Must staples that don't need to be marked kosher the rest of the year — milk, for instance — be marked "kosher for Passover," along with the matzoh? (As with all questions Jewish, it depends on who's answering.)

And yet Passover is the time of year when sales of kosher foods reach their peak, and when the greatest number of Jews follow some form of dietary abstention. A moment of generally happy reconnection with Jewish identity, Passover can move usually unob- servant Jews to consider keeping kosher year-round. With its many preparatory kitchen-cleaning requirements, it is also the most logi- cal time to make the switch.

The market for foods certified kosher has been steadily increas- ing for at least a decade. Menachem Lubinsky, a marketing consul- tant and the editor of *Kosher Today*, a trade magazine, estimates that of $500 billion in retail grocery sales last year, $185 billion was certified kosher — a rise since 1988 of about 285 percent. As of 2004 fully 85,000 products were certified kosher, compared with 18,000 in 1988. Much food — flour, rice, and other staples, and all produce — is kosher by definition, and need not bear a *hechsher,* or kosher symbol, although a lot of it does. A *hechsher* can be as much an indication that a manufacturer thinks certification will attract customers as that it produces kosher food.

Commercial kosher certification in this country has come a long way from its beginnings, in the early 1920s, when shoppers had to look hard to see if a product was officially kosher. The inconspicuousness was intentional. With increasing waves of immigrants requesting kosher foods, established (and non-Jewish) food manufacturers recognized a new market to be tapped. But they didn't want to lose any customers. So they asked the Orthodox Union, based in New York and today the largest certifying organization in the world (it certifies food in seventy-seven countries), to devise a symbol that did not show the word "kosher" or betray its meaning to those who might prefer to avoid "Jewish food." The symbol — a U inside an O — is still in use. Today's *hechshers* are practically blaring by comparison, and many mainstream producers now spell out the words "pareve," meaning neither dairy nor meat, and "kosher" itself.

The labeling is useful not only to those keeping kosher but also to many others who choose or need to control their diet. Vegetarians know that a product marked "dairy" or "pareve" contains no meat, and vegans and people who are lactose-intolerant know that pareve foods contain no dairy products. Seventh-Day Adventists, who are often vegetarian, are an important part of the kosher market, as are Muslims: all forms of pork are both *haram* (not allowed in the Muslim diet) and non-kosher, or *treif* (literally "unfit"). Observant Muslims will buy kosher meat in the absence of a halal butcher.

People are turning to kosher food not just because of a revival in religious observance but because anyone buying food today is rightly concerned with safety, especially the safety of meat, and kosher certification requires careful inspection. Animals that are visibly ill before slaughter are forbidden. (This would have eliminated the "downer" cow, unable to walk, that was the one confirmed carrier of mad cow disease in the United States; other safeguards include the prohibition of stunning before slaughter, which can spread brain and spinal fluids to meat.) Some animals are further examined after slaughter. "Glatt," a word meaning "smooth," signifies that the lungs of the animal have been found free of adhesions indicating possible cancer or other systemic disease. An animal rejected as glatt can be qualified as (plain) kosher, but many slaughterhouses simply sell that meat as non-kosher, so by default all their kosher meat is glatt. Although "glatt" has no meaning outside the slaughtering process, in the 1970s it became generally used to mean "extra kosher," as Lisë Stern explains in her recently published *How to Keep Kosher.*

Kosher certification does not, however, offer many of the guarantees that health- and environment-conscious consumers might want. Kosher food need not be organic. There is no clear rabbinical stance on genetically modified organisms, even if in theory the manifold rules against anomalous foods would seem to forbid them. This is a natural concern for "advocates of eco-kashrut," as Stern terms them in her book. (With kashrut being adopted by many young Jews, there is of course an eco-kashrut movement; you can read about it at earthkosher.com.)

And kosher food is often produced by multinational agribusinesses whose environmental and labor practices can be questionable. Hebrew National, for instance, known for its kosher hot dogs, is owned by ConAgra, a company practically synonymous with global agribusiness. (For reasons of slaughtering and certification methods, many Orthodox rabbis recommend against Hebrew National products.) Like all other industrially raised and packaged foods, kosher food can be full of trans fats (more unhealthful than butter, though pareve) and processed sugar. Lovers of "old" Coke take note: at Passover big-name sodas are made not with the usual corn syrup — cheap and insipid and, happily, not kosher for Passover — but with the far superior cane syrup.

Perhaps more surprising, certification rules seldom concern the conditions under which animals are raised, though the Torah does advocate the humane treatment of animals. Factory-farm veal, inhumane by almost anyone's standards, is officially kosher, although many rabbis recommend against consuming it or any other animal raised inhumanely. The Talmud does spell out the rules of slaughter. *Shochets,* trained slaughterers, must slit animals' throats cleanly and without hesitation, using a well-honed, nick-free blade. At the beginning of a slaughtering session the *shochet* blesses the process as commanded by God; the blessing is not for the animal or its life. Contrary to many people's belief, food certified kosher is not blessed by rabbis.

Apart from being assured of meat likelier to be safe, why bother buying kosher food, let alone keeping kosher? The answer for Jews is to obey God, pure and simple. As Judith Shulevitz, who is writing a book on the relevance of the Sabbath in modern times, put it to me recently, keeping kosher is meant to "carve holiness out of the physical world." It is not meant to be justified by claims for food safety or superior ethics. Such justifications have been forwarded since at least the time of Maimonides, who wrote in the mid-1100s, while a court physician to the sultan of Egypt, that both Jews and Muslims prohibited pork because the pig's "habits and food" are "very filthy and loathsome." Finding logic in the rules of kashrut is a frustrating task, as the anthropologist Marvin Harris entertainingly recounts in his book *The Sacred Cow and the Abominable Pig*. Citing numerous examples of circular, anachronistic logic, Harris explains that attempts to apply modern knowledge of hygiene and disease and zoology to the Middle East of biblical times are usually fruitless. (Harris notes, for example, that the knowledge that undercooked pork may cause trichinosis dates only to 1859.)

In her seminal essay "The Abominations of Leviticus," from *Purity and Danger*, the anthropologist Mary Douglas discouraged theologians and anthropologists alike from using modern scientific thinking to justify biblical prohibitions. Douglas posited that what underlay the rules of kashrut was the desire to establish and maintain order (or "seder"). Kashrut was meant not to safeguard the health of Jews but to bring them closer to holiness, by keeping them separate from other tribes and religions.

The very root of the word "holiness," Douglas pointed out, means "set apart." She concluded,

> The dietary laws [were] like signs which at every turn inspired meditation on the oneness, purity and completeness of God. By rules of avoidance, holiness was given a physical expression in every encounter with the animal kingdom and at every meal.

Keeping kosher is at heart a spiritual choice, then, and separation and the inexplicable are its essence. The practical consequences of that choice provide daily challenges, and daily connections to the spiritual.

The biggest challenge is the first: converting a kitchen. Stern gives friendly and practical instructions in her book, along with the advice that if you're thinking of making the switch, Passover is a good time to do it. Observant Jews must clean their kitchens top to bottom anyway, to excise all traces of *chametz*, or bread and leavened foods. Most American Jews, following the advice of US rabbinical organizations, also use separate Passover dishes, like the ones my family hauled up from the basement before the first seder. These two new sets of dishes, one for milk and one for meat, are in addition to the two sets of dishes used the rest of the year. Jews in other countries simply *kasher*— or "make kosher" — their everyday dishes for the holiday, usually by immersing them in boiling water (Stern quotes an Israeli friend who asked, "Who had four sets of dishes?").

The annual ritual of cleansing and separation is a smaller-scale version of a changeover to kosher, a more-stringent procedure that requires days of pantry purging and thorough cleaning of cabinets and drawers; you must also boil metal cookware and make sure you have two of everything (wooden spoons, knives, broiling pans). Labeling cabinets and drawers is helpful, and so is color coding, a tradition familiar from the red (meat) and blue (milk) dish towels and soap pads of my childhood. Stern traces the widespread use of color coding to the soap manufacturer Israel Rokeach, who developed a kosher soap (made without animal fat) in his native Poland and produced blue and red versions of it in 1890s New York.

Not everything in a non-kosher kitchen can be converted. Most toaster ovens, for instance, cannot survive the scorching heat necessary to *kasher* them, as stoves and regular ovens can; buy a new one. With this requirement as with all others, Stern is careful to say, Consult a rabbi. There is no single authority and no one rule.

Stern leavens (if I may) the book with reminiscences of her childhood, when, as a displeased nine-year-old who liked bacon, she was made to participate in her parents' decision to go kosher, as part of an attempt to add meaning to their lives. I already knew Stern to be an expert baker; we met when she worked at this magazine, and we later collaborated on baking and candy recipes for a book I wrote on coffee. She's also an active member, with her husband and three children, of a Cambridge synagogue. Her account of how her initial resentment turned to acceptance and then to enthusiasm may mirror what others newly converted to kashrut feel.

Daily challenges become second nature; daily deprivations are surprisingly few. And habits become ingrained. My sister does not keep kosher — nor do I — but she recently told me that it would never occur to her to mix milk or butter with meat in her kitchen, and the only time I countenance it in mine is for the ultra-*treif* pork simmered in milk. My stepmother, who did not grow up in a Jewish home, chose to keep kosher when she married my father, and says that after twenty years the one rule of kashrut she still resents is not mixing milk and meat dishes in a single dishwasher load, which she finds both illogical and wasteful.

She enjoys experimenting with recipes in the Jewish cookbooks I've sent her over the years. The reigning queens of the genre, Joan Nathan, Claudia Roden, and Faye Levy, have written numerous books demonstrating the sometimes astonishing international scope of Jewish food, most but not all of it kosher. Judy Zeidler, a sophisticated cook and traveler, has written many books of up-to-date recipes that happen to be kosher (*The Gourmet Jewish Cook, The 30-Minute Kosher Cook*), taking the only sensible approach: her recipes are wide-ranging and good, and don't call for fake versions of ingredients like cream, butter, and bacon, which are almost always unsatisfactory and awful-tasting. Maggie Glezer, the author of the comprehensive *Artisan Baking Across America,* recently published *A Blessing of Bread,* with two dozen recipes for challah, and instructions for making matzoh — though you'd have to be very flexible in personal observance to call it kosher for Passover.

My favorite book on Jewish cooking, frequently in and out of print since its 1981 release, miraculously appeared in the mail while I was researching this article, in a fresh reprint with a slightly revised title: *Classic Italian Jewish Cooking.* The author, Edda Servi Machlin, grew up in Pitigliano, a small hill town in southern Tuscany, where her father was the rabbi and *shochet*. This is a great cookbook, on a par with Marcella Hazan's books in clarity and in promoting a wide understanding of and reverence for Italian food. It has inspired many of my travels throughout Italy, and I once made a pilgrimage to Pitigliano, which she lovingly evokes as a pre-war model of comity between Jew and gentile.

Machlin includes numerous Passover recipes, including chicken soup with peas and homemade egg noodles made with Passover flour, and a showpiece dish of lamb chops with chicken meatballs and spinach (the San Francisco author Joyce Goldstein fruitfully mined similar territory in *Saffron Shores: Jewish Cooking of the Southern Mediterranean*). But the annual conundrum that sends Passover cooks to bookstores is dessert, and Machlin supplied the cake that has become my family's favorite at seders — torta del re, or king's cake, an elegant almond torte that is fresh-tasting from lemon peel. It inspires that most desired end-of-seder-meal exclamation: "This doesn't taste like Passover!"

For a cake that will yield twelve thin slices, line the bottom of a ten-inch springform pan with parchment or wax paper, grease it, and coat it with matzoh meal (or bread crumbs outside Passover). Preheat the oven to 325° with a rack placed in the middle. Beat five egg whites with a pinch of salt until they are stiff, and set them aside. In a large bowl beat at medium speed five egg yolks, adding one and a quarter cups of sugar in a slow stream, until the yolks are lemon-colored, three to five minutes. Gradually fold in two and a half cups (ten ounces) of blanched almonds, chopped very fine but not ground, along with the grated rind of one lemon, a teaspoon of vanilla extract, and, if desired, a teaspoon of almond extract. The nuts will gum up the airy yolk mixture, but persevere; stir to make a coarse, hard paste. Work in a third of the beaten whites to lighten the paste, and then fold in the remaining whites as delicately as possible. Pour the batter evenly into the prepared pan and place in the center of the rack. Bake for one hour without opening the oven door. Then turn off the heat and leave the cake in the oven, with the door ajar, for ten to fifteen minutes. Remove the pan from the oven and invert it onto a cooling rack. When the cake is thoroughly cool (wait at least thirty minutes), release it upside down onto a serving plate. Sift confectioner's sugar (be sure it's kosher for Passover, meaning made with potato rather than corn starch) on top, and decorate with toasted sliced almonds if you like. The root of holiness may be separation, but this is a cake that can unite the most kosher-skeptical of cooks.

THOMAS LYNCH

Our Near-Death Experience

FROM *The New York Times*

IMAGES OF THE PAPAL WAKE dominated the news this week: the
dead man's body vested, mitered, laid out among his people in St.
Peter's Square, blessed with water and incense, borne from one station to the next in a final journey. Such images — along with the
idea that millions of people would wait for hours merely for a
chance to pass by the body itself — may have given pause to many
Americans for whom the presence of the dead at their own funerals has become strangely unfashionable.

For many bereaved Americans, the "celebration of life" involves
a guest list open to everyone except the actual corpse, which is often dismissed, disappeared without rubric or witness, buried or
burned, out of sight, out of mind, by paid functionaries like me. So
the visible presence of the pope's body at the pope's wake and funeral strikes many as an oddity, a quaint relic. How "Catholic" some
will say, or how "Italian" or "Polish" or "traditional"; how "lavish" or
"expensive" or "barbaric." Such things were said when Diana, Prin-
cess of Wales, died and when Ronald Reagan did.

In truth, what happened in Rome this week, like what happens
in Michigan or Manhattan or Mozambique when one of our own
kind dies, is a deeply human event, unique to our species — this
going the distance with our dead. Cocker spaniels do not bother
with this, neither do rock bass, nor rhododendrons, nor any other
thing that lives and dies.

But we do. Wherever our spirits go, or don't, ours is a species that
down the millenniums has learned to deal with death (the idea of
the thing) by dealing with the dead (the thing itself) in all the flesh

and frailty of the human condition. We process grief by processing the objects of our grief, the bodies of the dead, from one place to the next. We bear mortality by bearing mortals — the living and the dead — to the brink of a changed reality: heaven or Valhalla or whatever is next. We commit and commend them into the nothingness or somethingness, into the presence of God or God's absence. Whatever afterlife there is or isn't, human beings have marked their ceasing to be by going to the tomb or the fire or the grave, the holy tree or deep sea, whatever sacred space of oblivion to which we consign our dead. Humans have been doing this for forty thousand years.

I've been doing funerals for almost forty.

I came up burying Presbyterians and Catholics, devout and lapsed, born again and backslid. Baptists, Orthodox Christians, an occasional Zen Buddhist, and variously observant Jews. For each of these sets, there were infinite subsets. We had right old Calvinists who drank only single malts and were all good Masons and were mad for the bagpipes, just as we had former Methodists who worked their way up the Reformation ladder after they married into money or made a little killing in the market. We had Polish Catholics and Italian ones, Irish and Hispanic and Byzantine, and Jews who were Jews in the way some Lutherans are Lutheran — for births and deaths and first marriages.

My late father, himself a funeral director, schooled me in the local orthodoxies and their protocols as I have schooled my sons and daughter who work with me. There was a kind of comfort, I suppose, in knowing exactly what would be done with you, one's ethnic and religious identities having established long ago the fashions and the fundamentals for one's leave-taking. And while the fashions might change, the fundamental ingredients for a funeral were the same: there is someone who has quit breathing forever, some others to whom it apparently matters, and someone else who stands between the quick and dead and says something like "Behold, I show you a mystery" or "Do not be afraid" or "Goodbye."

Late in the last century more homegrown doxologies became more popular. We boomers, vexed by the elder metaphors of grief and death, wanted to create our own. Everyone was into the available "choices."

So we started doing more cremations — it made good sense. Folks seemed less "grounded" than their grandparents, more "scattered" somehow. "Bridge Over Troubled Water" replaced "How

Great Thou Art." And if Paul's Letter to the Romans or the Book of Job was replaced by Omar Khayyam or Emily Dickinson, what harm? After great pain, a formal feeling comes, and rings as true as any sacred text. A death in the family is, as Miss Emily describes it: First — chill — then stupor — then the letting go.

Amid all the high fashions and fashion blunders, the ritual wheel that worked the space between the living and the dead still got us where we needed to go. It made room for the good laugh, the good cry, and the power of faith brought to bear on the mystery of mortality. The broken circle within the community of folks who shared blood or geography or belief with the dead was closed again. Someone brought the casseroles, someone brought the prayers, someone brought a shovel or lighted the fire. Everyone was consoled by everyone else. The wheel that worked the space between the living and the dead ran smooth.

For many Americans, however, that wheel is not just broken but off track or in need of reinvention. The loosened ties of faith and family, of religious and ethnic identity, have left them ritually adrift, bereft of custom, symbol, metaphor, and meaningful liturgy or language. Times formerly spent in worship or communion are now spent shopping or Web-browsing or otherwise passing time. Many Americans are now spiritual tourists without home places or core beliefs to return to.

Instead of Methodists or Muslims, we are now dead golfers or gardeners, bikers or bowlers. The bereaved are not so much family and friends or fellow believers as like-minded hobbyists and enthusiasts. And I have become less the funeral director and more the memorial caddy of sorts, getting the dead out of the way and the living assembled for a memorial "event" that is neither sacred nor secular but increasingly absurd — a triumph of accessories over essentials, stuff over substance, theme over theology. The genuine dead are downsized or disappeared or turned into knickknacks in a kind of funereal karaoke — bodiless obsequies where the finger food is good, the music transcendent, the talk determinedly "life affirming," the accouterments all purposefully cheering and inclusive and where someone can be counted on to declare "closure" just before the Merlot runs out. We leave these events with the increasing sense that something is missing.

Something is.

Just as he showed us something about suffering and sickness and dying in his last days alive, in death Pope John Paul II showed us something about grieving and taking our leave. The good death, good grief, good funerals come from keeping the vigils, from bearing our burdens honorably, from honest witness and remembrance. They come from going the distance with the ones we love.

CHARLES MARTIN

After 9/11

FROM *The Hudson Review*

We lived in an apartment on the ridge
Running along Manhattan's northwest side,
On a street between the Cloisters and the Bridge,

On a hill George Washington once fortified
To keep his fledglings from the juggernaut
Cumbrously rolling toward them. Many died

When those defenses failed, and where they fought
Are now a ball field and a set of swings
In an urban park: old men lost in thought

Advance their pawns against opponents' kings
Or gossip beneath a sycamore's high branches
All afternoon until the sunset brings

The teenagers to occupy their benches.
The park makes little of its history,
With only traces of the walls or trenches

Disputed, died by, and surrendered; we
Tread on the outline of a parapet
Pressed into asphalt unassertively,

And on a wall descending to the street,
Observe a seriously faded plaque
Acknowledging a still unsettled debt.

What strength of memory can summon back

That ghostly army of fifteen-year-olds
And their grandfathers? The Hessians attack

And the American commander folds;
We could have watched those losers made to file
Past jeering victors to the waiting holds

Of prison vessels from our Tudor-style
Apartment building's roof.
                                    When, without warning,
Twin towers that rose up a quarter mile

Into a cloudless sky were, early one morning,
Wreathed in the smoke from interrupted flight,
When they and what burst into them were burning

Together, like a secret brought to light,
Like something we'd imagined but not known,
The intersection of such speed, such height —

We went up on our roof and saw first one
And then the other silently unmake
Its outline, horrified, as it slid down,

Leaving a smear of ashes in its wake.
That scene, retold from other points of view
Would grow familiar, deadening the ache:

How often we saw each jet fly into
Its target, with the same street-level gasp
Of shock and disbelief remaining new.

Little by little we would come to grasp
What *had* occurred, our incredulity
Finely abraded by the videotape's

Grim repetitions. A nonce community
Began almost at once to improvise
New rituals for curbside healing; we

Saw flowers, candles, shrines materialize
In shuttered storefronts for the benefit
Of those who'd stopped the digging with their cries

And those who hadn't. None came out of it,
None would be found still living there, beneath
The rubble scooped up out of Babel's pit:

From the clueless anonymity of death
Came fragments identified by DNA
Samples taken from bits of bone and teeth,

But that was later. In those early days
When we went outside, we walked among the few
Grieving for someone they would grieve for always,

And walked among the many others who,
Like ourselves, had no loss as profound,
But knew someone who knew someone who knew

One of the ones who fell back as he wound
A spiral up the narrow, lethal staircase
Or one who tumbled helplessly to the ground,

The fall that our imaginations trace
Even today: those whom we most resembled,
Whose images we still cannot erase. . . .

On the third night, the neighbors reassembled
For a candlelight procession: in the wind,
Each flame, protected by a cupped hand, trembled

As though to mimic an uncertain mind
Struggling toward some insufficient word —
What certitude could our searching find?

Those who had come here to be reassured
Would leave with nothing: nothing could be said
To answer, or *have* answered, the unheard

Cries of the lost. Yet here we had been led
To gather at the entrance to the park
In a mass defined by candles for the dead,

As though they were beyond us in the dark
And with them were those others, who had been
Surrendered here, marched off, forced to embark

On one of the prison ships they perished in,
All now restored to us in a sublime
Confirmation of the pattern, the design.

But none appeared to mock *this* paradigm:
All that has come before us lies below
In layer pressing upon layer. . . .
                                        Time

Is an old man telling us how, long ago,
As a child in Brooklyn he went out to play,
And prodding the summer earth with his bare toe

Discovered a bone unburied in the clay,
From one of those whose rotting corpses filled
The hulks that settled into Wallabout Bay;

Time is the monument that he saw built
To turn their deaths into a victory,
Its base filled with their bones dredged out of silt;

Time is the silt grain polished by the sea,
The passageway that leads from one to naught;
Time is what argues with us constantly

Against the need to hold them all in thought,
Time is what places them beyond recall,
Against the need of the falling to be caught,

Against the woman who's begun to fall
And the woman who is watching from below;
Time is the photo peeling from the wall,

The busboy, who came here from Mexico
And stepped off from a window ledge, aflame;
Time is the only outcome we will know,

Against the need of those lost to be claimed
(Their last words caught in our mobile phones)
Against the need of the nameless to be named

In our city built on unacknowledged bones.

WILFRED M. MCCLAY

The Secret of the Self

FROM *First Things*

CONSIDER THE OBITUARY COLUMN in your local newspaper —
not the obituary of anyone famous but just an ordinary obituary of
an ordinary person from an ordinary place.

Consider it first as a surviving family member or friend, the one
who has to gather the information for the obituary and select the
appropriate facts. Many of us have had this experience and know
how difficult and unsatisfying the process can be. The right balance between the competing demands of tenderness, respect, justice, loyalty, and candor is hard to find.

Consider, as well, what photograph of the deceased should be
used to accompany the text. Rightly or wrongly, we grant enormous
weight to the *image* in forming our enduring sense of the person.
What image, in what setting and at what age, should be provided?
Should the photograph be formal and artful, soberly and self-
consciously posed? Or casual and spontaneous, a blithe and impromptu slice of life? Should it record youth, or maturity, or old
age?

The sophisticated response to this string of questions is to assert
that there is no such thing as a human totality or essence, and leave
it at that. There is no unitary self, only — as Emerson once put it —
a series of surfaces upon which we skate. But such a glib and
weightless jibe, while it may be good enough for the seminar room,
is no help. Obituaries must still be written, and photographs provided, because one's respects must be paid, and there are better
and worse ways of going about it. The roughness of the judgments
that life forces upon us does not excuse us from responsibility for
making them.

Life rarely resembles a Hollywood movie, in which the hero goes out in a blaze of glory, leaving a trail of smiles, admiration, harmony, and contentment in his wake. The actual end of most human lives is sad, painful, sometimes grueling, profoundly embarrassing, and pathetic, often leaving emptiness, loss, regret, relief, and other contradictory and disturbing emotions in its wake. And so one would never pick a deathbed photograph to accompany an obituary. (Indeed, it probably reveals something important about our age's sensibilities that we have come to find unthinkably ghoulish and unpleasant the once-venerable idea of creating a death mask as a memento of the departed.)

But why would one then feel bound to use an old-age photograph instead? Why not make the photograph stand as an idealized representation of the departed, not in a state of decline or debility, but at the pinnacle of physical strength and beauty — even if the face being rendered thereby is a face from thirty or forty years ago, a face much more attractive and cheerful, but one that almost no one still living would recognize?

We can see the logic in that choice and yet ask: what is really being memorialized by such a photograph? Doesn't such a choice imply that the aged are merely living on the downhill slope of life and that our essential nature is actually realized in youth or early adulthood, and that nothing worth representing or acknowledging is gained by subsequent experience — as though there were some brief and shining moment, at around the age of thirty-five, that one was at one's peak, was fully oneself, even if it hardly seemed thus at the time? One sometimes notices that women who die in their seventies and eighties are nevertheless represented in their obituaries by pictures taken in their twenties or early thirties. Is this merely an example of all-too-human vanity at work? Or is there an implicit judgment about when a woman is most fully herself? When we judge that a man is "past his prime," does that statement carry a larger significance about the way we understand the relative dignity of life's passages?

A picture may be worth a thousand words — but there are many things a picture can simply never do. No single moment is ever going to capture the essence of a human being. No one can translate four dimensions into two — or imagine what individuals look like *sub specie aeternitatis,* as they must appear in the eyes of God. Great portrait painting may gesture toward the larger frame within which an individual life moves and has its being. But plain obituary photographs claim no such ingenuity. Indeed, what makes them so poignant is precisely their artlessness. It is as if their subjects make a silent plea to us, a modern restatement of Thomas Gray's "Elegy in a Country Churchyard," asking us to keep faith with them by remembering the unrendered reality of their lives, filling in the silences, completing their stories in our hearts.

An obituary always falls short of what we would like it to be — and yet, it is better than nothing. When we write one, we believe we are remembering something discrete and doing something more than recording a list of items on a curriculum vitae. We are, in some sense, striving for a God's-eye view: not just people at particular moments in their lives, but people in their distilled essence, both as they were known and as they knew, or tried to know, themselves. We are attempting to represent a *soul,* something whose nature is greater and deeper than any particular instance can adequately show.

Our age, of course, prefers to speak of selves. "Souls" seems a term too laden with metaphysical implications to pass through customs. But it is striking to note how poorly the word "self," even though it is one of the cardinal terms of our discourse, serves us as a marker for that thread of essential continuity in the individual life that we acknowledge and commemorate in the obituary. An obituary is not, or not only, about a self. The self is too changeable and contingent and interior a thing for that, and too tied to a romantic view of the isolated and autonomous individual, to tell us adequately about the individual. The self is a movable and malleable target, one that adapts to changing circumstances, revising its constitution repeatedly over the course of an individual life, taking on strikingly different colorations at different times.

And it is, in some fundamental way, unreachable. Indeed, the self can even be thought of as something that doesn't match our lives exactly, coming into being after birth, as in the psychological development of a very young child, and ceasing to exist before death, as in cases of severe dementia or mental impairment. Yet even when a sense of self seems to have departed entirely from an individual we know — and this disappearance itself is often hard to ascertain, since the self is so irreducibly a subjective and interior phenomenon, and is so remarkably protean and resilient — there is something else that remains. What is one to call it?

That something else, I would contend, is better described by the term "person." It is the person, not merely the self, that we attempt to capture in the obituary. It is the person, not the self, that is not only the home address of our consciousness, but the nexus of our social relations, the chief object of our society's legal protections, the bearer of its political rights, and the communicant in its religious life. To put it another way, it is the person, not the self, whose nature is inextricably bound up in the web of obligations and duties that characterize our actual lives in history, in human society — child, parent, sibling, spouse, associate, friend, and citizen — the positions in which we find ourselves functioning both as agents and acted-upon.

The concept of the self, so steeped for us in romantic individualism, once seemed the most stable thing of all, the resting place of the Cartesian *cogito* and the seat of conscience. The young Emerson could still believe that introspection was the royal road to the universe's secrets, so that the commands to "know thyself" and "study nature" were different ways of saying the same thing. But in the long years since Emerson, the link between self and nature has broken down, leaving us to soldier on alone in exploring the dim and misty marshlands of ungrounded subjectivity. The self has proven a highly unstable concept, having a tendency to dissolve on closer examination into a kaleidoscopic whirl of unrelated colors and moods, an ensemble of social roles, a play of lights undirected by any integrative force standing behind them all.

The concept of person, however, extending all the way back to its Latin roots (*persona*), accepts the social nature of the human individual, and the necessity of social recognition, without ever regarding the individual as reducible to these things. In a word, it stands nearer to the facts of social existence. It is a less vivid but more fundamental concept. A self is what I *experience*. A person is what I *am*.

"The person" has not fared especially well at the hands of modern attempts to write about history, which have generally sought to locate historical explanations in the workings of large structures, impersonal forces, and social groups rather than the vagaries and razor-edged contingencies of individual character and agency.

Some of this has to do with the enduring quest to make history resemble a science, a vision that took hold in earnest in the nineteenth century and has never entirely lost its appeal among academic historians. And as Alexis de Tocqueville observed, some of this has to do with the profound intellectual changes characteristic of a democratizing world, changes that alter both the subject matter of history and the historian's manner of approach to it. Historians who write in an aristocratic age tend, Tocqueville believed, "to refer all occurrences to the particular will and character of certain individuals." But those historians who write in a large modern democracy tend to make "general facts serve to explain more things," so that "fewer things are then assignable to individual influences." Ironically, the same democratic age that exalted the value of the individual also rendered that individual a prisoner of aggregate forces, with little or no power to control or affect the events of his day.

Tocqueville's comments seem especially germane in the present context, for he was very concerned that the democratic historian's emphasis on "general facts," while not entirely wrong, was prone to exaggeration, and therefore could become dangerously misleading. Although the change in historical circumstances made necessary a change in the manner of historical analysis, the extent of that change could easily be overstated. The historians who devoted all their attention to general causes were, he thought, wrong to deny the special influence of individuals, merely because such influence was more difficult to track than had been the case in earlier times.

He saw this not only as an explanatory problem but as a psychological and spiritual one. By promoting such distortions, these writers were creating false images of the human situation in both past and present, which could have the disastrous effect of depriving "the people themselves of the power of modifying their condition," thereby encouraging a kind of fatalism and paralysis of will, and a steady contraction of the human prospect. While the historians of antiquity "taught how to command," those in our own time, he complained, "teach only how to obey." They produce works in which "the author often appears great, but humanity is always diminutive." The belief that individual human agency should be factored out of history was, he feared, a self-fulfilling dictum, since the factored-out would come to believe it themselves.

While this generalizing tendency Tocqueville described was gathering strength, the main currents of modern Western thought in other disciplines, such as philosophy and literary studies, were moving in the opposite direction, toward an ever-tighter embrace of antinomianism and radical subjectivity. Yet the paradox was only a seeming one, for the two opposites went together. What, after all, could be more logical, in a sense, than the impulse to resist the coercive, domineering force of the increasingly organized and mechanized external world of the nineteenth century — ordered and disciplined and measured on every side by clocks, factories, whistles, telephones, maps, telegraphs, railroads, state bureaucracies, large business corporations, and Standard Time Zones — by withdrawing into a zone of inner freedom, by cultivating and furnishing a large and luxuriant interior realm, insulated from the world's tightening grip? It is no paradox that we use the term "modern" to refer both to the external material and social forces that transformed the world, and to the internal intellectual and expressive movements that wrestled with, and often deplored, the human costs of that same transformation. They were two facets of the same phenomenon.

And yet, the seeming gulf of this opposition helps explain much about the ways in which the dualism of "individualism" and "collectivism" came to be understood for much of the twentieth century. It helps explain why so much of the energy of American social and cultural criticism, past and present, has been devoted to the sustained critique of nearly any perceived force of political power or social conformism — power elites, corporate magnates, hidden persuaders, would-be traditions, and other suspect cultural hegemonies — that might inhibit the full expression of the self as an autonomous or relatively unconditioned historical actor.

Our age has lost none of its appetite for fables of personal liberation, and it tends to side with the rebels Roger Williams and Anne Hutchinson, or with the precepts of Emersonian self-reliance, or with the antinomian moral fables offered repeatedly by movies. We are asked to side with the put-upon individual, cast as an unjustly thwarted soul yearning to breathe free, and we are instructed to hiss at the figures of social or political authority, whose efforts to maintain order establish them as monsters and enemies of humanity.

Yet autonomy, like the self that purports to exercise it, turns out to be elusive and unreliable, never quite delivering what it promises. Even the most energetically "unencumbered self" is always already a "person" enmeshed in social, intellectual, and institutional frameworks that structure and enable the ideal of autonomy. But the liberatory preoccupations of so much modern scholarship and thought have made it difficult to move beyond the amorphous and untenable concept of self to the sturdier and more tenable concept of person. Indeed, one could argue, following the historian Christopher Shannon, that the agenda of modern cultural criticism, relentlessly intent as it has been upon "the destabilization of received social meanings," has served only to further the social trends it deplores, including the reduction of an ever-widening range of human activities and relations to the status of commodities and instruments, rather than ends in themselves.

One would be a bold prophet indeed to predict that this tendency will exhaust itself anytime soon. But things will start to change when we insist upon seeing the human person as the focal point of historical inquiry, the cynosure of historical meaning, the fleetingly visible figure to be sought in history's lavish carpet. The study of history is arid and incomplete unless it is understood as a work about (and by) individual human beings — and, moreover, a story whose substance and manner of telling are matters of moral significance. A shift from "self" to "person" can strengthen that endeavor. It can rescue the individual from being smothered by giant structural explanations, the prospect that Tocqueville feared. But it also can rescue the individual from being let loose into a whirling centrifuge of subjectivism and indeterminacy, a prospect even more inimical to historical understanding.

The recovery of the idea of the human person will necessarily entail a reappropriation of neglected religious and other long-standing moral and spiritual normative traditions. As Charles Taylor has argued in his magisterial study *Sources of the Self,* the coherence and integrity of the human person rests upon a moral foundation, on a set of presuppositions about the structure and teleology of the moral universe. A moral disposition toward one's world, and a prior assent to certain moral criteria, are the preconditions of there being any psychological order and consistency at all in a human personality. Health is built upon morality, and not vice versa.

The concept of moral responsibility, which therapy would seek to banish or marginalize, turns out to be essential and inescapable. There is no value-neutral way of being happy and whole.

Martin Buber's 1938 essay "What Is Man?" is still remarkably fresh and clarifying, stressing the "dialogic" and relational qualities for which Buber had become famous with his great 1936 book *I and Thou*. For Buber, the human person was reducible neither to the discrete features of individualism nor the collective ones of social aggregates, let alone the vagaries of language and discourse. The study of man, Buber asserted instead, must start with the consideration of "man *with* man." If you begin there, "you see human life, dynamic, twofold, the giver and the receiver, he who does and he who endures, the attacking force and the defending force, the nature which investigates and the nature which supplies information, the request begged and granted — and always both together, completing one another in mutual contribution, together showing forth man."

Or, as the French Neo-Thomist Jacques Maritain put it nearly a decade later, "There is nothing more illusory than to pose the problem of the person and the common good in terms of opposition," for in reality, it is "in the nature of things that man, as part of society, should be ordained to the common good." The problem of the person "is posed in terms of reciprocal subordination and mutual implication." Here one finds no concession either to the romance of the heroic atomic self or to the historiography of vast impersonal forces, or to the putative opposition between them.

One might go further and point out that the concept of "person" helps us understand human dignity as something deriving from the fact of one's intrinsic being — rather than from the extent of freestanding autonomy, the "quality of life," that a person might demonstrate. Such a view would stand in the longer Western tradition of individualism, affirming the diversity of legitimate human roles and ranks in society as we find it. At the same time, it would be in direct competition to the increasingly influential view that the dignity of any individual life is dependent upon the competency of the individual, as though a self with a poor quality of life has a life not worth living.

One thing seems clear, however. We need to rescue the idea of individual dignity from its captivity in individual psychology and postmodernist subjectivity. And this is what the word "person" begins to accomplish. It reaffirms the core meaning of individualism with its insistence upon the ultimate value of the individual human being. But it also embraces the core insight of communitarianism: the recognition that the self is made in relationship and culture, and the richest forms of individuality cannot be achieved without the sustained company of others. And it would build upon Tocqueville's further insight that it is in the school of public life, and in the embrace and exercise of the title of "citizen," that the selves of men and women become most meaningfully equal, individuated, and free — not in those fleeting, and often illusory, moments when they escape the constraints of society, and retreat into a zone of privacy, subjectivity, and endlessly reconstructed narratives of the "self."

Henry James's celebrated story "The Figure in the Carpet," a characteristically multilayered and inscrutable tale, relates the quest of an earnest young literary critic for the hidden meaning, "the undiscovered, not to say undiscoverable, secret," animating the voluminous work of an eminent novelist named Hugh Vereker. What was sought by all critics, but grasped by none, was "the general intention" behind all of Vereker's books, their unifying meaning. The critics and Vereker's other readers, though consistently mystified, were yet certain that "the thing we were all so blank about was vividly there. It was something . . . in the primal plan, something like a complex figure in a Persian carpet."

The story is a masterpiece of ambiguity, impossible to reduce to a single stable interpretation. Indeed, it can even be read as a mockery of the whole literary enterprise, pairing dull and uncomprehending readers who ploddingly manage to miss the obvious, with clever authors (both the fictional Vereker and the actual James) who feel compelled to play the trickster, taunting their readers with the hint that there is something — indeed, the whole point of it all — that they don't get.

Predictably, many recent critics, brilliantly managing to combine indeterminacy with reductionism, think the story is all about homosexuality and the epistemology of the closet. There are even Oz-like moments when one suspects that all the elaborate concealments exist to conceal precisely nothing, and the story is an exer-

cise in mockery, put forward by an author who himself felt perpetually misunderstood and undervalued. Yet such a bitter and
nihilistic interpretation is very hard to sustain in the end, and one
is left instead with the sense that the search for a unifying idea —
for the figure in the carpet — is a quest too compelling to refuse.
The name "Vereker," after all, suggests some relationship to the
truth.

And so the story teaches us something about how to look for
such things — if not necessarily to know when we have found them
— and to know what kinds of secrets are worth pursuing. The great
literary critic Frank Kermode wrote of "The Figure in the Carpet"
that "Vereker's secret — 'the thing for the critic to find' — is not,
we infer, the sort of thing the celibate and impotent may look for
when they speculate about sex. It is a triumph of patience, a quality
pervading the life of the subject, like marriage. It is not the subject
but the treatment, which is why it is a suffusing presence in all
Vereker's work, and not a nugget hidden here or there. It is a matter of life and death and a matter of jokes and games. The error of
criticism is a ludicrous one; it is also tragic."

We should avoid such errors in searching for the figure, for the
human person. The suffusing presence will not be disclosed in a
single fact-nugget, or by a dark secret, pulled from a personal diary
or a police file or a divorce testimony or how-to manual. Instead, it
is the sort of complex secret that reposes in plain view, an abiding
condition that can only be seen, if at all, by standing still and looking, until the pattern emerges and makes meaningful the life of the
subject.

It may be as hard to detect as the atmosphere. Or the enveloping
climate of marriage. Or the light that rings the ordinary images of
ordinary faces on the local paper's obituary page — or the shad-
owy depths beneath their smiles. Seeing it may well be a gift of
grace. Yet such are the lights and shadows, and figures in the carpet, for which we should search.

RICHARD JOHN NEUHAUS

Our American Babylon

FROM *First Things*

ONCE UPON A TIME — it was the 1976 bicentennial of the American founding, to be precise — I wrote a book on the American experiment and the idea of covenant. *Time* magazine picked up on it and reported, "On the day of judgment, Neuhaus wants to meet God as an American."

That's not quite right. What I wrote is that I *expect* to meet God as an American. And that for the simple reason that, among all the things I am or have been or hope to be, I am undeniably an American. It is not the most important thing, but it is an inescapable thing. Nor, even were I so inclined, should I try to escape it. It is a pervasive and indelible part of what is called one's "identity." Among American thinkers, and not least among American theologians, one frequently discerns an attempt to escape one's time and place. It is a very American thing to try to do. We are never more American than when we believe we have transcended being American. America is, after all, as some like to say, the world's first "universal nation."

The theologian Robert Jenson has employed to fine effect the phrase "the story of the world." The story of Israel and the Church, he writes, is nothing less than the story of the world, and the world is today lost in its confusions because it has "lost its story." I would add that, for those of us who are Americans, we are *as Americans* part of the story that is the story of the world. Moreover, America itself — this nation that the founders called an experiment and, like any experiment, may succeed or fail — is part of the story that is the story of the world. Of the many ways of thinking about America — economic, political, cultural, etc. — there is today a striking scarcity of thinking about America theologically.

It was not always so. Not so long ago, American intellectuals, including American theologians, spent considerable time thinking about their place as Americans. But in the last half century or so, we have largely lost our story and our place in the story of the world. Theologians, too, have succumbed to the false-consciousness of having transcended the American experience, which is expressed, more often than not, in a typically American anti-Americanism that is relished and imitated by others, notably by European intellectuals. As in the writing of biography, or of history more generally, one cannot think truly about a story with which one is not sympathetically engaged. Love is sometimes blind, but contempt is always blind.

Perhaps we should from the start attend to one common misunderstanding. To think about the American experiment theologically, or to suggest that God is not indifferent to the American experiment, in no way implies that people who are Americans are "special" in the sense of occupying a superior place in God's concerns and purposes. The Christian tradition gives us to understand that a beggar on the streets of Calcutta is in the view of God, *sub specie aeternitatis,* as important as the president of the United States. As for the proud pretensions of worldly powers, Psalm 2 tells us that God holds them in derision, laughing them to scorn. And yet, it is precisely God's concern for everyone, including the littlest and the least, that warrants our belief that He takes an interest in realities that affect billions of people on earth. America and its role in the world is such a reality.

To the God who marks every sparrow that falls, *everything* matters. God is infinite and his capacity for concern is inexhaustible. To propose that He cares more about one people than another is both unseemly and theologically incoherent. To God and to its five million citizens, the Kingdom of Denmark "matters" as much as the United States of America. But the Kingdom of Denmark is not, insofar as we can measure consequence, as consequential for human history as is, for better and for worse, the United States. Our subject is the stories within the story of the world, which is to say human history, which is to say the events and forces that influence and engage people who are the object of God's infinite concern.

Any suggestion that one nation is more "special" to God than another is excluded. The people of Israel and the Church joined to Israel are His elect people, but God is no respecter of nations. At the same time, neither is He indifferent to, among other things beyond numbering, the political configurations that may hinder or serve His purposes. It is by no means the decisive thing, but neither is it a trifling thing, that we Christians in America are *American* Christians. We have a measure of responsibility for this country and its influence in the world. As do Danes for Denmark, Japanese for Japan, Kenyans for Kenya, and on and on. Because America impinges upon them all, they, too, have more than a passing interest in how the American story within the story of the world is told.

Thought that is real and not merely, as Cardinal John Henry Newman put it, "notional," is thought that is sympathetically *situated* in time and place. The Letter to the Hebrews reminds us that Christians have here no abiding city. In the third eucharistic prayer of the Mass we pray, "Strengthen in faith and love your pilgrim Church on earth." We Christians are a pilgrim people, a people on the way, exiles from our true home, aliens in a strange land. There is in all the Christian tradition no more compelling depiction of our circumstance than Saint Augustine's *City of God*. Short of the final coming of the Kingdom, the City of God and the earthly city are intermingled. We are to make use of, pray for, and do our share for the earthly city. Here Augustine cites the words of Jeremiah urging the people not to fear exile in Babylon: "Seek the welfare of the city where I have sent you into exile, and pray to the LORD on its behalf, for in its peace you will find your peace."

It is often forgotten how very much of a Roman Augustine was. The *City of God* is, among other things, a sustained argument with pagan interlocutors whom we might today call "public intellectuals," in which Augustine is contending for the superiority of the Christian philosophy and understanding of history. It is sometimes suggested that Augustine knew he was writing in the ruins of a collapsing empire that he dismissed as terminally corrupt. In fact, he wrote, "The Roman Empire has been shaken rather than transformed, and that happened to it at other periods, before the preaching of Christ's name, and it recovered. There is no need to despair of its recovery at this present time. Who knows what is God's will in this matter?" Knowing that we do not know God's will does not mean that we do not think about God's will in this and all matters, for, as Augustine writes in the same text, "It is beyond anything incredible that God should have willed the kingdoms of men, their dominations and their servitudes, to be outside the range of the laws of His providence."

The Christian disposition toward exile in Babylon, wherever that Babylon may be, is nicely caught in the second-century *Letter to Diognetus,* in which it said of the Christians that "though they are residents at home in their own countries, their behavior there is more like that of transients; they take their full part as citizens, but they also submit to anything and everything as if they were aliens. For them, every foreign country is a homeland, and every homeland a foreign country."

Taking their full part as citizens in the foreign country and homeland that is our American Babylon, Christians have, at least until fairly recently, tried to understand the part of the American experiment within what Augustine calls the laws of God's providence. In this they followed the precedent of the Great Tradition of Christian thought in other times and places.

As Oliver O'Donovan reminds us in *Desire of the Nations* and his more recent *The Ways of Judgment,* "Constantinianism," far from being a term of opprobrium, represents a considerable Christian achievement of that place and time. The distinguished historian Robert Louis Wilken convincingly argues that the toleration and later establishment of the Church was not a corruption in which, as it is sometimes said today, the Church ended up "doing ethics for Caesar." When, in A.D. 390, Saint Ambrose excommunicated the Christian Theodosius for his massacre in Thessalonika, he was holding Caesar accountable to the ethics of the Church. Similarly, what is often dismissively referred to as medieval "Christendom" can be seen as a creative coordination, for its time and place, of the tensions between, and the mutual interests of, the earthly city and the City of God.

In the light of this long and complex tradition, we can view the distinctive ways in which American Christians have tried to understand the American story — the ways in which (if one is permitted that barbarous phrase) they "did theology" about America. The first Puritan settlers understood themselves to be, in Perry Miller's happy phrase, on an errand into the wilderness. The image was that of God's chosen people on the way to the promised land, and they were the New Israel. Sometimes they and the New World *were* Jerusalem, having escaped the captivity of the Babylon of the Old World and, most particularly, having escaped the Babylon of Catholicism and of the insufficiently Protestantized Church of England.

With these Puritan beginnings, American thinking about America radically reversed the image of exile. The Church of the *Letter to Diognetus* and of Augustine became Babylon, and the foreign country unqualifiedly the Christian homeland. In the Puritan imagination, America became Jerusalem, and even, in the more utopian flights of theological imagination, the New Jerusalem.

After his visit to this country, G. K. Chesterton famously remarked that "America is a nation with the soul of a church." The remark is both famous and true. America, he said, is about "making a home for vagabonds and a nation out of exiles." It is a "home for the homeless." It is a temporary home, to be sure, but a happy refuge for pilgrims along the way. Every human being, said Chesterton, can become an American by accepting a political creed. And the great thing about that political creed is that it leaves one free to accept a higher creed and pledge a higher allegiance to a country where we will, at last, be homeless no more.

In the absence of an ecclesiology that tethered them to the Church through time, for many American Protestant thinkers the nation with the soul of a church became their Church. That was true then, and it is true now. More than three hundred years later, in yet another reversal, some theologians today depict America itself as Babylon. But, like their Protestant forebears, they, too, have no Church in continuity with the Christian story through time. It is not enough to have the soul of a church. American Protestants have a tendency to forget that, in the biblical image, the Church is not the *soul* of Christ but the *body* of Christ. With this in mind, we can better understand Harold Bloom's argument that "the American religion" is gnosticism. Religious gnosticism goes hand in hand with ecclesiological docetism. The result is less the Christian story than the free-floating and ambiguously Christian experience untethered from an ecclesiology that, as Newman would say, is not notional but real.

But I get ahead of myself. After the Puritan errand into the wilderness came the national founding. With very few exceptions, it

was presided over by men who understood themselves to be serious
Christians. Even Jefferson — whom ideological secularists depict
as the chief, if not the only, founder — was much more of a Chris-
tian than is generally allowed. (See, for instance, Michael Novak's
On Two Wings, or James Hutson's *Religion and the Founding of the
American Republic.*)

In order to advance a principle of freedom, and in order not
to threaten the religious establishments of the several states, the
founders did a historically unprecedented thing. In the first provi-
sion of the First Amendment, they declared that the national government abdicated control of religious belief and practice. It would
take almost two hundred years — the Supreme Court's *Everson* decision of 1947 is the usual reference here — for religious freedom
to be radically recast as the government's "neutrality" between religion and irreligion, much to the benefit of irreligion. The consequence is what has been described as the naked public square. By
that phrase is meant the enforced privatization of religion and religiously informed morality, resulting in the exclusion of both from
the government of "We the People" who stubbornly persist in being a vigorously, if confusedly, religious people.

In rebelling against what claimed to be legitimate authority of
the British crown, the founders appealed to the laws of nature and
of nature's God, making the argument that they were acting upon
self-evident truths about inalienable rights with which we are endowed by the Creator. The inspiration of the errand into the wilderness resonates in The Great Seal of the United States of America printed on the back of every dollar bill, declaring this America
to be a *novus ordo seclorum* — a new order for the ages. Again, the
ecclesiological intimations appear: here is a new church, and one
hears in the background the voice of the one who promised that
the gates of hell shall not prevail against it. Thus was born what
some call the American civil religion, a religion that is intricately
intertwined with the religion that most Americans call Christian.

The church of the *novus ordo seclorum* had a thin public theology. As
political philosopher Leo Strauss observed, its founding principles
were "low but solid." Perhaps too low and not solid enough. To
change the metaphor, the new order was not wired for first-princi-
ple questions such as the humanity and rights of slaves of African
descent. As it is not wired for today's questions about the humanity

and rights of the unborn child and others who cannot assert their rights. These are the questions at the vortex of what we call the culture wars. In the 1860s the church of the *novus ordo seclorum* was shattered by the bloodiest war in our history, and from that catastrophe emerged the greatest theologian of the civil religion. Lincoln's second inaugural address, with its profound reflection on the mysteries of providence, is in some ways worthy of Saint Augustine — except, of course, without Augustine's Church and therefore without the communal bearer of the story of the world by which all other stories, including the story of America, are truly told.

American theology has suffered from an ecclesiological deficit, leading to an ecclesiological substitution of America for the Church through time. Alongside this development, and weaving its way in and out of it, is a radical and vaulting individualism that would transcend the creaturely limits of time, space, tradition, authority, and obedience to received truth. Here the prince of apostles is Ralph Waldo Emerson, and it is little wonder that he is revered by Harold Bloom as the font of what he calls the American Religion. Here there is no doctrine other than what Emerson calls "the doctrine of the soul."

The many today who say they are interested in spirituality but not in religion are faithfully following in the tradition of Emerson's battle against tradition and the idea of the authoritative. Consider his powerful 1838 address to the divinity students at Harvard:

> Let me admonish you, first of all, to go alone; to refuse the good models, even those which are sacred in the imagination of men, and dare to love God without mediator or veil. Friends enough you shall find who will hold up to your emulation Wesleys and Oberlins, Saints and Prophets. Thank God for these good men, but say, "I also am a man." Imitation cannot go above its model. The imitator dooms himself to hopeless mediocrity. The inventor did it, because it was natural to him, and so in him it has a charm. In the imitator, something else is natural, and he bereaves himself of his own beauty, to come short of another man's.

Surveying what he views as the corruptions of historic Christianity with its doctrines, rituals, and traditions of authority, Emerson declares, "The remedy to their deformity is, first, soul, and second, soul, and evermore, soul."

Emerson was surely right to say "imitation cannot go above its model," and the many who have followed him have, in fact, fallen far short of the Emersonian model. Witness the fate of what used to be called "liberal religion" in the form of Unitarian-Universalism or visit the shelves upon shelves in the "spirituality" section of your local bookstore. One can agree with Harold Bloom that gnosticism is the right word for it.

At the same time, there were other American Christians who, remembering the words of Jesus that the servant is not above his master, did not aspire to go above their model. The latter part of the nineteenth century, when almost all Protestants called themselves evangelicals, the nation witnessed the impressive construction of the "Benevolent Empire" in what is commonly designated the third great awakening. The social gospel movement, led by formidable figures such as Walter Rauschenbusch, embraced the goal of "Christianizing America and Americanizing Christianity." Once again the note is struck that America is not only a nation with the soul of a church but *is* the church. This self-understanding was soon to be shattered by the fundamentalist-modernist clash of the first part of the twentieth century, giving rise to the conviction that theology, so rife with conflict and divisiveness, must give way to something like a public philosophy.

Here the most notable figure is John Dewey who died in 1952 at age ninety-two, having presided for six decades as perhaps the most influential public intellectual in American life. Like so many liberal reformers of his time, Dewey was only one step away from the Protestant pulpit. *A Common Faith,* published in 1934, proposed a distinctively American religion that would leave behind the doctrinal and ecclesiological disputes of the hoary past and embrace all people of good will in the grand cause of progressive social reform. In what was deemed to be a post-Christian era, here was a new *novus ordo seclorum* with America as the elect people in the vanguard of leading history toward its liberal consummation.

Today, Richard Rorty, the grandson of Rauschenbusch, claims the mantle of Dewey. The common faith of the elect people lives on. In his 1998 *Achieving Our Country,* Rorty writes that Dewey and his soul mate Walt Whitman "wanted [their] utopian America to replace God as the unconditional object of desire. They wanted the struggle for social justice to be the country's animating principle, the nation's soul." He quotes favorably the lines of Whitman: *And I call to mankind. Be not curious about God. / For I who am curious about each am not curious about God.* "Whitman and Dewey," Rorty writes, "gave us all the romance, and all the spiritual uplift we Americans need to go about our public business." In this he sets himself against other leftist thinkers whom he accuses of a "semi-conscious anti-Americanism which they carried over from the rage of the late 1960s."

Radical Christians' understanding of America's part in the world-historical scheme of things is very different, but Rorty shares with those radical Christians of an anti-American bent a belief that America is at center stage in the cosmic drama. For the followers of Rorty, America replaces God as "the unconditional object of desire," while for radical Christians, America is the antichrist in pitched battle against God's purposes through time. Both are quintessentially American in their indifference to Augustine's City of God, intermingled with the earthly city and on pilgrimage toward the End Time, and in their indifference to the Church of Augustine that sustains that pilgrimage.

There have been other efforts to establish a public philosophy quite apart from overarching claims of providential purpose. To cite an outstanding instance, thirty-four years ago John Rawls published *A Theory of Justice.* It will be remembered that, in this intricately reasoned work, Rawls proposed that reasonable persons motivated by self-interest and risk aversion and unencumbered by a knowledge of their place in the world could deliberate behind a "veil of ignorance" and agree upon the principles of a just society.

Rawls, to his great credit, helped revive an interest in political philosophy. Like Aristotle, and against the thinkers for whom politics is all procedure to the exclusion of ends, he understood that politics is the deliberation of how we ought to order our lives together. But his "oughtness" was assiduously insulated from what he called "comprehensive accounts" of history and the world, resulting in an esoteric theory of little use to the democratic deliberation of the question of how we ought to order our lives together. In that sense, Rawls is very un-American. From the Puritan beginnings to the founding, from Emerson and Lincoln to Rauschenbusch and Dewey, Americans have been embroiled in comprehensive accounts, trying to make sense of the story of America within the story of the world.

Stephen Webb has recently published a little book titled *Ameri-*

can Providence: A Nation with a Mission. It is deserving of much more attention than it has received. Nor should we be ignoring the important contributions of Reinhold Niebuhr and his brother H. Richard Niebuhr, especially the latter's *The Kingdom of God in America.* Reinhold was, I believe, much more of a Christian and much more of a Christian thinker than some of his contemporary critics allow. In many ways his sensibility might aptly be described as Augustinian. A half century ago and more, both Niebuhrs were in the long tradition of theologians wrestling with the story of America within the story of the world. Reinhold in particular was perhaps too much impressed by what he called the irony of American history. So skeptical was he of the pridefulness that often accompanied the idea of a national mission — one thinks, for instance, of the notion of "manifest destiny" and the purposes to which it was sometimes put — that he failed to engage constructively the irrepressible devotion to a national story, a line of devotion that runs from the errand into the wilderness to Martin Luther King Jr.'s "beloved community" to Ronald Reagan's "city on a hill" and George W. Bush's second inaugural on America's appointed task in advancing freedom and democracy in the world.

There was another theologian who has an important place among those who have thought deeply about the American experiment: John Courtney Murray. Father Murray, who died in 1967, is best remembered for his part in the Second Vatican Council's declaration on religious freedom. But his 1960 book *We Hold These Truths* is an unavoidable point of reference in discussions about America and providential purpose. He had the greatest admiration for the American founders, and admired most of all the modesty of their intention. This constitutional order, he insisted, rested not upon "articles of faith" but upon "articles of peace." Unlike so many others, Murray never confused America with the Church. As a Catholic, he already had a Church that claimed his prior allegiance. That Church is universal — as in "catholic" — and she has centuries of experience with nations, including nations with universal aspirations, that lay claim to that prior allegiance. We see again and again that, without a Church — not notional but real — that transcends the American experience, the American experience becomes one's church.

James Madison wrote in his famed *Memorial and Remonstrance* that those who enter the political community must have a prior allegiance to God and the laws of God. That allegiance is prior in both time and priority. For Madison and so many others, however, that allegiance was not instantiated in a community that claimed priority to the political community. Thus, again, America itself became their de facto church. Indeed the fundamental charge of anti-Catholics in American history is that Catholicism requires a "dual loyalty" — an allegiance to America *and* a prior allegiance to the Church. That was, and is, exactly right. A prior allegiance is not necessarily a conflicting allegiance. Murray argued that the Catholic allegiance complemented and reinforced the allegiance to the American experiment. In this he agreed with the *Letter to Diognetus* that America is both homeland and foreign country.

Already in 1960, Murray saw that the Protestant establishment, and not least its theological establishment, had wearied of thinking about America in terms of divine providence. In *We Hold These Truths,* he anticipated a day when Catholics would have to catch the fallen flag of this *novus ordo seclorum.* Murray envisioned a democracy in which citizens are "locked in civil argument" about how we ought to order our life together. He believed that the genius of this American experiment, grounded in what he called the American Proposition, is to have provided the procedures and to have cultivated the habits by which the argument could continue until the final coming of the promised Kingdom — a coming uniquely anticipated in the eucharistic life of the Church.

Along the way to the Kingdom, he proposed that politics — the deliberation of how we ought to order our life together — be guided by natural law. Natural law is by definition not the property of any one religion or denomination, although it has been the providential task of the Catholic Church to guard and to propose again and again the truths of nature and nature's God that were assumed by the American founders. "From the beginning," wrote the second-century Saint Irenaeus, "God had implanted in the heart of man the precepts of the natural law. Then He reminded him of them by giving the Decalogue."

The American founders, without exception, agreed. In the vision of John Courtney Murray, public discourse guided by appeal to natural law — and accompanied by the presence of a Church that effectively challenged democracy's idolatrous aspirations to ultimacy — could provide a public philosophy for sustaining the

American experiment in producing as just and free a society as is possible in this our Babylonian exile from our true homeland.

Talk about a public philosophy for the American experiment strikes many today as nonsensical or utopian. In their view, a common public discourse has been shattered, leaving only the shards of myriad constructions of reality. Abandoning the idea of moral truth, politics is no longer the deliberation of how we ought to order our life together but is now, in the phrase of Alastair MacIntyre, warfare carried on by other means. All politics is combat politics. There is no longer, some say, a common American culture, and we should stop pretending that there is. There are only subcultures. Choose your subculture, take up its grievances, contentions, and slogans, and prepare to do battle against the enemy. Liberated from the delusion that we and our opponents can together say "We Hold These Truths," we are urged to recognize the futility of being locked in civil argument and accept the fact that there is no substitute for partisan victory.

Such, we are told, is our unhappy circumstance, and many think it not unhappy at all. They relish the battle, with no holds barred, no compromise, and their opponents' unconditional surrender as the goal. Our circumstance is not entirely new. Today's culture wars, as they are aptly called, bear striking similarities to the moral and political clashes prior to the Civil War. I recently had occasion to revisit Walter Lippmann's *The Public Philosophy*, on the fiftieth anniversary of its publication. There he describes a circumstance — before the civil rights movement, before Vietnam, before the cultural and sexual revolutions, before *Roe v. Wade*, before wave upon wave of critical theory and deconstructionisms — not entirely unlike our own. That was a long time ago. It has been a long time since we have been locked in civil argument premised upon the confidence that we together "Hold These Truths." Incidentally, Lippmann's proposed remedy, to the extent he proposes a remedy, is a recovery of natural law. Although Lippmann was, however ambiguously, a Jew, Reinhold Niebuhr thought the book was altogether too Catholic.

It must be admitted that over these fifty years the churches have been of little help in restoring a politics of democratic deliberation about how we ought to order our life together. Those churches — once called mainline, and now more aptly oldline and, increasingly, sideline — have planted the banner "Thus Saith the Lord" on the cultural and political platform of the Left. The evangelical Protestant insurgency has often planted the same banner on the cultural and political platform of the Right.

For the purposes of this reflection, it matters little that those on the Right have greater political potency. With notable exceptions, both are enemies of a religiously informed public philosophy for the American experiment; both contribute to the political corruption of Christian faith and the religious corruption of authentic politics.

As for the leadership of the Catholic Church in this country, it oscillates between, on the one hand, a touching desire to be accepted by the oldline, and, on the other hand, cobelligerency with evangelicalism on great moral and cultural questions. But there are also, let it be said, some Catholics, including bishops and theologians, who remember that the Church is to be the "contrast society" of Madison's prior allegiance. As such a contrast society, the Church is not above the fray, but neither is she captive to the fray. Her chief political contribution is to provide a transcendent horizon for our civil arguments, to counter the confusion of the political penultimate with the theological ultimate, and to insist that our common humanity with God's gift of reason is capable of a common deliberation about how we ought to order our life together.

And so we return to the beginning. When I meet God, I expect to meet him as an American. Not most importantly as an American, to be sure, but as someone who tried to take seriously, and tried to encourage others to take seriously, the story of America within the story of the world.

The argument, in short, is that God is not indifferent to the American experiment, and therefore we who are called to think about God and His ways through time dare not be indifferent to the American experiment. America is not uniquely Babylon, but it is our time and place in Babylon. We seek its peace in which we find our peace as we yearn for and eucharistically anticipate the New Jerusalem that is our pilgrim goal. It is time to think again — to think deeply, to think theologically — about the story of America and its place in the story of the world. Again, the words of Augustine: "It is beyond anything incredible that God should have willed the kingdoms of men, their dominations and their servitudes, to be outside the range of the laws of his providence."

KATHERINE PATERSON

Are You There, God?

FROM *Harvard Divinity Bulletin*

NEARLY TWENTY-FIVE YEARS AGO, I was speaking in a small town that I will not name except to say it was a long way from Cambridge, Massachusetts. In the audience was a professor of children's literature from a nearby university. The professor spoke to me after the talk and in the course of the conversation asked me if I knew that my latest book at the time, *The Great Gilly Hopkins,* was on the restricted shelf in her local public library. Any child who wanted to check out the book needed to bring in written permission from home.

"I didn't mean to upset you," she said. "And if it's any comfort, sometimes our town can be a funny place. Just a few weeks ago I realized that I needed a copy of Judy Blume's new book, *Forever,* to use in my adolescent literature class. I went to the local bookstore and looked at the shelves of adolescent fiction. It wasn't there. With some trepidation, I searched the children's shelves, but it wasn't there either. I started out of the shop, only to be stopped by the clerk. 'May I help you?' she asked. 'I don't think so,' I said. 'I was looking for a copy of *Forever* by Judy Blume, but you don't seem to have it.' 'Oh, yes, we do,' she said and took me to the religion shelf, and there it was, sitting right next to Judy Blume's other book on religion, *Are You There, God? It's Me, Margaret.*"

I must say I had fun imagining the mother who didn't want her child exposed to Gilly Hopkins taking her to the local bookstore to purchase an inspirational book about eternal things, titled *Forever.*

The irony for me is that I see *The Great Gilly Hopkins* as perhaps the most explicitly Christian of all my novels.

I was at a conference and was being led to the platform for my talk when I was stopped in the aisle by a young woman. "Wait, wait," she said. "I'm writing a dissertation at the University of Chicago on Southern settings in children's literature and I have to know: Who is Maime Trotter?"

The woman leading me to the platform was not pleased by the interruption and took my arm to get me away from the young woman, so I called out to her, "Godddd." I couldn't tell from the look on her face if they believed in God at the University of Chicago, but I was sure they didn't think she spoke with a Southern accent.

To tell the truth, however, I didn't realize how close kin *Gilly Hopkins* was to the parable of the prodigal son until I had finished it. And from the number of times it has been challenged by my fellow Christians, its Christian theme of redemption seems to be a well-kept secret. In fact, I am often congratulated that my books *aren't* the obvious product of a Christian writer.

So what does it mean to both me and my reader not only that I was born into a Christian missionary family, but also that I've consciously and deliberately chosen to live out my life as a person of faith? How does that shape what I write?

First of all, I don't think I'm all that different from most children's writers I know. All of us, who are serious about what we do, write out of our own deepest selves. We don't poke religious convictions or humanistic philosophy or moral messages into a story to be pulled out by the reader like plums from Jack Horner's Christmas pie. Because our stories come from deep inside, our books will reveal, willy-nilly, who we really are. As C. S. Lewis once said, "The book cannot be what the writer is not."

It is your privilege as reader to decide who you think I am, but now I will try to say who I think I am, and I see myself as a person who believes God *is* there, and that the creator of all things is, as the Bible declares, the God of justice and steadfast love. And yes, I do believe in moral values, which is one reason I have rejoiced at the commitment services and marriages of gay friends and, yes, I am wholeheartedly for life. The German poet and novelist Hermann Hesse, musing on the commandment "Thou shalt not kill," said: "We kill at every step, not only in wars, riots, and executions.

We kill when we close our eyes to poverty, suffering, and shame. In the same way all disrespect for life, all hardheartedness, all indifference, all contempt is nothing else than killing. With just a little witty skepticism we can kill a good deal of the future in a young person. Life is waiting everywhere, the future is flowering everywhere, but we only see a small part of it and step on much of it with our feet."

I pray that I will not be one of those who steps on life — any person's life. I want my morality to be defined not in negatives, but in positives. I want to be, in the words of the Anglican priest Martin Smith, a co-creator with God.

What, exactly does that mean for my life as a writer for the young? In the Genesis story as Smith reminds us, God creates by speech. And it is by language that we humans, created in God's image, make meaning. "We give voice to the images and metaphors," Smith says, "and the chaos that surrounds us gives way to narrative, to a story."

Perhaps few modern poets do this better than Mary Oliver. One Sunday in early Lent, our co-pastor brought one of Oliver's poems to share with our adult class. The poem is titled "White Owl Flies Into and Out of the Field." Having read this poem, I don't think I can think of death in the same way ever again. "What a wonderful, wonderful image!" I said to Carl. "Yes," he said, "that was what I thought, but Gina [his wife and our co-pastor] said, 'That's all very well unless you're that little mouse running across the field.'"

But isn't that exactly the point? We *are* that mouse. We human beings scrabble through life, unseeing, unhearing, and suddenly the owl is swooping, down upon us. That is not the time to say to the mouse, "Never mind, sweetie. It's all part of a grand and beautiful design." It is probably not the moment for a sermon at all. In the midst of suffering, in the face of death, we are not often supported by argument or consoled by discourse, but we may, indeed, we often are, comforted by art. I know that on September 11, a day of fear and terror, I finally had sense enough to turn off the TV and put on a CD of Brahms's *German Requiem.*

But I'm guessing most of us don't rate ourselves as a Mary Oliver, much less a Johannes Brahms. I'm a writer for children. What is my role as maker of meaning in a world gone mad?

It was a week after September 11. We were finally having to give up the last faint hope that Peter, our son John's brother-in-law and close friend, would be found unconscious in a hospital or wandering senseless in a distant locale. I looked at my calendar and was distressed to see that I was slated to speak to middle-school students in Hinesburg, Vermont, the next day. What was I going to say to twelve- and thirteen-year-olds in the midst of this grief and terror, which had not only our extended family but also our whole nation in its death grip? Finally, I decided to start by reading them a passage from *Bridge to Terabithia*, which I had written out of another time of family grief and tumult:

That night as he started to get into bed, leaving the light off so as not to wake the little girls, he was surprised by May Belle's shrill little "Jess."

"How come you still awake?"

"Jess. I know where you and Leslie go to hide."

"What d'you mean?"

"I followed ya."

He was at her bedside in one leap. "You ain't supposed to follow me!"

"How come?" Her voice was sassy.

He grabbed her shoulders and made her look him in the face. She blinked in the dim light like a startled chicken.

"You listen here, May Belle Aarons," he whispered fiercely. "I catch you following me again, your life ain't worth nothing."

"OK, OK." — she slid back into bed — "Boy, you're mean. I oughta tell Momma on you."

"Look, May Belle, you can't do that. You can't tell Momma 'bout where me and Leslie go."

She answered with a little sniffling sound.

He grabbed her shoulders again. He was desperate. "I mean it, May Belle, you can't do that. You can't tell nobody nothing!" He let her go. "Now, I don't want to hear about you following me *or* squealing to Momma ever again, you hear?"

"Why not?"

"'Cause if you do — I'm gonna tell Billy Jean Edwards you still wet the bed sometimes."

"You wouldn't!"

"Boy, girl, you just better not try me."

He made her swear on the Bible never to tell and never to follow, but still he lay awake a long time. How could he trust everything that mattered to him to a sassy six-year-old? Sometimes it seemed to him that his life was delicate as a dandelion. One little puff from any direction, and it was blown to bits.

"I don't know about you," I told those children, "but I'm feeling a lot like a dandelion today." I could see them visibly relax. Here was an adult willing to tell the truth. We can't make meaning for anyone, much less for the young, unless we are first willing to tell the truth.

Otherwise we are like Pangloss, Candide's false mentor, who in the face of earthquake, inquisition, war, and pestilence merrily insists that all is well, all is for the best in this the best of all possible worlds. One look at the morning newspaper and a glib and foolish optimism will strike us as obscene. The world our children live in, the one we cannot protect them from, is a world where evil and suffering and injustice are rampant. It is useless to pretend to children that all is well in our world. But cynicism is the easy way out for writers confronted with the world as it is. And there are writers for the young as well as the old who choose this route. But we who are people of faith must seek against all odds to wring meaning out of what it would be easier and, in the world's eyes, more realistic, to dismiss as meaningless.

Freud says we are infantile to seek for meaning in life, perhaps even neurotic to try. But it's not Freud we are arguing with. If the God of the Bible *does not exist,* there is no contest. It is precisely *because* we have faith, *because* we believe in a God of justice and steadfast love, that we find ourselves in a painful, sweating wrestling match in which the adversary is God.

I have told this story many times; it is the story I went on to tell that morning in Hinesburg. I feel the need to tell it again in this context, because I think it says what I, as a writer, often do, often must do, and that is to use art to somehow make sense for myself something that makes no sense otherwise — it is my way of demanding a blessing from the Divine Adversary with whom we are, in times of crisis, locked in mortal combat.

The story begins a little more than thirty years ago. The small school that our children attend is closed and all the students are moved to a much larger elementary school across town. David, our second grader, is miserable. In the little school he was both the class artist and the class clown. In his new school he is simply weird. Every day he comes home and declares that he is "never, never going back to school and you can't make me." And I, his mother, who had been in fifteen different schools by the time I was eighteen and had been initially despised at nearly every one, am overidentifying with my seven-year-old, probably exacerbating his misery, but, nevertheless getting him up every morning and grimly pushing him out the front door, fearing that his unhappiness will never end.

Then one afternoon, our bright funny little boy that I was sure was gone forever walks into the house. "Me and Lisa Hill are making a diorama of *Little House in the Big Woods*," he announces cheerily. I had never heard the name before, but from then on I am to hear hardly any other name. "Now I'd like to promise you girls," I say when I'm talking to children, "that I was thrilled that my son's best friend was a girl. But unfortunately, all I could think was 'They thought he was weird before. If his best friend is a girl, he'll never fit in.'"

But then I meet Lisa, and my worries evaporate. Anyone would be fortunate to have her for his best friend. She is bright, imaginative, and funny. She laughs at his jokes and he at hers. She is the only girl daring enough to invade the second-grade boys' T-ball team. She and David play together after school in the woods below her house and talk to each other in the evenings on the phone.

"It's your *girlfriend*, David," his older brother says.

But David takes the phone unperturbed. Girlfriends are people who chase you down on the playground to grab you and kiss you. Lisa is no more a "girlfriend" than Rose Kennedy is a Playboy Bunny.

On an August morning, the phone rings. It is a call from the Hills' next-door neighbor. "I thought you ought to know," Mrs. Robinson says, "that Lisa was killed this morning." While the family was on vacation at Bethany Beach, on a day when the lifeguards sensed no danger from thunder far off in the distance, a joyful little girl, dancing on a rock above the beach, was felled by a bolt of lightning from the sky.

How am I to make sense of that to my eight-year-old son? I can't make any sense of it for myself. David tries. One night after his prayers, he tells me that he has figured out why Lisa died.

"It's not because Lisa was bad," he says. "Lisa wasn't bad. It's because I'm bad. And now God is going to kill Mary [his little sister] and you and Daddy and Lin and John . . ." — going down the list of his family and loved ones, all of whom God will kill in punishment for his real and imagined sins.

This is not the God I know — not the God we thought we had

taught our children about, but this was one child's painful struggle to find meaning. Which is why, finally, I began to write a story. I was trying to make sense of a tragedy that didn't make sense. As a writer, I know that a story needs to make sense. It has to have a beginning, a middle, and an ending, and when you come to the ending, you look back and even if it is unexplainable intellectually, emotionally you know you have made the journey from chaos to order, from senselessness to meaning. Often you find yourself at a total loss when someone asks you what your book is about. You can't put it into a neat verbal summary, because if you, the writer, have done your job, the whole story *is* the meaning.

I know my gift is limited. I know I cannot stand toe-to-toe with philosophers or theologians and solve for myself or anyone else the problem of evil, either natural or moral, but we who are writers can tell a story or write a poem, and where rational argument will always fail, somehow, miraculously, in metaphor and simile and image, in simple narrative, there are, in the words of Barry Lopez, both "healing and illumination."

We write stories not because we have answers, but because we have questions. The writing of the story *is* the wrestling with the angel. Rabbi Heschel has said, "Art is boring unless we are surprised by it." And a wrestling match is fixed, it is a cheat, if you know in advance how it is going to turn out. The writer may have some notion of the ending of the plot, but she is seeking for much more than plot. We write to struggle for sense, for a meaning, which we do not already know, and the first reader who is, of course, the writer herself, will inevitably be surprised by the blessing wrested from the angel.

I've heard more than once the dictum that the difference between a book for children and one for adults is that a book for children must end in hope. But hope is not something to be tacked on like the tail on the donkey at a birthday party. Hope like faith and love must come from the depths of the writer or it is little more than wishful thinking.

In a baccalaureate address at Stanford University this year, the activist theologian Jim Wallis said to the graduates: "When I was growing up, it was continually repeated in my evangelical Christian world that the greatest battle and biggest choice of our time was between belief and secularism. But I now believe that the real battle, the big struggle of our times, is the fundamental choice between cynicism and hope. The choice between cynicism and hope is ultimately a spiritual choice, and one that has enormous political consequences."

Among my pantheon of heroes are those teachers who, going into impossible situations every day, daily make the choice for hope.

Between sessions at a middle school in a southern city, one of those heroes came up to me with a reluctant student in tow. The boy who was taller than both me and the teacher walked with a slump. "Ask Mrs. Paterson your question, Reginald," the teacher urged.

Reginald wouldn't look me in the eye, but he did manage to mumble out his question: "I want to know how come you wrote *Gilly Hopkins.*"

I did not take the time to tell him the story in full detail — he might well have grown a beard waiting. But I did tell him that I wrote it because my husband and I had been asked to serve as temporary foster parents and, although I thought I was at least an average mother of our own four children, I felt I had flunked out as a foster mother. When I asked myself why, I heard myself saying things like: "Well, I can't deal with that problem, they'll only be here for a few weeks," or "Thank goodness, they'll only be here for a few weeks." And what I was saying, what I was doing, was treating two human beings as though they were disposable. People aren't disposable.

Reginald gave me a quick look, as though to check out whether or not I was on the level.

I continued. "That's why crimes are committed — that's why wars are fought — because somebody thinks somebody else is disposable. And we know, don't we, Reginald, that no one on this earth is disposable." I knew he was listening now. "So," I said, "I wrote the book to figure out what I would be like if I felt other people thought I was disposable. And I thought I might be very angry."

Reginald gave a hint of a nod in my direction.

"See, Reginald," the teacher said gently. "That's what I was trying to explain to you the other day. You can use writing to deal with your feelings. To figure out things for yourself."

"That's what writers are always doing," I said.

"Reginald has a lot of really tough problems to face," his teacher said. "We've been talking about how he can do that. I told him I thought writing about it might help."

"That's what I do," I said.

And the amazing thing I have learned, time after time, is this: when I am willing to give the deepest part of myself, whether admirable or not, when I am willing to share my own struggle, my own wrestling, readers are able to respond to what I have written from their own deepest core.

It was about sixteen years ago that I was asked to speak to a book club that was discussing a book of mine. This reading group was made up of prisoners incarcerated in the Chittenden County Correctional Center in Burlington, Vermont. Twenty-four inmates had read *The Great Gilly Hopkins* and wanted an opportunity to talk with the author about it.

One of the young men said that when he was a teenager he had lived briefly in a foster home with a foster mother who was really kind to him. She had wanted him to read the book at that time, but, he sort of shrugged: "I was a kid that didn't want anybody telling me what to do. I guess that's why I ended up in here. Now that I've read the book," he added, "I know what she was trying to tell me."

"Just out of curiosity," the instructor asked, "how many of you were ever in foster care?"

Every single prisoner raised a hand.

As part of the program, each participant was given a paperback copy of the book, so at the end of the session, the inmates lined up to have their books autographed.

"What's your name?" I asked a young man handing me his book.

"It's not for me," he said. "It's for my daughter. Her name is Angel."

It had been an emotional afternoon, but that one sentence was the one that haunted me for years. Finally I began to write my fourteenth novel, about a child whose father is in prison.

But one idea, as I often tell students who ask about ideas, doth not a novel make. If you try to write a book based on a single idea, you are not likely to get beyond the third chapter. It takes more than one strand, sometimes many, to weave the fabric of a story.

At least a dozen years after that day in the prison, I was in California and a friend gave me a copy of a small magazine, which her husband was editing. On the back of the magazine was a dramatic photo of supernova remnant Cassiopeia A and under the picture this quotation:

"When the Chandra telescope took its first image in August of this year, it caught not just another star in the heavens, but a foundry distributing its wares to the rest of the galaxy.

"Silicon, sulfur, argon, calcium, and iron were among the elements identified from Chandra's X-ray image. 'These are the materials we are made of,' said the project scientist."

The thrill that every writer recognizes went through my body. I knew I had an idea for a book in that quotation. Eventually, I recognized it as the missing strand I had needed to write Angel's story. What would it mean to a child that the world has discarded as waste material to learn that she is made of the same stuff as the stars?

One of my great frustrations as a writer of stories for children are the adults who are afraid to entrust meaning making to the young. This results in book banning and challenging. But even those of us who love a book want to make sure our children catch on to the message the book has for us. We can hardly resist the temptation to explain the meaning of the story. But I beg you, resist. The story belongs ultimately, not to the writer, not even to you the caring adult, but to the young reader.

In her book *When God Is Silent,* Barbara Brown Taylor speaks of the narrative style of Jesus and points out "how *courteous* it is, how respectful of the listener."

"Story and image," she goes on to say, "both have great pockets of silence in them. They do not come at the ear the same way advice and exhortation do — although they are, I believe, even more persuasive. Perhaps that is because they create a quiet space where one may lay down one's defenses for a while. A story," she says, "does not ask for decision. Instead, it asks for identification, which is how transformation begins."

Despite the genealogies, the laws, the exhortations included, the Bible comes to us chiefly as story — the story of God and humankind. And what for the Christian is the climax of the story? Incarnation. God with us. God identifying with us, and that is where the transformation occurs.

Not long ago I was asked to speak to a group of public-school teachers who would be taking their classes to see a production of the play *Bridge to Terabithia*. I spent more than an hour explaining how the book came to be written and rewritten and then how Stephanie Tolan and I adapted it into the play their classes would see. There was the usual time of questions, at the end of which a young male teacher thanked me for my time, then said: "But I want to take something special back to my class. Can you give me some word to take back to them?"

I was momentarily silenced. After all I had been talking continuously for nearly an hour and a half; surely he could pick out from that outpouring a word or two to take home to his students. Fortunately, I kept my mouth shut long enough to realize what I ought to say —

"I'm very biblically oriented," I said, "and so for me the most important thing is for the word to become flesh. I can write stories for children and young people, and in that sense I can offer them words, but you are the word become flesh in your classroom. Society has taught our children that they are nobodies unless their faces appear on television. But by your caring, by your showing them how important each one of them is, you become the word that I would like to share with each of them. You are that word become flesh."

That day long ago in the Chittenden prison, one of the inmates asked me: "Do you think Gilly would have made it if there had been no Maime Trotter?"

"I don't know," I said. "I just don't know."

If you ask me what message a book of mine contains, I'll get testy, but that doesn't mean I have nothing I want to say to my readers. What I hope to say to isolated, angry, fearful youth — to all the children who feel that their lives are worthless in the eyes of the world is: you are seen, you are not alone, you are not despised, you are unique and of infinite value in the human family. As a writer, I can try to offer children a chance to make sense of their own lives through the words of a story, but I can't stop there, thinking that my task is done. Nor, I dare say, can you. It is up to each of us not simply to write the words, but to be a word of hope made flesh.

Seven Penitential Psalms

FROM *Poetry*

1

Pain's first casualty is proportion.

So my brother, juror in a child pornography trial,
Browses my shelves while the Easter lamb roasts

And, coming on Weston's nudes of his son
Paired with a text describing how Neil at eight

Is "moulded with reedlike flow of unbroken line"
— The exposures framed so the torso, Pentelic marble,

Ends with arm buds and the stem of the penis —
Slams the book and storms out,

Shaken that I own such things.

2

The damaged man licking sauce from his spoon —
Why do I feel stricken sitting in the same café,
Watching his unbridled relish in the mess?
He's showing me a secret I don't want to see.
The toughest shell conceals the tenderest meat.

My friend rejects aids to help him hear
Because they transmit chat he's never
Learned to filter out. How do we bear

Any sense without muting its tone?
The cuff of meat around the marrow bone.

3

The clergy who rejected Caravaggios's "Death of the Virgin"
For showing the bare soles of Mary's feet
Could hardly conceive the Holy Mother
Straining like a ewe in labor with the Lamb of God.

Yet Luke writes that the inn was full and the birth outdoors.
A beast's entry. No bed for Heaven's Queen but a nest of straw;
The babe's head haloed but, if we take the incarnation at its word,
Breaching the labial tissue crowned in beads of blood.

The first mystery is spirit housed in meat. And the miracle —
That you love the brutal creature eating from your breast.

4

"Nice day," she remarks of the glacier-sharp noon beyond the
    window,
"A nice day, under glass." Backhoeing a new well, her son's

Unearthed a Venetian Whiteheart, the beads-for-beaver currency
Once swapped here by the river, six glass nubs per finished pelt.

Resembling a drop of arterial blood, it's crossed three centuries
And countless palms to this snub of cotton in the vitrine by
    their TV.

He lets me hold it, and the red seed plunges me into a vitreous
Humor where we're all flecks floating in the eye of God.

Then drafts whistle through their window's glazing. Like glass,
My faith's both brittle and liquid, ever shattered or shifting shape.

5

The devil, weeping for help, is plaintive.
He calls us by name and it's unclear what we should do.
I say "should," because if there really is a devil
Gulping in fevered sobs under the bed,
Mustn't there be a God who shut him in our house?

Are we to show pity for the pitiless,
Prove his nature to bite won't stifle our nature
To comfort his wounds? Or is giving the whimpering
Little fiend a blanket and cup of milk a sin?
Which hell do we want to burn in if we're wrong?

6

There was a horse farm, long white paddocks, beside the railroad.
Can you see where this is going? Those horses were beautiful and
   — wet clover,
Loose fence posts — hard to keep safe. The day two mares and a
   gelding
Stopped an express (no humans hurt, train delayed while the
   track was cleared),
My brother slipped off to the scene. He craved blood, I think,
   because he'd
Reached the age that needs to feel beyond doubt that the world
   is real.

A boy, ten or twelve, on a bike; some horses; a train.

From the blue it comes back, and when I recall his crazy bravado,
   describing
What remained of the giants that once lipped apples from our
   palms, I'm surprised
At my rage: Who'd put horses there? Who a railroad? Who a boy?

7

Such frenzy! All this fluster, no stillness at the root.
Always weeping, raging, driving backhoes, giving birth. . . .

You love illuminated books because they're crammed, like your
Little verse, with busyness. You want the world's
Shards on velvet, so you've built a reliquary out of words.

Ach, peddler, you're no better than the friar
Hawking pig-knuckles as the bones of a saint.

You want a form that will hold the river's water
So it glitters, miraculous as tears?

First, smash the vial. First, swallow the shards.

MATTHEW POWER

The Lost Buddhas of Bamiyan

FROM *Harper's Magazine*

NEAR SUNDOWN, atop TV Hill in Kabul, I am surrounded by a squabbling group of children, bright-eyed, rotten-toothed, dressed in ragged *salwars* with hands out, crying: *Howdy! Howdy! Howdy!* I root through my pockets and find nothing but a handful of American coins, pennies and nickels, and lint, and I hold them up and point at Lincoln and Jefferson and FDR and say, *America*, and they echo, *Merik, Merik*, and push each other, laughing and grabbing for the unspendable coins. Their tiny hands, filthy, cracked like mud plaster, deeply etched by sun, are far older than mine, are scale models of crones' claws. In the falling breeze, a boy tries with one hand to maintain the loft of a paper kite played out on a length of audiotape, twisted helically like a strand of DNA, while his other hand thrusts into the elbowing throng around me.

The sun, obscured all day behind a ceiling of low-slung clouds, splits the bank a finger's breadth above the horizon and floods the Kabul Valley with ethereal light, sharply tracing the shadow of the ridgeline far across the grid of streets below: Chicken Street, Flower Street, Passport Lane (the city is named practically, as TV Hill's broadcast towers attest).

A handful of construction cranes perch like watchful herons across the valley floor. The nacreous light, shocking, fleeting, vanishing, casts the leafier enclaves (where Western aid groups pay Manhattan rents to ex-Taliban landlords in Peshawar) in deeper shadow. The new mud-brick slums that inch up the hillsides, built by some of the city's one and a half million returnees since the fall of the Taliban, are imbued with a magnificence that would not stand up to closer inspection. It is as if the day's allotment of beauty were compressed into a few moments, before another night falls with its punctuation of barking street dogs, rumbling Humvees, the echoes of muezzins, and the occasional slamming door of a rocket attack in another part of town.

Howdy! Howdy! Howdy! And the children scatter through the dusk like poplar leaves. Line upon line of peaks, spurs of the Hindu Kush, catch the light and reveal themselves at theatrical distances, relentlessly unfurling like rows of sharks' teeth. Somewhere beyond them, hidden in a valley a hundred miles into the wall of mountains to the northwest, is the question mark, the rubble pile, the twin emptiness and stone keyhole I came here to peer into: Bamiyan.

The images have haunted me since March 2001, a time now part of another age, when an obscure one-eyed cleric named Omar gave the order that the massive 1,500-year-old Buddhas of the Bamiyan Valley be destroyed. Hadn't the Prophet himself, the old iconoclast, smashed the idols in the Kaba'a? There was a grainy news loop, and an international condemnation, and a great fluttering of op-ed pages. There was Mullah Omar taunting: "All we are breaking are stones."

And then there was September, and the world found more pressing concerns with Afghanistan. Sometime that fall I saw a wall painting in a gallery in lower Manhattan of two giant Buddhas standing in the smoking pits of the World Trade Center towers. Perhaps it was a stretch to make a parallel: two temples of commerce, two long-abandoned symbols of worship. The monuments of civilizations in their twilight and their loves.

I arrived in Kabul on the Ariana flight from Delhi, where I had come across the stewardesses smoking cigarettes by the bathroom as we crossed the Hindu Kush, and on landing I watched from the window of the plane as a de-mining team underwent its work alongside the runway. I was soon met by my guide and translator, a young Afghan medical student named Najib, possessor of an infectious laugh, recurrent malaria, and a rockabilly pompadour. There was a crush at arrivals, herded by Afghan soldiers in smart new uniforms and bootleg Oakleys: sunburned, walrus-mustached, potbellied "defense consultants" from Virginia smoked by the carousel; women in burkas and high heels milled about; old bearded men in turbans just back from Mecca carried five-gallon jugs of holy water; an Afghan businessman in a sharp suit waited to see how badly his golf clubs had been treated by the baggage handlers. (The grassless greens of the Kabul Golf Course are once again open for business. Players carry a section of AstroTurf with them on the course.) All have arrived at this caravansary of the jet age, a Silk Road stopover of the New World Order, to place their bets on the future.

Afghanistan is a shattered country, a place that has never properly been whole, the crossroads of marching armies and the overlapping frontier of rival empires. Osama bin Laden might be the best thing that's happened to the country in years: he prodded the Western world once again to halfheartedly invest in its construction. Terror was the Afghan oil: it seeped from the ground, it brought the world's notice. Despite all the nation-building rhetoric of the international community, few Afghans expect this degree of engagement, limited as it is, to last for long. But while the game is in town, the locals want nothing more than to get back to their centuries-old pastime of cleaning out every foreigner who passes through.

Kabul has reinvented itself to a remarkable degree in three years. Whereas early invocations of Paris in the twenties may have been wishful hyperbole, plasma TVs, satellite dishes, and even a single temperamental ATM have all popped up in the city like Martian landers. When Afghanistan's only ATM is out of commission, there is the currency bazaar, where traders at open tables stacked with Vegas-size sheaves of bills sit with calculators and satellite phones to compute up-to-the-second exchange rates for rials, dollars, rupees, euros, and afghanis. Behind the gruesome wheelbarrows of sheep's heads at the Titanic market, a thousand jerry-rigged stalls in the drought-cracked bed of the Kabul River, a cinephile can pick up *Titanic, Rambo III, Fahrenheit 9/11,* and a host of other pirated DVDs for one hundred afghanis each.

Kabul supports a glut of construction projects, restaurants, car dealerships, and a dual economy sustained by the thousands of international aid workers now living in the city. Afghans, though not benefiting nearly as much as the hordes of Westerners who have come here to work, are getting as big a piece of the pie as they can. Particularly the elite expat returnees, many of whom bring home the money and business acumen of twenty-five years in London,

Sydney, Toronto, or Los Angeles. The average income of an Afghan may be forty dollars a month, but a lone UN worker can easily spend that much on dinner at one of the Thai, Italian, or Croatian restaurants that have sprung up in Kabul. There are ten-dollar margaritas at The Elbow Room, and a martini-shaped pool at the Peacock Lounge. All the best restaurants hunker behind iron gates with armed guards in the tonier neighborhoods of Wazir Akbar Khan and Shar-e-Naw. After a speakeasy-style window slides back and one's foreignness is ascertained, a pleasure garden of tiki torches, pretty waitresses, and imported wine manifests like an opium dream, with dinner conversation in a half-dozen languages and the bill going to the NGO's expense account. But sorry, no credit cards yet.

There are plenty of places to spend money in Kabul, as a walk down Chicken Street illustrates. Once the destination for stoned backpackers hopping overland along the K's (Kabul, Kashmir, Kathmandu) to Kuta in Bali, Chicken Street is now a treasure trove of Soviet kitsch, overpriced carpets, and racks of rusting Enfield rifles from the 1800s supposedly given to the mujahedeen by the CIA. In a shop window there is a rug woven with a tableau of the twin towers aflame superimposed over a map of Afghanistan, the planes in poor perspective crashing into them, with an aircraft carrier sliding up to the towers' base, launching a missile. Lest anyone be confused over the political intent behind the iconography, an American flag and an Afghan flag are joined by a dove bearing an olive branch, beneath the curious inscription: THE TERRORS WERE IN THE AMERICAN AFGHANISTAN.

When the Taliban abandoned the city in November 2001, the Western press delighted in stories of the people of Kabul digging TV sets up from their backyards and blasting Bollywood music, of liberated women casting off their burkas, and of children flying kites with impunity. Kabulis became the clichéd poster children for the successes of the war on terror, the backdrop for Bush's pseudo-Lincolnian invocations of a new birth of freedom in the Muslim world. There were celebrations, and Najib describes people filling the streets, riding on the roofs of trucks, shouting. The Taliban vanished like smoke in the night, but the burkas, for the most part, have not come off, and Najib tells me that 60 percent of women in Kabul, and 98 percent outside, still wear the coverings in public.

Women in burkas beg throughout the center of town, lean billowing into sudden dust storms, squat by the kebab stands thrusting sickly infants at well-heeled passersby, tug on shirtsleeves calling out, *Baksheesh, baksheesh.* This is nothing new, I'm told, but the numbers have risen in direct proportion to the foreign presence here. An extraordinarily persistent burka trails me for twenty minutes through a traffic jam, tapping at the taxi window like a pigeon in a behavioral experiment.

But as mendicants, the "shuttlecocks," as a Pakistani journalist I meet calls the burka panhandlers, are not alone: in June, Jaap de Hoop Scheffer, the NATO secretary-general, told member nations at a summit meeting in Istanbul that he felt "like a beggar," that Afghanistan had a sixth of the NATO forces provided to Kosovo. Afghanistan may be the first NATO mission outside Europe, but its inability to provide peacekeeping forces for the bulk of the country is a mark of shame upon the operation. The vast majority of the 8,000-strong international military presence here, called ISAF (International Security Assistance Force), patrols only within the city limits. The sixteen thousand American troops in the country are largely headquartered at the former Soviet airbase at Bagram (the one place in the country that has built a Burger King). Germans, Canadians, Greeks, Poles, Latvians — there are thirty-six countries represented. At the US compound, gangs of grubby street kids beg for pens and candy outside a blast wall of dirt-filled containers built by Kellogg Brown & Root, while inside, a series of well-tended neighborhood streets houses the occupying armies, and Afghan gardeners tend rosebushes and apple trees. The press conferences in front of a forest of international flags are a good show, but there is little doubt that if they could, the Western nations would gladly sweep the fragments of Afghanistan back under the rug once again.

Today, all assessments of the situation in Afghanistan are framed in terms of *inside* Kabul and *outside* Kabul. *Inside,* Kabul is growing and relatively safe. There is real cultural ferment and progressivism in the city, with a growing indigenous press and a Top 40 station sponsored by a condom company that enjoys over 80 percent market penetration. Radio Arman, which means "hope" in Dari, was founded by three Afghan siblings who grew up in Australia and Japan during the years of war. Despite the fact that they had no experience running a station, they decided that radio was the way to go in a country with 66 percent illiteracy. With a Top 40 list of Bollywood and Ricky Martin and J-Lo lorded over by Ahmad Zahir, the Afghan Elvis, Radio Arman echoes throughout the capital, in every taxi, every bazaar stall, every transistor radio dangling from a bike's handlebars.

Outside Kabul, a vast and lawless country the size of Texas belongs to a medieval collection of fiefdoms, where guns rule and the economy is built on an annual harvest of three thousand six hundred tons of raw opium. And forget poppies: dozens are killed in tribal wars fought over the annual pistachio harvest. Six dollars a kilo for pistachios is no joke in Afghanistan. The rebuilding of the country has begun in Kabul, but there are few indications that it will spread much farther anytime soon, particularly from whatever central government is formed in the capital. For all their cruelty, the Taliban are the subject of a whispered nostalgia in some quarters, because of the relative stability they offered to 90 percent of the country.

But even in the city, echoes of the dark years are everywhere. Najib takes me across town to the soccer stadium, where many of the Taliban's amputations and executions were conducted. Olympic rings are now hung on its facade, and a group of boys in mismatched uniforms kicks a ball across the heavily irrigated field. It is the first green grass I have seen in Afghanistan. I had once seen a picture from this very field (grassless then) of a laughing boy holding up a bouquet of severed hands, tied together at the thumbs. Najib tells me of an afternoon here, not four years ago, when he and his friends came and sat in the stands, as a woman in a burka was led out onto the field and made to kneel, and how a Talib had put a Kalashnikov to her head and "crack, she fell like a sack of flour dropped from a truck."

The election, America's great experiment in Afghan nation-building, is on everyone's mind. Later I have a conversation with Hafeez Mansor, an opposition-newspaper editor and spokesman for a loose coalition of warlords ("I do not prefer the term 'warlords,'" he tells me. "They are 'tribal leaders.'") He catches the anti-Karzai skepticism precisely: "Karzai is like a can of Coca-Cola whose Coca-Cola has been drunk, and now keeping the empty can will just be self-deceiving, not anything else. We'll have more insecurity, the reconstruction will be hurt, the international community will be ill-reputed even more, and it is possible Afghanistan will be converted to another Iraq. The result is clear — someone who cannot make one step without his foreign bodyguards, how would he get the votes of the people?"

At a voter-registration station on the outskirts of the city, a lone guard sits smoking by the gate, his Kalashnikov leaning against a wall. Throughout the summer, election workers around the country have been attacked, from poll workers gunned down in far-flung provinces to a busload of women bombed on the way to a registration center. Inside there is a roomful of men lining up to register, making their thumbprints and getting Polaroids for voter ID cards. There is another room for the women, almost all in burkas, and they lift them briefly to get their photos snapped. Some refuse, forbidden by their families to have a portrait, and are given IDs with only thumbprints. UN-designed election posters festoon the walls, showing men and women balanced on scales, both slipping votes into locked boxes; another shows a line of women in burkas, amputees, Tajiks, Hazaras, and Pashtuns casting their lot for democracy. It all seems unimpeachably good and just, the stuff of heartwarming political advertisements, and in Bamiyan, on October 9, in the shadow of the enormous empty niches of the twin Buddhas, thousands lined up in an early autumn snowstorm to mark their ballots.

We leave Kabul at sunrise, the first light catching on the still-shuttered shops that line the road out of town. Everywhere there are huge billboards of Ahmed Shah Massoud, the Northern Alliance leader killed by Al Qaeda just before 9/11, who in his martyrdom has become some combination of Che, Patton, and Bob Marley. Someone clearly hopes for some of the star power to rub off on Karzai, whose billboards are almost always adjacent to Massoud's. It is a classic exercise in brand building, as broad recognition of Karzai's face will be key when the largely illiterate populace stamp their votes next to their selected candidate's portrait in October.

The road is perfectly smooth fresh tar, built on contract by the Americans to connect Kabul with Bagram air force base, but at the city's edge the delimitations of the Western reconstruction are immediately apparent. Shattered houses, walls, and granaries line the road for mile after mile across the Shomali Plain, which was the scene of some of the worst fighting under the Soviets and the Taliban. Land-mine warnings dot the roadside, with painted check marks on walls meant to declare areas cleared. With ten to fifteen million mines, not to mention unexploded mortar shells, cluster bomblets, and artillery rounds, Afghanistan is among the most heavily mined countries in the world.

Everywhere along the road new infrastructure is built upon, or out of, the fragments of three decades of war. A bridge crossing a clear stream is anchored by the bombed-out shells of Soviet armored vehicles filled with rocks. A prefab Bailey bridge built by the US Army spans a river above the skeletal remains of its predecessor. Gardens of sunflowers are edged with whitewashed artillery shells; tank treads lie unfurled across the road through villages as speed breakers.

We make a sharp left off the main highway and leave whatever has recently been made new in Afghanistan far behind. The road, if it can be called that, is an unpaved nightmare of potholes, frost heaves, and hummocks that screech along the underbelly of the van. It is like driving up a creek bed, and we rarely break ten miles an hour. The road winds up narrow valleys as the peaks of the Hindu Kush loom overhead, and men with mountainous turbans and creased faces lead donkeys by the roadsides. Mud-brick tribal compounds rise up in grim medieval solidity, rifle ports at their corners. Life is concentrated around water, a thin green line between the unrelenting aridity of the mountains and the culture that has subsisted here for centuries. The logic of the poppy trade, in a country where so little can be grown, is hard to miss.

To instill real change in a place so determinedly traditional, with so little uniting infrastructure, seems nearly impossible. Whenever we pass a burka-clad woman walking by the roadside, alone or with her husband, she stops and turns away, looking out over the orchards and fields of the valley bottoms. In the villages turbaned merchants sell almonds and dried mulberries and apricots from piles spread on burlap sacks. Often along the route, the rusting hulks of Soviet tanks lie frozen, their barrels still pointed in ambush at a far bend of the road, the words AFGHAN TOURISM ORGANIZATION, BAYMAN HOTEL stenciled on their sides in testament to a resurgence of entrepreneurial spirit. The makeshift billboards mark every tank for fifty miles, in an ironic enticement for the trickle of weekending UN workers, journalists, and NGO people who travel to Bamiyan during the summer months.

The valley bottoms, cut into fertile steps planted with walnuts

and almonds and apples, are surrounded by dun-colored sandstone cliffs. Hazara boys, the Shia Muslim and Asiatic descendants
of Genghis Khan, stand by the roadside, holding out bags of fresh
apricots, running after the van in clouds of dust. I buy a bag, the
fruit so perfectly ripe that the stone rattles inside like a drum.

In a Pashtun village farther on, there is not a single woman on
the streets, and crowds of fierce-looking Pathans with black beards
and mascara-ringed eyes stare at me. "Don't worry, you look like a
Panjshiri," my guide tells me, but despite my month's worth of
beard I'm not fooling anyone. We take tea and horrid sugar-coated
mulberries and make small talk with the men. Boys riding sidesad-
dle idly switch donkeys down the street, and merchants fan the flies
away from heaps of raisins. A child swings from the barrel of a
blasted Soviet tank as if it were a jungle gym. I ask the owner of the
teashop why there are no women walking around the town. "Why
do they need to go out? If they want something, we bring it for
them. If they want to see somebody, we arrange a visit. That is our
duty."

Up toward a high pass, we scramble through unrepaired wash-
outs from the spring rains. The difficulty of the road drives home
the primary fact preventing Afghanistan from being truly unified
or modernized. The geography is mind-bogglingly severe, the easi-
est way between two points scarcely ever a straight line. The road
from Kabul to Herat requires a thousand-mile detour through Kandahar. For all its illustrious history as a crossroads of civilization
and artery of the Silk Road, today's Afghanistan has scarcely any
sealed roads tying it together, which only serves to compound the
regionalism, tribalism, and warlordism that dominate the country.
The driver, clearly irked that his new van is being pounded to
pieces on the road, curses loudly in Dari every time the chassis bottoms out on a rock, and stops frequently to inspect the damage.
Finally, after eleven hours of driving, a red sandstone precipice
rises hundreds of feet above the road, topped by the ruined ramparts and citadels of the ancient fortress of Shahr-i-Zohak, which
has guarded the entrance of the Bamiyan Valley for eight hundred
years.

When the Chinese Buddhist pilgrim Hiuen Tsiang reached the
Kingdom of Bamiyan in A.D. 632, he found a thriving commercial

and religious nexus of the Silk Road. Situated in a high valley in the center of the Hindu Kush, Bamiyan had strategic control over a number of mountain passes that connected trade routes from China, India, and Persia. Buddhism had thrived in Afghanistan since the second-century rule of the Buddhist convert and philosopher-king Kanishka and had reached its apogee by the time of Hiuen's arrival. I imagined him arriving on a bell-clear afternoon like this, walking with a staff down a dirt trail along the valley's lower contours and coming over a rise to see for the first time the wheat fields and orchards, a teeming bazaar of Indian spices and Chinese silks and dried fruits, strings of Bactrian camels and yaks at rest. Above it all, carved into a sandstone cliff face towered over by 18,000-foot peaks, stood the colossal Buddhas: the universe, mapped in the human form, cut from the living rock.

> To the northeast of the royal city there is a mountain, on the declivity of which is placed a stone figure of Buddha, erect in height 140 or 150 feet. Its golden hues sparkle on every side, and its precious ornaments dazzle the eyes by their brightness. — the journals of Hiuen Tsiang

The enormous Buddhas were gilded and decorated with lapis or perhaps ocher. The whole matter, even of their original appearance, is cloaked in mystery, and the conclusions of scholars are largely inferential. The arms were wooden armatures covered over with stucco and painted, the hands in one of the Buddha's mudras, symbolic hand gestures that indicated the lesson the Buddha meant to impart: *dharmacakra,* the gesture of teaching; *varada,* the gesture of compassion; *ab-haya,* the gesture of fearlessness. Some art historians believe that the great alcoves in which they stood were painted with frescoes of the heavens, an eternally blue sky cut from stone. The colossi could have been adorned with sheets of reflective mica, or had stanchions of flame planted on their shoulders during ceremonies.

The world stood then, as it does now, at a momentous juncture. The very same year that Hiuen entered Bamiyan and described its wonders in his journal, the Prophet Muhammad died in Mecca at the age of sixty-three. Within a few centuries the lapping tide of Islam swept over Afghanistan, and by the tenth century Buddhism had been abandoned in the Hindu Kush. But the colossi remained for a thousand years, sentinels of a world that had vanished, their golden hues scoured away by drifting snows, the painted heavens of their frescoes, with their flights of geese and red clouds blistered by the swell of frosts, chipped away by the steel arrowheads of Genghis Khan and the cannons of the Mughal emperor Aurangzeb. The stone ears (from which once depended bright jewels brought by caravans as tribute for the right of passage) echoed with the passing drumbeats of the British and Soviet empires in their ruin.

The Buddhas stood, carved in deep relief, 125 and 180 feet tall, dressed in stucco tunics cut in the fashion of the armies of Alexander, which had passed through the region a millennium earlier en route to the Khyber Pass. Bamiyan was a fusion of Greek, Indian, Persian, and Chinese, at its peak as vibrant a marketplace of ideas and goods as existed anywhere on the planet. How different is today's Kabul, again a frontier of the clash of civilizations, a destination for mercenaries and visionaries and refugees returning home?

Meaning faded with the years in the cliff kingdom of Bamiyan, and the Buddhist monasteries and their handed-down rituals passed away and withdrew to the high Himalayas and the Tibetan plateau. The great statues, recast in local memory, were thought to be the pagan kings of a vanished empire, an Ozymandian attempt at immortality that decayed a bit with each passing season. Locals called the larger Buddha Solsol, meaning "year after year." The smaller, which they imagined to be a woman, was called Shahmama, the kingmother. The living decide upon meaning, and the Hazaras of Bamiyan (their name, derived from a Persian term for the Mongol hordes, means "thousand riders") presided over a valley of ghosts. The heavily mined ruins of Shahr-e-Gholghola, the City of Screams, watches over Bamiyan from the east; in 1221 it was betrayed by the king's daughter to Genghis Khan, who in turn massacred every last inhabitant. When a group of archaeologists came to the valley in the 1950s to study the Buddhas, they found the base of the larger one walled in with mud brick, turned into a sheepfold and granary by local farmers, whose flocks bedded down in the echoing alcove.

Fifteen centuries they stood, the largest rock-cut figures of the standing Buddha in the world, until March 2001, when the decree of a Taliban jirga stated that they were idolatrous and un-Islamic. The final straw, it was reported at the time, was an offer by a group of European envoys of money to protect and preserve the sculptures. The Taliban, then one of the world's most isolated regimes (recognized only by the Saudis, Pakistan, and the United Arab Emirates), craved legitimacy more than anything else, and in a blind fury that the West cared more about a bunch of crumbling stones than a million starving Afghans, called for the Buddhas' immediate annihilation. Days of antiaircraft and cannon fire were followed by placed dynamite charges that tore the statues from the cliff face. The Taliban were so proud of their handiwork that they brought a Western press junket into Bamiyan, and within weeks they were selling photo calendars of the destruction in the bazaars of Kabul and Kandahar. Fifty cows were slaughtered at the site to atone for the delay in the statues' destruction, and rumor had it that Bin Laden himself had come to watch the final demolition.

Even prepared by hours of expectation, I am shocked by my first view of the town of Bamiyan. Around a bend of road the valley opens wide amid shining fields of wheat, and past copses of willow and poplar the cliff-face city reveals itself. There are hundreds of caves along the mile-long facade, a latticework of temples, galleries, and monastic residences eroded to resemble Swiss cheese. At the center of the complex, set half a mile apart, are the huge empty alcoves, cast in deep shadow by the dazzling mountain light, like arched doorways into the heart of the mountains.

The presence of absence is overwhelming, like returning to New York in the final smoking months of 2001, before the meaning of Ground Zero was hijacked by jingoistic sentiment, political opportunism, and the selling of ghoulish tchotchkes. It was palpable: the vibrations of collapse reverberated between Bamiyan and New York like the humming tines of a tuning fork. At the bottom of each alcove lay a compact pile of sandstone rubble like the sweepings of some monstrous broom. T. S. Eliot's heartbroken summation of the role of poetry in the modern world comes to mind: "these fragments I have shored against my ruins." There is nothing against the back walls of the alcoves but ragged, crumbling sandstone and the ghostly outline of the Buddhas' forms.

At the Bamyan Hotel, the satellite dish sits propped up by the whitewashed cog of a tank wheel. Out back, a half-dozen tanks rust in a wheat field, with wildflowers poking up between their treads. The hotel proprietors are building a row of yurts to offer the hoped-for swarms of tourists a more authentic Bamiyan experience (even though yurts aren't native to this part of the Hindu Kush). There are few other guests, except for a shy, friendly US State Department employee with a vague job description, a side arm, and a cortege of Nepali Gurkhas shadowing him at all times. The quiet Americans have returned to the Hindu Kush.

At dinner I meet Edmund Melzl, a fedora-wearing and walrus-mustached German restoration expert. Melzl is employed by ICOMOS, the International Council on Monuments and Sites, a UN agency that works to preserve and protect world heritage sites. Bamiyan, in a textbook example of bureaucratic afterthought, was named a world heritage site by UNESCO in 2003 and listed as "threatened."

Melzl is here to coordinate a team of international experts in the restoration of the Buddhas. This will involve, in a humpty-dumpty exercise without parallel, the sorting and cataloging of every fragment in the niches. The sedimentary stone of Bamiyan, laid down by millions of years of floods and then carved out by the valley's river, has a geologic profile, a map of layers as precise as DNA, by which the fragments can be reordered. In the alcove of the 180-foot Buddha, there are more than 4,000 fragments, some weighing as much as 100 tons. So the first work is counting the pieces, then figuring out how to put them back together. Melzl's goal, ultimately, is to rebuild the Buddhas as they were in early 2001, using only the pieces from the niches, in accordance with UNESCO's 1964 Venice Charter. "Even the parts that have been reduced to sand we will use."

I ask why, when so much of Afghanistan is barely functioning, when there are no roads, health care is abysmal, and the entire country is reverting to medieval narco-statehood, the international community should be concerned with so costly and difficult a project. "Reconstruction like this is a crucial part of identity and reconciliation," he tells me. "The Taliban wanted to erase history here. If the Afghans have no sense of their past, they will have no future. The Frauenkirche in Dresden was finished fifty years after the end of the war. The sixteenth-century Mostar bridge, in Bosnia, has now been rebuilt using traditional methods. The people here want the Buddhas back."

*

The desire to rebuild, and quickly, has led to a host of suggestions with varying degrees of viability and an air of argument reminiscent of the debate over the 9/11 memorial. A photogrammetrist in Zurich has created a near-perfect 1/200th scale model of the great Buddha by using software to turn archival photographs into a 3-D map. The governor of the province, a former warlord, has threatened to reconstruct the Buddhas in concrete to boost tourism, calling the sculptures his people's introduction to the world. An Italian sculptor wants to carve the Buddhas anew farther along in the cliff. A mysterious Japanese billionaire is said to have his own rebuilding plan: to commission an installation artist to project the sculptures as holograms into the empty niches. There are, of course, no Buddhists around to ask, but for most people in Bamiyan the prospect of rebuilt sculptures attracting even a fraction of the town's former tourist bounty is extremely tempting.

However far-fetched a tourism renaissance seems now, the people of Bamiyan are holding out hope. The prevailing logic in town is *if you build it, they will come*. In the new bazaar half a mile from the mine-sown ruins of the medieval market destroyed by the Taliban, they sell grainy postcards of the Buddhas in the sepia light of a foliage-tinged autumn in the 1970s, and the Lonely Planet guidebooks have rereleased their Central Asia guide, urging backpackers to *get there first*. There is a refreshing brand of hucksterism in Bamiyan's bazaar, the natural tendency of a marketplace to do the things that it was meant to do: buy, sell, argue, have tea, engage in the commerce of living. But the alcoves can be seen from the market, and everyone says the same thing from behind their piles of walnuts or money or DVDs: bring them back.

Melzl's restoration plan for the Buddhas is painstaking and dangerous work. The Taliban had antiaircraft emplacements in the cliff face, and had planted hundreds of mines around the Buddhas and in the network of paths and caves that surrounded them. Melzl tells me that the Taliban, in destroying the Buddhas, also placed antitank mines at the bottom of the niches so that falling pieces of stone would hit them and be further pulverized, making the restoration work a de-mining project as well. Even the empty niches, fissured by earthquakes and the high explosive blasts that brought the Buddhas down, were threatened with collapse last winter, when a team of Italian engineers came and shored up the walls with tons of concrete and injected epoxy resin. It is a deeply ironic endeavor that resonates throughout the rebuilding of Afghanistan: the struggle to save empty holes from disintegration.

The problems of rebuilding, even if all the extant pieces can be reordered, are immense. The greater Buddha had been missing its legs for centuries, so even among the fragments there would be nothing to create static support for the thousands of tons of stones above. They certainly couldn't be anchored to the brittle sandstone at the back of the niche, so Melzl envisions some sort of steel support armature to hold the massive weight. "Normally," he says, "everything is possible." He shows me a packet of pictures he took on his first trip here, in 1958. The 180-foot Buddha looms in towering perspective, the stucco folds of its tunic as even and delicate as ripples on a pond. Parked at the base is Melzl's Volkswagen bug. "The road was actually better then," he tells me.

Across the valley at his office in a disused mosque, Melzl gives me a pair of jeweler's glasses and a fragment of the stucco lathe that once formed the Buddha's garment. It is a fragile lime plaster, mixed with filaments of straw and wool to give it tensile strength. I hold in my hands the work of some laborer fifteen hundred years past, the wool of a sheep and the straw of a threshed harvest from not long after the fall of Rome.

Little is known about the Kingdom of Bamiyan at its peak, not even the precise dates of the carving of the Buddhas. The vast wooden scaffolding, the echoes of hundreds of picks and chisels realizing the huge bodies from the stone, can only be dimly imagined. Besides the journals of Hiuen Tsiang and a few others, there are no historical accounts. Almost all that is known has been inferred and theorized by scholars working from art-historical evidence: fragments of frescoes and rock carvings. Fieldwork in Bamiyan was almost impossible after the Soviet invasion, and after the Taliban's depredations most of the evidence was lost forever. Carved fragments from the rubble piles are said to have turned up on the black market in Tokyo, Zurich, and Los Angeles. The cultural, economic, and religious life of the valley is largely extrapolated from other Buddhist centers in China and India, but the enormity of the original undertaking implies the importance of Bamiyan, with countless workers carving the statues and monastic cave complexes over decades.

In his description of the colossal Buddhas, Hiuen Tsiang also mentions a third Buddha at Bamiyan: "To the east of the city . . . there is a [monastery], in which there is a figure of Buddha lying in a sleeping position as when he attained Nirvana. The figure is in length about 1,000 feet or so." There is nothing anywhere in the valley that fits this description, a prostrate Buddha the size of the Chrysler Building, represented at the exact moment of his death. A journalist I met in Kabul thought the story was apocryphal, or perhaps it was a natural rock formation that looked like the Buddha in a certain slant of light. Half a mile from Melzl's office, near the empty niche of the smaller Buddha, the Afghan-French archaeologist Zemaryalai Tarzi leads a dig beneath a buckwheat field in an attempt to find the third Buddha.

Tarzi is a compact, clean-shaven man, with a floppy hat and fingerless bicycling gloves. He speaks perfect French — Tarzi has lived in France since before the Soviet invasion. He leads me around the dig site, a grid of square holes occupied by a small army of dust-covered local laborers armed with shovels, picks, and brooms. "We have found the wall of the monastery mentioned in the journals," he says, pointing to a swept-off ridge of mortared river stones. So far the dig has uncovered fragments of pottery and seven terra cotta Buddha heads. If his calculations are correct, the remains of the huge sculpture — which was likely built of mud brick — extend from where we stand for a thousand feet eastward. "Perhaps we are near its feet."

The Hazara diggers in their pits, Tarzi tells me, have moved down through time, past the Islamic period and into the Buddhist, brushing away layers of history and the accretions of centuries. The newly dug holes are time machines; the piled dirt tells a story in layers of meaning, revisited for the first time in millennia. All Afghan history, Sikander and the terrible Khan and all who have gone to their gods like soldiers, all of the frail human mark against unraveling time, can be read like a core sample in the cut bank of soil. The tanks sinking into the wheat fields are just the newest additions to the archaeological record. Tiny fragments of fired clay turn up like flotsam tangled in seaweed. But shards of pottery can never really recall the totality of human loss, the heft of hammers and shovels, the fearful gathering up of family and belongings to flee one direction or another from the onrush of history. I kick up a .50-caliber shell in the soil, perhaps Soviet, perhaps Taliban, and when I shake out the dust and blow across its top it makes a low whistle.

Tarzi was in France when he heard that the Buddhas had been destroyed. "On that day I became a militant for Afghan culture." I bring up the reconstruction project going on less than a mile from here, and Tarzi sneers. Melzl had mentioned that the two men weren't on speaking terms. Tarzi is opposed to any reconstruction. "In a conference I said we have to leave the two niches empty like two sinister pages of Afghan history. To underline the folly of human beings, and for the future generations to see what happened here. You could reconstruct them in Las Vegas — you have more tourists there."

The planners of the memorial at Ground Zero, two voids left where the towers had stood, came to essentially the same conclusion as Tarzi. Often in Buddhist art, the presence of the Buddha is indicated by the placement of other figures in relation to a void in the picture, a reflection of the emptiness that is the essence of the Buddha's nature. The towering voids in the cliff face exude a presence and a mystery in their emptiness, visible from everywhere within the valley. In the niche of the smaller Buddha, all that remains besides the 125-foot shadow is a fragment of the Hellenistic robe, carved rippling in stone high on the wall, a shred caught on a thorn in a giant's passing.

A worker from the hotel, a toothless, sunburned old man named Abdul Hamid, has driven with us out to Tarzi's dig. An ethnic Hazara and a Shia, Hamid says his tribe suffered extensively under the Taliban, with thousands killed in Bamiyan and Mazar-e-Sharif in reprisals when the fortunes of the civil war shifted. One of a handful of Hazaras who had returned to Bamiyan after it fell, he says he had seen Arabs and Pakistanis, dressed in white in the days before the sculptures were destroyed, and that the Taliban had done it to please them.

"When the Taliban exploded the Buddha idols, I was living in Bamiyan. Inside the city we own a small café, and that's where I was, about a kilometer away. At first, the Taliban had placed their artillery on the hill. Every day they were shooting more than twenty shells at the idols, but they did not destroy them completely. Hazara men were hung by ropes from above and forced to place explosives in the holes in the idols' sides. One of them suffocated because of the rope, the way he was hung. The others I don't know what happened. At that time we were in the city, and we climbed on the roofs of our houses and watched. There was a thunderous sound, and the dust raised to the sky. This is something that we never expected."

Whatever the Taliban had in mind in Bamiyan, nine months later they were routed and left Afghanistan in essentially the same state they had left the Buddhas. Today the Afghan people and the international community have plenty of ideas on how to put things together, but hope and reality have diverged. The flawed elections, in which Karzai swept to victory on the wings of Blackhawk helicopters and the American PR machine, were nevertheless crucial to a sense of Afghan reconciliation and unity. Karzai, declared a victor at the same time as Bush, won 55 percent of the national vote, but in Bamiyan the electorate swung three to one to Mohammed Mohaqeq, a Hazara chieftain who immediately after the election vowed never to recognize the legitimacy of the Karzai government.

The elections were in a sense concrete Buddhas: a quick, sloppy fix, a deep compromise of possibility, a nice postcard to show the folks in the swing states at home. But how many ways can you rearrange a pile of rubble and call it whole? How can a country so broken be made complete? In Bamiyan, where the shattered plaster folds of the Buddhas' robes were echoed in the burka pleats of the women who lined up in the snow to vote, the election was a movement — fitful, stumbling, uncertain — into a new era. But what is the alternative? It is an existential dilemma: something must be done; nothing can be done. The world cannot afford to let Afghanistan lie in ruins as a monument to darkness.

We walk up from the dig site, along the base of the cliff. In a few places along the way we climb paths and enter the caves. Inside, a series of galleries contain fragments of devotional frescoes. The faces and hands of the figures in the paintings have been methodically shot off, the bullets reducing the plaster to powder and gouging deep into the sandstone walls. Enough of the remaining painting has been left to indicate the handiwork of vandals, as if defacing made the message clearer than wiping the stone clean. So few clues to reconstruct a world: a fold of robe, a tracing of cloud, a pair of disembodied feet surrounded by chewed-up rock.

At the bottom of the 180-foot Buddha, behind a chicken-wire

fence, the pile of shattered stones is ten feet high, some the size of Melzl's Volkswagen. The Sisyphean nature of Melzl's task is immediately apparent: to reorder this, to make of this once more something whole, something comprehensible — how could that be done? It is a broken pile of rocks, seemingly interchangeable with the broken rocks that litter this entire country. The outline of the Buddha, fifteen stories high, is traced against the back of the alcove like a photonegative, a radiation shadow left by an atomic blast. Abdul leads the way, and we follow a series of switchbacks up a scree slope.

Just off the path are small stones painted red. *Uncleared mines.* Evil little things, injecting fear directly into the earth, like a lottery of ill luck and desolation. They make the ground itself traitorous. A UN pamphlet I read earlier noted the warning signs: overgrown paths, unfilled fields, orchards of ripe fruit dropping unpicked to the ground. I imagine the moment a mine seizes the body and tears it like fresh bread, and I follow exactly in Abdul's footsteps.

Climbing higher up the cliff face, we enter a doorway carved into the stone wall of the cliff and step out of the brilliant light of the Hindu Kush. Following a tunnel carved by hand centuries ago, the old man ahead moves through bands of light and darkness as he passes narrow slits cut in the wall. The daylight behind fades, and we are in full darkness, feeling our way farther into the mountain. And then we come out to a ragged hole in the stone, 180 feet high in the back of the vast alcove, above where the Buddha's head had been. Far below lies the rubble pile, its meaning shattered and now in the process of being remade. Looking out, the frame of the alcove's arch perfectly composes the scene: ruins of the mud-brick bazaar, the new market, high-walled compounds and stands of willow by the winding river, waving green-gold wheat fields, smooth sandstone foothills towered over by the saw-edge peaks of the Hindu Kush that tear the clouds like raw silk.

Perhaps Hiuen Tsiang, whose writing outlasted the stone he described, had stood just here atop the Buddha's house-size head. Hiuen would have looked out from under the great stone arch beneath the painted branches of a bo tree, or maybe a painted heaven, contemplating its twin sky arching over Bamiyan. So much and so little has changed. There is a fresh cut in the hillside across where the Bamyan Hotel is building an annex for the tourists who have not yet returned. A boy with a donkey passes below and a woman in billowing burka carrying water. I am looking out from where the Buddha's gargantuan head had hung. Over a thousand years ago the monks of a vanishing order had ascended here in prayer, echoing the Buddha's life journey in a rite of circumambulation, a walking circle that was meant to renew the world. And even then, across a thousand miles of mountains and desert, at Mecca the Kaba'a was similarly circled, in a covenant with the great unknown.

Maybe the Buddhas *were* just stones, carved by an empire that would shortly be swallowed whole by history, and whose true motives and dreams have since been lost. Built with tributes offered for safe passage along the trade routes, perhaps they were an attempt at status and immortality by a forgotten emperor, or just a shill's draw for the passing caravans. They were images of God but they were built by humans, with the frailties and desires of humans.

Bamiyan had witnessed the great mixing of the world, the cross-pollination of civilizations. Maybe the reconstruction now can recreate the genius of that vanished moment; maybe the signal of Radio Arman will make it even out here. Today there are as many people of goodwill who have arrived in Afghanistan wanting to help as profiteers who have come to get their cut. For every journalist-trainer brought by nonprofits like the Institute for War & Peace Reporting there is a contractor who has come to build a compound. Whether the interests of both, and the will of the Afghan people, can bring something out of the wreckage remains to be seen. So afraid of ideas, the Taliban didn't even understand what they were wrecking. The Buddha can't be killed. Something of humanity and eternity had been put into the statues, and had remained, and, even destroyed, still remains. Omar, with his dynamite and artillery, could no more tear it down than Kellogg Brown & Root can build it back up.

A scattering of sand and pebbles, kicked loose by my foot, rattles down the empty cliff face and falls on the pile below, my own accidental contribution to entropy, the rearrangement of particles and meaning. The landscape of the Bamiyan Valley, of all Afghanistan, is defined by erosion: the slow wearing of wind and water and the rapid dissolution of war. In their niches, the statues had been protected from one and not the other, but they would have come to the same place eventually: the final victory of gravity and time. The huge alcove catches an edge of the wind, seeming almost to breathe, and I sit a long time looking out. In the stillness, it is difficult to conjure the fire and the smoke, the whistle of the shells and the thunder of collapse, the wash of blood that has rippled out from Afghanistan like a pebble dropped into a well. A cliff swallow glides in to the sheltering alcove and rises on an updraft without a wing beat. It levitates a moment, as if painted into the landscape, before returning to its nest of mud and straw built just where the Buddha's head had been.

LOUIS SIMPSON

Ishi

FROM *The Atlantic Monthly*

Ishi, the last of his tribe,
walked out of the forest.
He was dying of starvation.
A home was found for him,
the Anthropology Museum,
and harmless occupations.

He helped the hospital nurses
clean their instruments.
He showed Professor Kroeber
his tools: a pot for cooking,
a rope, a basket,
a bow and arrow.

*

Ishi liked to walk to town
and ride the trolley.
Kroeber took him to the opera.
Instead of watching the show
Ishi turned his chair around
and looked at the crowd.

The first airplane he saw
made exploding noises.
"American man go up
in sky," he said, and laughed,

like an ancient Roman,
not to be astonished by anything.

*

Ishi died of tuberculosis.
He was buried with five arrows,
"some things of a personal nature,"
and left the noisy world
as quietly as he came,
taking the forest with him.

GEORGE STEINER

Ten (Possible) Reasons
for the Sadness of Thought

FROM *Salmagundi*

Schelling: *Ueber das Wesen der Menschlichen Freiheit* (1809)
"Dies ist die allem endlichen Leben anklebende Traurigkeit, die
aber nie zur Wirklichkeit kommt, sondern nur zur ewigen Freude der
Ueberwindung dient. Daher der Schleier der Schwermut, der über die
ganze Natur ausgebreitet ist, die tiefe unzerstörliche Melancholie alles
Lebens."

"Nur in der Persönlichkeit ist Leben; und alle Personlichkeit ruht auf
einem dunkeln Grunde, der allerdings auch Grund der Erkenntnis Sein
muß."

("This is the sadness which adheres to all mortal life, a sadness, however, which never attains reality, but only serves the everlasting joy of
overcoming. Whence the veil of depression, of heavy-heartedness which
is spread out across the whole of nature, hence the profound, indestructible melancholy of all life."

"Only in personality is there life; and all personality rests on a dark
ground, which, however, must also be the ground of cognition.")

Schelling, among others, attaches to human existence a fundamental, inescapable sadness. More particularly, this sadness provides the somber ground on which consciousness and cognition
are founded. This somber ground must, indeed, be the basis of all
perception, of every mental process. Thought is strictly inseparable
from a "profound, indestructible melancholy." Current cosmology
provides an analogy to Schelling's belief. It is that of "background
noise," of the elusive but inescapable cosmic wavelengths which are

the vestiges of the Big Bang, of the coming of being into being. In all thought, according to Schelling, this primal radiation and "dark matter" entail a sadness, a heaviness of heart *(Schwermut)* which is also creative. Human existence, the life of the intellect, signifies an experience of this melancholy and the vital capacity to overcome it. We are, as it were, created "saddened." In this notion there is, almost undoubtedly, the "background noise" of the biblical, of the causal relations between the illicit acquisition of knowledge, of analytic discrimination and the banishment of the human species from innocent felicity. A veil of sadness *(tristitia)* is cast over the passage, however positive, from *homo* to *Homo sapiens*. Thought carries within itself a legacy of guilt.

The notes which follow are an attempt, wholly provisional, to understand these propositions, to grasp, tentatively, some of their implications. They are necessarily inadequate because of the spiral whereby any attempt to think about thinking is itself enmeshed in the process of thought, in its self-reference. The celebrated "I think, therefore I am" is finally an open-ended tautology. No one can stand outside it.

We do not really know *(in Wirklichkeit)* what "thought" is, what "thinking" consists of. When we try to think about thinking, the object of our inquiry is internalized and disseminated in the process. It is always both immediate and out of reach. Not even in the logic or delirium of dreams can we reach a vantage point outside thought, an Archimedean pivot from which to circumscribe or weigh its substance. Nothing, not the deepest probes of epistemology or neurophysiology, has taken us beyond Parmenides' identification of thought with being. This axiom remains at once the wellspring and boundary of Western philosophy.

We have evidence that processes of thought, of conceptual imaging, persist even during sleep. Some modes of thinking are totally resistant to any interruption whatever, as is breathing. We can, for short spells, hold our breath. It is by no means clear that we can be *thoughtless*. There are those who have labored to achieve this condition. Certain mystics, certain adepts of meditation have aimed at vacancy, at an entirely receptive because void state of awareness. They have aspired to inhabit nothingness. But such nothingness is itself a concept, charged with philosophical paradox and, where it is achieved by directed meditation and spiritual exercises, as in Loyola, emotionally replete. Saint John of the Cross characterizes the suspension of mundane thought as brimful of the presence of God. A true cessation of the pulse-beat of thought, exactly like the cessation of our physiological pulse-beat, is death. For a time, a dead person's hair and nails continue to grow. To the best of our understanding, there is no prolongation of thought however brief. Hence the suggestion, in part gnostic, that only God can detach Himself from His own thinking in a hiatus essential to the act of creation.

To revert to Schelling and the assertion that a necessary sadness, a veil of melancholy attaches to the very process of thought, to cognitive perception. Can we try and clarify some of the reasons? Are we entitled to ask why human thought should not be joy?

1

So far as we are aware, so far as we can "think thinking" — I will come back to that awkward phrase — thought is limitless. We can think of and about *anything*. What lies outside or beyond thought is strictly *unthinkable*. This possibility, itself a mental demarcation, lies outside human existence. We have no evidence for it either way. It persists as a hidden category of religious and mystical conjecture. But it can also figure in scientific, cosmological speculations, in the concession that a "theory of everything" lies outside and beyond human understanding. Thus we can think/say: "this problem, this topic surpasses our cerebral potentialities either at present or forever." But within these ill-defined, always fluid, and perhaps contingent confines, thought is without end, without any organic or formally prescriptive stopping point. It can suppose, imagine, assemble, play with (there is nothing more serious and, in certain regards enigmatic, than play) *anything* without knowing whether there is, whether there could be anything else. Thought can construe a multiplicity of universes with scientific laws and parameters wholly different from our own. Science fiction generates such "alternatives." A well-known logical conundrum postulates that our own universe is only a nanosecond old and that the sum of our memories is incised in the cortex at the moment of birth. Thought can theorize that time has a beginning or none (there is a despotic sophism in the ruling that it makes no sense to ask about the moment *before* the Big Bang). It can produce models of space-time as bounded or infinite, as expanding or contracting. The class of counterfactuals — of which "if" clauses, optatives, and subjunctives are the grammatical encoding — is incommensurable. We can deny, transmute, "unsay" the most obvious, the most solidly established. The scholastic doctrine whereby the one and only limitation on divine omnipotence is God's inability to change the past is unconvincing. We can readily both think and say such change. Human memory performs the trick daily. Thought-experiments, of which poetry and scientific hypotheses are eminently representative, know no boundaries. That humble monosyllable "let" which precedes conjectures and demonstrations in pure mathematics, in formal logic, stands for the arbitrary license and unboundedness of thought, of though manipulating symbols as language manipulates words and syntax.

Human thought reflects on our own existence. We suspect, though we do not know for certain, that animals cannot do this, even where primates share some 90 percent of our genome. We can model, we can devise mathematical expressions for, the "heat-death" of our universe by virtue of the thermodynamics of entropy. Or, on the contrary, we can advance arguments for eternal life, for resurrection — an appalling thought — or cyclical mechanisms of "eternal return" (as in Nietzsche). Not only innumerable ordinary men and women, but the begetters of religions, metaphysicians such as Plato, and certain psychologists, such as Jung, have rejected the axiom of finality, of psychic zero after corporeal demise. Thought can roam at liberty across the entire gamut of possibilities. It can, even prior to Pythagoras, wager on the transmigrations of the human soul. There is, there can be no verifiable evidence either way.

The infinity of thought is a crucial marker, perhaps *the* crucial marker of human eminence, of the *dignitas* of men and women as Pascal memorably declared ("thinking reeds"). It distinguishes what is signally human in the human animal. It enables the grammars of our speech to articulate remembrance and futurity, though we pause only rarely to take in the logical fragility of the future tense. Thought entails man's mastery over nature and, within certain restrictions such as infirmity and mental affliction, over his own being. It underwrites the radical freedom of suicide, of bringing thought to a voluntary, freely timed halt. So why the inescapable sadness?

The infinity of thought is also an "incomplete infinity." It is subject to an internal contradiction for which there can be no resolution. We shall never know how far thought reaches in respect of the sum of reality. We do not know whether what seems open-ended is not, in fact, absurdly narrow and beside the point. Who can tell us whether much of our rationality, analysis, and organized perception are not made up of puerile fictions? For how long, to how many millions, was the earth flat? We are indeed able to cogitate and phrase "ultimate questions" — "how did the cosmos come into being; is there any purpose to our lives; does God exist?" This impulse to questioning engenders human civilization, its sciences, its arts, its religions. But nothing identifies Marx more closely with enlightenment innocence than his affirmation that mankind only poses those questions to itself for which there will be an answer. It is the opposite which comes closer to the truth. It is "jesting Pilate." On absolutely decisive fronts we arrive at no satisfactory, let alone conclusive answers however inspired, however consequent the process of thought, either individual or collective, either philosophical or scientific. This internal contradiction (*aporia*), this destined ambiguity is inherent in all acts of thought, in all conceptualizations and intuitions. Listen closely to the rush of thought and you will hear, at its inviolate center, doubt and frustration.

This is a first motive for *Schwermut,* for heaviness of heart.

2

Thought is uncontrolled. Also during sleep and, presumably, unconsciousness the current flows. Only very rarely are we in control. The pulse of thought looks to be manifold and many-layered. It can originate at somatic and psychosomatic depths far beyond the reach of introspection (thoughts can rise out of deep-buried pain or pleasure). It is, very possibly, a prelinguistic phenomenon, a thrust of psychic energies prior to any executive articulation. But trapped in the great prison-house of language we arrive at no plausible, let alone "translatable" notion of what unspoken, unspeakable thinking could be like (does the deaf-mute come any closer?).

It is just conceivable that the unspoken meaningfulness of music, so obviously somatic in some of its key components, provides some analogy. The levels which depth-psychology, such as psychoanalysis or hypnosis, identify as subconscious, let alone unconscious, are, so far as they surface in words, images, dreams, or symbolic representations, superficial. They fall far short of the crust in the geophysics of the human psyche. And even at the surface, there is only intermittent control.

At each and every moment, acts of thought are subject to intrusion. A limitless congeries of external and internal elements will interrupt, deflect, alter, muddle any linear deployment of thought (Dante's *moto spirituale*). The stream is incessantly muddied, dammed, and diverted. A sudden sight or sound, however marginal, any tactile experience, a wisp of tiredness or boredom, the wedge of sudden desire, will appropriate a thought-response. Sensory phenomenality (*Sinnlichkeit*) in its incommensurable aggregate and confusion, can master and redirect thinking at virtually every moment in our lives ("it slipped my mind"). Daydreaming, pathological misprisions — to be "out of one's mind," a precisely meaningless proposition — are merely accented, identifiable forms of perpetual discontinuities, of inherent drift. Soliloquies of concealed or unwanted thought go their anarchic ways underneath articulate, cognitively apprehended speech. Though it may be that the creative artist or visionary can sometimes dip into these deep and turbulent eddies. By far the greater volume of recall and forgetting lies at the blurred edges of willed thinking. The winds of thought — an ancient simile — their sources beyond recapture, blow through us as through innumerable cracks. Kafka heard "great winds from under the earth."

Is it, in fact, possible to "think straight"? Can thought be made laserlike? Only at the price of trained, disciplined concentration and abstention from diversion. A number of activities depend on this narrowing and "monotone." The mathematician at his analysis and proof seems able to shut off and out the world, sometimes for hours on end. As does the chess master at his board or the formal logician at his lemmas. At crucial stages at his worktable, the watchmaker behind his magnifying glass, the surgeon operating, suspend all inattention. We knit our brows, the virtuoso musician closes his eyes. Contemplatives, masters of meditation, and their acolytes testify to spells, sometimes of astounding length, of absolute compaction, of an ingathering of the psyche so exclusive of any dispersal that it allows a single, total intentionality. It may be that Bach's solo partitas translate such "singularities"; but so does the suspension of breath of the marksman waiting to kill.

Such purities, such shafts of unwavering thought are accessible only to the relatively few, and their normal span is brief. They can occur at the summits of human excellence, as in what we know of Spinoza's methods, or at trivial levels, as in the circus-arts of the memory acrobats capable of learning by heart and regurgitating extended series of random numbers or names. There is evidence, though fitful, that the implicit powers of ultimate concentration can burn out at a fairly young age. First order pure mathematics and theoretical physics are the prerogative of the young. Which does suggest that the generative means involved are in some vital regard neurophysiological, indeed "muscular." There is documentation, although too often anecdotal, to suggest that totalities of concentration comport not only temporary exhaustion but long-range mental collapse (notably in chess masters and pure mathematicians or mathematical logicians). Prodigies in mnemonics rarely mature.

This allows the hypothesis whereby the involuntary, polymorphic wash of common thought is a safeguard. It acts as a conservation of mental reserves in what may be virtually a neurological sphere. It enables us to respond more or less adequately to the spontaneous, often shapeless demands and stimuli of the everyday. The bursts of concentration in undeflected thinking, the coercion of absolute focus, may carry the risk of subsequent mental exhaustion or impairment. There is monomania in certain intensities of thought (lasers can burn). It is, nonetheless, a monomania without which many peaks of human understanding and accomplishment would not be feasible. Archimedes did not desist from his analysis of conic sections, though that focus meant death. Far, far more often than not, however, ordinary thinking is a messy, amateurish enterprise.

A second cause of *unzerstörliche Melancholie* (of "indestructible melancholy").

3

Thinking makes us present to ourselves. Physical sensations, notably pain, are instrumental. But to think of ourselves is the main constituent of personal identity. I cannot think that I am not except in a fantasized, merely verbal game. The cessation of thought, even where madness is active, is simultaneously, tautologically that of the *ego*.

No one, nothing can verifiably penetrate my thoughts. To have one's thoughts "read" by another human being is nothing more than a figure of speech. I can altogether conceal my thoughts. I can mask and falsify their outward expression as I can that of my mien or body language. Hired mourners howl with grief over the remains of clients unknown to them. Even torture cannot elicit beyond doubt my inmost thoughts. No other human being can think my thoughts for me. This is the determinant reason, the ontological crux why no other man or woman can "die for me" in any literal sense. No one else can assume my death. I can die with, but never "for," the other, however inalienable our bonds, our kinship. The blind, the deaf-mute, the immobilized victim of paralysis or motor-neuron disease can harbor, formalize, and expound thoughts which reach to the edge of our universe. Thoughts are our sole assured possession. They make up our essence, our at-homeness or estrangement from the self. Their inwoven pressure is such that we may at times labor to hide them from our awareness, to silence them internally by means which psychology qualifies as amnesia or repression. It is doubtful that they remain irretrievable. I breathe therefore I think.

There follows a consequence whose enormity — in the proper sense of that word — is taken strangely for granted. No closeness, be it biological (identical or Siamese twins *may* represent a limit-case), emotional, sexual, ideological, be it that of a lifetime of shared domestic or professional coexistence, will enable us to decipher beyond uncertainty the thoughts of another. The quest for telepathic communications and simultaneities is an attempt, almost certainly futile, to overcome this often maddening or tragic inhibition. As is the resort to truth drugs in various obscenities of interrogation. The beloved lies in our arms, the treasured child in our embrace, the best friend clasps our hand. Yet we have no indubitable proof as to the thoughts being generated, registered inwardly at the relevant moment. So frequently in erotic union the current of thought, of the intensely imagined, pulses elsewhere. We make inner love to another. Under the adoring smile of the child, of the intimate friend, there can be the truth of boredom, indifference, or even repulsion. The ability to lie, to conceive of and enact fictions is organic to our humanity. The arts, social conduct, language itself would be impossible without it. As Jonathan Swift so astutely allegorizes it, perfect truthfulness, perfect transparency of thought belongs to the animal kingdom. Men and women endure by virtue of recurrent disguise. But the mask is worn underneath the skin.

Yet observe the paradox. This inaccessible core of our singularity, this most inward, private, impenetrable of possessions is also a billionfold commonplace. Although expressed, voiced or unvoiced, in different lexical, grammatical, and semantic forms, our thoughts are, to an overwhelming degree, a human universal, a common property. They have been thought, they are being thought, they will be thought millions and millions of times by others. They are endlessly banal and shop-worn. Used goods. The components of thinking in even the most private, personalized acts and moments in our existence — in sex, for example — are clichés, interminably repeated. They enlist, most saliently in an age of mass media or in one of restricted literacy, identical words and images. Our performative ecstasies, our taboo scenarios or approved rhetoric of sentimentality are shared, synchronically, with numberless other men and women. They are a mass-market merchandise labeled by the endlessly reiterative commonplaces of our language, our culture, our time and milieu. The phrase "sexual commerce" has a palpable connotation in our current structures of mass consumption and public explicitness.

All this is an inescapable consequence of language. We are born into a linguistic matrix which is historically inherited and communally shared. The words, the sentences we use to convey our thinking, either internally or externally, belong to a common currency. They render intimacy democratic. In embryo, as it were, the dictionary inventories the near-totality of both actual and potential thought. Which, in turn, is made up of combinatorial assemblages of and selections from prefabricated counters. It may be that the grammatical rules and precedents on offer (the pieces in the Lego kit) predetermine, place constraints on, the vast majority of our acts of thought and articulations of consciousness. The potentialities of construction are manifold, but also repetitive and bounded.

In consequence, true originality of thought, the thinking of a thought for the first time (and how would we know?) is *exceedingly* rare. As Alexander Pope famously observed, it is the verbal form not the content which gives an impression of novelty. Language and diverse symbolic codes may indeed articulate a thought, an idea, a conceptual image with unprecedented force, completeness, or economy. The performative shock may be intense. But there is absolutely no way of knowing, let alone proving, that that very thought has never been emitted before, albeit in a less adequate, even defective or almost "mumbling," guise. It may have occurred to sub- or illiterate men and women, to the deaf-mute or the cerebrally impaired who very simply took no notice of it. It may be that in the pure and applied sciences, in technology, cumulative and collective development, the exchange of conjectures and refutations, generates a *novum organum*. Yet even here much is rediscovered or arrived at simultaneously by different individuals and teams. The theory of natural selection, of calculus, of DNA provide well-known instances. With his genius for awe, Einstein professed that he had had only two genuine ideas in his entire life.

In the "humanities," taking that word in its widest circumference, in philosophy, the arts, literature, political and social theory, what we call "originality" is almost always a variant or innovation in form, in executive means, in the available media (bronze, oil paints, electric guitars). Such innovations and enabling discoveries are of immense significance and prodigality. They shape much of our civilization. But how many are "original" in any rigorous sense? How many are an authentic mutation? A new thought-act, an imagining without discernible precedent, is the ambition, acknowledged or not, of writers, painters, composers, thinkers. It can be realized outside dreams only where the relevant idiom is itself made new. Where there is some reorientation of the available deluge of ordinary language and shared formal conventions. Poets have indeed striven to create new languages, as in Dada and certain experiments in futurism. The products have been more or less incomprehensible trivialities. Where verbal modes are new, who is to understand them? In what sense have metaphors been invented and by whom? The inventory of myths, of the "great stories" on which Western literature feeds is that of a structure of themes and variations. Quantum leaps are (magnificently) rare. It *may* be that

Sophocles "thought up" the Antigone legend, though there were actual political-military precedents to suggest it. So far as we know, the Don Juan motif was a "find," datable in time and place, with almost immediate and ubiquitous echo. But these inceptions are infrequent.

Such thinkers and begetters of argument as Plato, Aristotle, Paul of Tarsus, Saint Augustine *may* have developed the linguistic and conceptual instruments with which to formulate and make widely accessible thoughts, images, metaphors of radical originality. This, however, is by no means certain. We may be stunned by the apposition in Sartre's "*le sale espoir*" and find no previous public utterance of this irony. But it is exceedingly doubtful that his was the first intellect or sensibility to experience this notion and communicate it to himself. When Giordano Bruno characterizes as new the concept of an unbounded, multiple cosmos, when Saint-Just proclaims "happiness to be a new idea in Europe," they are being eloquently rhetorical. Neither proposition was without precedent, some of it millennially ancient. Was romantic love truly invented in Provence during the twelfth century?

Thinking is supremely ours; buried in the uttermost privacy of our being. It is also the most common, shopworn, repetitive of acts. The contradiction cannot be resolved. A third reason for an *anklebende Traurigkeit* (for a "sorrow which adheres to us").

4

We have seen that there can be no final verification for the truth or error of subjective thought, for its sincerity or falsehood. What of public, systematic thinking, of that pursuit of objective truths which, since Parmenides, has been held to be the excellence of man in the West?

The values, logically formal or existential, diffuse or rigorous, which attach to the word "truth" are enmeshed in historical, ideological, psychological coordinates often arbitrary ("truth on one side of the Pyrenees" as Pascal put it). Even the experimentally demonstrable and empirically applicable truths of the sciences are underwritten by theoretical, philosophical presuppositions, by fluctuating "paradigms" always susceptible of revision or discard. Where it addresses, where it invokes "truth," thought relativizes this criterion in the moment in which it adverts to it. There is no escape from this dialectical circularity. As a result, the history of truth, a concept which itself negates any absolute status — the absolute has no history — ranges from the most dogmatic, "revealed" fables to the most extreme skepticism and the modernist move, already implicit in classical skepticism, "anything goes." However consequent, however scrupulous in its self-examination, a thought-act can postulate its attainment of truth solely where the process is tautological, where the result is a formal equivalence, as in mathematics or symbolic logic. All other statements of truths, doctrinal, philosophic, historical or scientific are subject to error, falsifiability, revision, and erasure. Like those "super-strings" in today's cosmology, "truths" vibrate in manifold dimensions inaccessible to any final proof (indeed, there is no clear view as to what such a "proof" could be). Existential thinking, the proceedings of thought in intellectual and daily life, cannot "break through" to any self-evident, incontrovertible, everlasting realm of truth. Yet it is just this realm which revealed creeds, which metaphysics as in Plato, Plotinus, or Spinoza, promise and labor to attain. Thus there is in abstract thought, in epistemological methods a latent ground bass of nostalgia, an edenic myth of lost certitudes (we hear it, with poignant integrity, in a thinker such as Husserl). To think is to fall short, to arrive somewhere "beside the point." At very best, thought breeds what Wallace Stevens called "supreme fictions." Einstein would have it otherwise: "The creative principle resides in mathematics. In a certain sense, therefore, I hold it true that pure thought can grasp reality as the ancients dreamed" (where "dreamed" may be a more than Freudian lapse). To which one of the most authoritative of today's cosmologists replies: "even within the basic domain of the basic equations of physics our knowledge will always be incomplete."

The more fierce the pressure of thought, the more resistant the language in which it is encased. Language, as it were, is inimical to the monochrome ideal of truth. It is saturated with ambiguity, with polyphonic simultaneities. It delights in fantastication, in constructs of hope and futurity for which there is no proof. Perhaps this is why the great apes have hesitated to develop it. Human beings could not endure without what Ibsen called "life-lies." Thought limited to logical propositions, best expressed nonverbally, or demonstrable factualities, would be madness. Human creativity, the life-giving capacity to negate the dictates of the organic, to say "No" even to death, depend integrally on thinking, on imagining counterfactually. We invent alternative modes of being, other worlds — utopian or hellish. We reinvent the past and "dream forward." But indispensable, magnificently dynamic as these thought-experiments are, they remain fictions. They nourish religions and ideologies, the *libido* is brimful of them (Shakespeare's "lunatics, lovers and poets"). Language constantly seeks to enforce dominion over thought. In the stream of thought it generates whirlpools, which we call "mental disorders" and those logjams known as obsessions. Yet the interference, the incessant "muddying of the waters" are also those of creativity. In this tidal surge, the act of pure concentration, the attempt to purge consciousness of its vital fictions, of the open-eyed hallucinations of desire, intent, or fear, are, as we noted, exceedingly rare. They exact a discipline profoundly contrary to natural language, though available to mathematics and symbolic logic. When Einstein appeals to "pure thought," it is precisely these he has in mind. Certain eminent philosophers have, in turn, attempted to make their linguistic articulations as "mathematical" as possible, as immune as possible from the mutinous joy of natural speech. But how many Spinozas, how many Freges or Wittgensteins are there, and to what degree have even these ascetics of truth prevailed? At twilight, Socrates sang.

This fundamental antinomy between the claims of language to be autonomous, to be liberated from the despotism of reference and reason — claims which are crucial to modernism and deconstruction — on the one hand, and the disinterested pursuit of truth on the other, is a fourth motive for sorrow (*Unzerstörliche Melancholie*).

5

Thinking is almost incredibly wasteful. Conspicuous consumption at its worst. Neurophysiological investigations have sought to localize and evaluate numerically "brain waves" emitted by the cortex. They have tried to identify the quanta of energy, the rhythm of electromagnetic pulses associated with moments and clusters of concentrated thought. It does seem plausible that there are in what

we call "thinking" components of neurochemical and electromagnetic energy, that the synapses in the human brain have their mea-
surable output (the study of cerebral lesions provides evidence).
But so far much remains conjectural and mappings are approximate. Intuitively, impressionistically, we do experience some analogy to muscular fatigue after sustained spells of sequential thought,
of reflection under pressure. Problem solvers in the exact and applied sciences, mathematicians, formal logicians, computer programmers, chess players, simultaneous translators report phenomena of exhaustion, of "burnout." Wartime cryptologists at their
decoding were among the first to register mental strain of extreme,
"physical" intensity. Again, however, our understanding of such
stress and of the mechanisms involved is rudimentary.

The point is this: thought processes, be they conscious or subconscious, the thought-stream within us articulate or unvoiced,
during waking hours or sleep — those rapid eye movements much
studied in recent decades — are, in overwhelming proportion, diffuse, aimless, dispersed, scattered, and unaccounted for. They are,
quite literally, "all over the place," which makes the idiom "scatterbrained" entirely valid. The economics are those of an almost monstrous waste and deficit. There may be no other human activity
more extravagant. We do not think about our thinking except in
brief spells of epistemological or psychological focus.

Very nearly the incessant aggregate and totality of thinking flits
by unnoticed, formless and without use. It saturates consciousness
and presumably the subconscious, but drains off like a thin sheet of
water on baked earth. Even the notion of "forgetting" is too substantive. That of which we may have been thinking an hour ago
may have left no trace whatever owing to contingent circumstances
or the interference effects of some task in hand. At best, it may
have been arrested in writing or encoded in some other modes of
semiotic markers. Japanese globetrotters are said to employ spe-
cialists who identify for them the locale of their own photographs.
But by far the iceberg mass of human thought vanishes unper-
ceived, unrecorded in the trash bin of oblivion. "Alms for oblivion." "What was I thinking when I said this or did that?" Or consider the banal disappointment when one awakes convinced of
having dreamt a major insight, an elusive solution, of having composed significant poetry or music only to find recollection helpless

and the bedside pad covered with meaningless scribbling. Which frustration and embarrassment does *not* prove that the effaced, lost thought or imagining was not of signal merit and importance. It is simply out of reach, erased as are millions and millions of other thoughts tiding through us in unfathomable waste.

This suggests the science fiction model of a society in which thinking is rationed. In which it is licensed only for certain hours or days and where such rations are distributed according to individual mental capacities and powers of concentration. A waste of thought would be regarded as vandalism or worse. Food, fuel can be rationed in wartime. The currency can be put under strict control. Why not regulate the infinitely valuable supply of thought, preserving it from waste and inflation? Science fiction, to be sure. Yet are attempts in that direction not the core of totalitarian systems, of despotic ideologies be they religious or political? Efforts to ration thinking, to constrict it within permitted, circumscribed channels are at the very heart of tyranny. Anarchic, playful, wasteful thought is that which totalitarian regimes fear most. It is the utopia of censorship to read not only the text, but the thoughts which underlie it or which it conceals. Hence the Orwellian trope of a "thought-police."

Though they contain hyperboles of proud modesty, Einstein's claim to have had only "two ideas" in his entire life, and Heidegger's maxim that all major thinkers have only one thought which they expound and reiterate throughout their works, may point to a vital truth. The significant thinker in the humanities or the sciences would be one who perceives and exploits a decisive insight or concept, who fixes on one crucial discovery or connection. It is he or she who invests almost avariciously in a seminal thought-act or observation, exploiting its full potential. Darwin seems to represent an exemplary instance. Whereas the numberless plurality of human beings, even if brushed as it were in transit by first-class thoughts, by radical notice, pays no especial heed, does not "grab a hold" or press on to performative realization. How many recognitions go to waste in the indifferent deluge of unattended-to thinking, in the un- or overheard soliloquy of everyday and "everynight" cerebral emission? Why are we unable to encapsulate, put in ordered storage and potentiality — as does an electric battery — the possibly fruitful voltage generated by the sleepless arcs and synapses of our mental being? It is, precisely, this infinitely spendthrift, ruinous generation which we cannot, as yet, account for. But the deficit is beyond reckoning.

A fifth reason for frustration, for that "dark ground" (*dunkler Grund*).

6

Thought is immediate only to itself. It makes nothing happen *directly*, outside itself. Fragile, disputed experiments in telekinesis have sought to show that thinking can produce minute material phenomena, effects of vibration or minimal displacement. Quantum physics, itself so enigmatic, has it that the act of observation alters the objective configuration of that which is being observed (Einstein found this supposition little short of monstrous). Here almost everything remains conjecture. Thinking has incommensurable consequences, but the inference of a direct continuum is, as Hume taught, inferential. It cannot be shown to be directly causal. The vast majority of habitual acts and gestures are "thoughtless." They are performed instinctively or via acquired reflexes. Famously, the millipede would come to a suicidal halt if it thought about its next step. A chilling reflection if ever there was one. Automatism is decayed thought. But even where an action is most carefully and consciously "thought out," where it follows on some internalized blueprint or an outward and articulate proposition, the sequence can only be inferred. Only God, so the theologians say, experiences no hiatus between thought and consequence. That which He thinks *is*. That there is a connection between thought and existential, pragmatic consequence is a rational postulate without which we could not conduct our lives. So far, however, we possess no working model of the chain of generative phenomena, of the presumably immensely complex translation of the conceptual need or desideratum into neurophysiological and muscular accomplishment. The neurochemistry which relates intention to effect can only be traced at rudimentary levels. In so many cases, it is as if cause comes after effect. Thought-acts seem to follow on unpremeditated, spontaneous enactments which thought then interprets and "figures" to itself in the past tense. (I wonder whether the spellbinding experience of déjà vu does not relate to this reversal.)

Far more often, there is obliteration: "I have no idea of why I did so and so. My mind is a total blank."

Interpositions between thought and act are as manifold, as diverse as is life itself. The shadows which fall between thinking and doing can never be exhaustively inventoried let alone classified. There are, in the most exacting of engineering or architectural constructs, minute deviations from design, from precise calibration. No painter, however skilled, can fully realize the transfer on to his canvas of his internal vision or of that which he believes he sees before him. Even in the strictest of forms, music embodies only partially the complex of feelings, ideas, abstract relations inward to its composer. The distance between felt pressures on sensibility, between the imagined and its linguistic utterance, is a mournful cliché, a commonplace of never-ending defeat since the inception not only of literature but of the most urgent and intimate of human exchanges. "I cannot put it into words," says the lover, say the grief-stricken; but also the poet and the philosopher. The intimation of barriers, of interference effects or "white noise" is disturbingly physical. Sentiment, intuition, intellectual or psychological illumination, crowd at the inner edge of language but cannot "break through" to complete articulation (though the great writer somehow works closer to that edge and to the pulses of the prelinguistic than do less privileged minds). Energies of recognition, metaphoric lightning flashes, and momentary comprehension vibrate just out of reach. Eurydice recedes tantalizingly into darkness. Within the turbulent, polysemic magma of conscious and subconscious processes, incessant thought or its wholly mysterious antecedents, nocturnal as well as diurnal, are only fragmentarily recuperable. Coming to the lit surface via the simplifying constraints of language, of coercive logic, this generative force is always inhibited and deflected. Hence the doomed labors of the Surrealists in quest of "automatic" writing or virgin modes of speech. The aleatory is already conditioned by imperatives.

Thinking does not, cannot make it so. Even the most prudentially gauged and focused motion of thought is "bodied forth" (Shakespeare's penetrating idiom) only imperfectly, only in part. The work of art, however sovereign, the political or military project, the material edification, the legal code or theological-metaphysical *summa* compromise with the ideal, with the necessary fiction of the absolute. A speck of chromatic impurity, all but imperceptible, remains in the black tulip, in the crystal symmetries of private or collective political, social design. The concept of perfection is an unfulfilled dream of thought, a conceptual abstraction, as is infinity. It is in the paradox of the existence within us of these two unattainable ideals that classical theology, in Anselm as in Descartes, locates its proof of the existence of God. Though *in extremis,* Wittgenstein spoke for every creative consciousness when he declared that the part of the *Tractatus* which mattered was that which remained unwritten.

Ineluctably, therefore, the totality of our futurities, of our projections, anticipations, plans — be they routine or utopian — carries within it a potential of disappointment, of prophylactic self-deception. A virus of unfulfillment inhabits hope. The grammars of optatives, of subjunctives, of every nuance of future tenses — these grammars being the irresponsible glory and morning light of the human mind — can never be guarantors. They do not entail and underwrite untainted fact. The odds may be overwhelmingly in our favor, induction may seem almost contractual and foolproof, but to expect, to await, to hope for is a gamble. Whose only certainty is death. The consequences of our expectations, of that impatience which we call "hope," fall short. Often they abort altogether (though there are dispensations in which they surpass our imaginings). Customarily, the anticipation, the projection, the fantasy and image exceed realization. If we hail experiences as "beyond our wildest dreams," these dreams have been cautionary and threadbare. A revealing emptiness, a sadness of satiety follows on fulfilled desires (Goethe and Proust are the unsparing explorers of this *accidia*). The celebrated gloom *post coitum,* the longed-for cigarette after orgasm, are precisely those which measure the void between anticipation and substance, between the fabled image and the empirical happening. Human eros is close kin to a sadness unto death. If our thought-processes were less urgent, less graphic, less hypnotic (as in the gusts of masturbation and daydreaming), our constant disappointments, the gray lump of nausea at the heart of being, would be less disabling. Mental breakdowns, pathological evasions into unreality, the inertia of the brain-sick may, in essence, be tactics against disappointment, against the acid of frustrated hope. Such are the failed correlations between thought and realization, between the conceived and the actualities of experience, that we can neither live without hope — Coleridge's "Work without hope draws nectar in a sieve, / And hope without an object cannot live" — nor overcome the bereavement, the mockery which failed hopes comport. "Hope against hope" is a powerful, but ultimately damning phrasing of the blight which thought casts on consequence.

A sixth *Ursache* or font for *tristitia*.

7

There are, we saw, two processes which human beings cannot bring to a halt so long as they are alive: breathing and thinking. In fact, we are capable of holding our breath for longer periods than we are able to abstain from thought (if that is possible at all). On reflection, this incapacity to arrest thought, to take a break from thinking, is a terrifying constraint. It imposes a servitude of peculiar despotism and weight. At every single instant in our lives, waking or sleeping, we inhabit the world via thought. The philosophic-epistemological systems which seek to explain and analyze this habitation fall into two perennial categories. The first characterizes our consciousness and awareness of the world as being that of perception through a window. This model, founded somewhat naively on an analogy with ocular vision, underlies every paradigm of realism, of sensory empiricism. It authorizes a belief, however complex or attenuated, in an objective world, in an "out there" whose ideal and material elements are conveyed to us by conscious or subconscious input and the placement of this input by intuitive, intellectual, and experimental means. The other epistemology is that of the mirror. It postulates a totality of experience whose only verifiable source is that of thinking itself. It is our minds, our neurophysiology which project what we take to be the forms and substance of "reality." Per se this is the irrefutable Kantian axiom: "reality," whatever it may consist of, is inaccessible. It eludes any demonstrable, assured grasp. It may amount to a collective hallucination, a common dream. Extreme, playfully grave versions of this solipsism suggest that we are ourselves "such stuff as dreams are made on," perhaps dreamt by a Demiurge or indeed, as Descartes speculates, by a demon. All thought about the world, all observation and understanding would be *reflection*, mappings in a mirror.

On one capital point these two opposed systems concur: the

glass, be it window or mirror, is never immaculate. There are scratches on it, blind spots, curvatures. Neither vision through it nor reflection from it can ever be perfectly translucid. There are impurities and distortions. This is the crux: there is interposition between ourselves and the world we inhabit. Conceptualizations, observations (as in the "uncertainty principle") are acts of thought. There are no innocent immediacies of reception, however spontaneous, however unthinking they seem. Theories of cognition, whether Descartes's, Kant's, or Husserl's, struggle heroically to situate a point of unpremeditated immediacy, a point at which the self meets with the world without any presuppositions, without any interference by psychological, corporeal, cultural, or dogmatic presumptions. Such "phenomenologists" strive to "see things as they are," to make out the truth of the world's presence and "thereness" either via the window or the mirror. But, as Gertrude Stein knew, there is no unwavering, reinsuring "there there." No Archimedian point or tabula rasa has ever been convincingly located. The identity of the "thinking reed," the obscuring ubiquity of thought-processes acts as a screen. Experience, where it would be naked and Adamic, is filtered and essentially compromised. The expulsion from Eden is a "fall into thought." Thus there is no element in existence which is not "sicklied o'er with the pale cast of thought."

In consequence, even the most inventive, capacious, orderly of human intellects and imaginations operates within indirections and limitations which it cannot truly define, let alone measure. Everywhere the masterlight of the mind abuts on obscurity. Are there neurophysiological, evolutionary limits to our conceptualizations and analyses of the world? Are there categorical bounds to human reason? Which are the inherent constraints — whether perceived or not — that predetermine the reach and clarity of our boldest conjectures (conjectures which may, in fact, be entirely inadequate to or even out of touch with the actualities of the cosmos)? What proof have we, what proof could we have, that the progress of empirical investigation and theoretical construction is limitless, that the speculative intellect will continue on its seemingly open-ended journey through "seas of thought." The most powerful of electron microscopes now appear to be nearing the limit of possible observation as, in haunting symmetry, are the most probing of radio telescopes. It is not that the light from remote galaxies does not reach us; it will *never* reach us in allegory of our solitude. How much of our proud science is also science fiction, a model whose only demonstrable *veritas* is that of mathematics, of mathematics playing its own entranced games?

There has always been ground for suspicion in regard to the seemingly incontrovertible axioms of logic and the syntax in which they are so despotically incised. Do these axioms, do the sacrosanct rules which govern contradiction, do no more than externalize the local particularities of hominid cerebration, the architecture of our cortex? Just as vision may be held to enact the anatomy and physiology of the human eye. Each and every one of us has experienced frustrations of awareness, barriers to understanding. We "run up," often viscerally, against impalpable but unyielding walls of language. The poet, the thinker, the masters of metaphor make scratches on that wall. Yet the world both inside and outside us murmurs words which we cannot make out. "Unheard tunes" are proclaimed to be the sweetest. Cézanne testifies in modest anger at the inability of his eye to penetrate in depth the landscape before him. Pure mathematics knows of the insoluble though there is no assured grasp of the source of such insolubility. The most inspired thinking is impotent in respect of death, an impotence which has generated our metaphysical and religious scenarios. (I will come back to this.) Thought veils as much as, probably far more than, it reveals.

A seventh reason for that *Schleier der Schwermut* ("veil of heaviness" of heart).

8

This opacity makes it impossible to know beyond doubt what any other human being is thinking. As I noted, we possess no indubitable insight into anyone else's thoughts. Again, we pay too little attention to this enormity. It should strike terror. No familiarity, no analytic cunning can ensure or verify "mind reading." Neither hypnosis nor psychiatric techniques nor "truth drugs" can extract in any verifiable way the thoughts of the other. His or her most vehement avowals, oral and written testimony under oath, naked confessions can deliver no fundamental, insured content. They may or may not express the most candid intent, the most purposed revelation. They may or may not disclose partial truths, fragments as it were of utmost sincerity and self-disclosure. They may or may not conceal felt meaning whether in *toto* or in part. Motions of disguise can range from the outright lie professed consciously to every shading of untruth and self-deception. The nuances of mendacity are inexhaustible. No laser of inquisitorial attention, no ear however acute, no cross-examination can elicit certitude. The mere question "what are you thinking, what have you in mind?" solicits answers which are themselves many-layered, which have, however unnoticed, passed through complex filters.

Hence the unsettled relations between thought and love. Hence the likelihood that love between thinking beings is a somewhat miraculous grace. Every man and every woman, every adult and every child uses what linguists call an "idiolect," this is to say a personalized selection out of available language with private, singular, perhaps untranslatable counters, connotations and references which the recipient in dialogue cannot wholly or with certitude interpret. We try to translate to each other. We so frequently get it slightly or grossly wrong. But even this partial or flawed intelligibility of all communication lies only at the surface. The idiolects of thought, the privacies of the unspoken are of a much deeper and intractable order.

Even in moments and acts of extreme intimacy — perhaps most acutely at such moments — the lover cannot embrace the thoughts of the beloved. "What are you thinking, what am I thinking as we make love?" This exclusion makes the vaunted fusion of orgasm and its rhetoric of unison arguably trivial. As Goethe liked to point out, numberless men and women have clasped in the arms of thought lovers, remembered, wished-for, fantasized other than those they are making love to. This cognitive interposition, this mental reservation, involuntary or deliberate, blurred or graphic, can chime like a derisive echo beneath the cries and whispers of ecstasy. We shall never know what deep-lying inattention, absence, repulsion, or alternative imagery deconstruct the manifest text of the erotic. The closest, most honest of human beings remain strangers, more or less partial, more or less undeclared to each other. The act of love is also that of an actor. Ambiguity is native to the word.

Thought is most legible, least covert during bursts of unchained, compacted energy. As in fear and in hatred. These dynamics, particularly on the instant, are difficult to fake, though virtuosos of duplicity and of self-control can attain greater or lesser concealment. The animals we deal with show us that our fears emit a distinctive scent. Perhaps there is a smell to hatred. Enlisting all levels of cerebral and instinctive thrust, hatred may be the most vivid, charged of mental gestures. It is stronger, more cohesive than love (as Blake intuited). It is so often nearer than is any other revelation of the self to truth. The other class of thought-experience in which the veil is torn apart is that of spontaneous laughter. At the instant in which we "get" the joke or chance on the comical sight, mentality is laid bare. Momentarily, there are no "second thoughts." But this aperture to the world and to others lasts only very briefly and has the dynamics of the involuntary. In this regard, smiles are almost the antithesis to laughter. Shakespeare was much concerned with the smiling of villains.

Overall the scandal remains. No final light, no empathy in love, discloses the labyrinth of another human being's inwardness. (Are identical twins, with their private language, truly an exception?) At the last, thinking can make us strangers to one another. The most intense love, perhaps weaker than hatred, is a negotiation, never conclusive, between solitudes.

An eighth reason for sorrow.

9

Bodily functions and thinking are common to the species. Arrogantly, *Homo sapiens* so defines himself. Strictly considered, each and every living man, woman, and child is a thinker. This is as true of the cretin as it is of Newton, of the virtually speechless moron as it is of Plato. As I noted, seminal, inventive, life-enhancing thoughts may, at any time and in any place, have been thought by the subliterate, the infirm, even the mentally handicapped. They have gone lost because they were not articulated or attended to even by the one who has done the thinking ("mute, inglorious Miltons" in a sense which extends far beyond literature). Like minute spores, thoughts are disseminated inward and outward a millionfold. Only a minute fraction survive and bear fruit. Hence the incommensurable waste which I have cited previously. But the confusion may reside elsewhere.

Our taxonomy, notably in the current political-social ambience, tends toward the egalitarian. Does this not disguise and falsify an obvious, but scarcely or uncomfortably noticed hierarchy? Vaguely, rhetorically we attach to certain acts of spirit and what we assume to be their consequences — the scientific insight, the work of art, the philosophic system, the historical deed — the label "great." We refer to "great" thoughts or ideas, to products of intellectual, artistic, or political genius. No less vaguely, we adduce "profound" as distinct from trivial or superficial thoughts. Spinoza descends into the mineshaft; the man in the street customarily skates at the banal surface of himself or the world. Can these polarities, together with the innumerable gradations between them, be lumped together under one indistinct rubric? Can the mind's flotsam and inchoate babble be covered by the same sloppy definition as the solution to Fermat's last theorem or the Shakespearean begetting of enduring metaphor or mutations of sensibility? What factitiousness — picked up from the outset by caricaturists and vulgarians — inhabits Rodin's *Thinker*?

All of us conduct our lives within an incessant tide and magma of thought acts, but only a very restricted portion of the species provides evidence of *knowing how to think*. Heidegger bleakly professed that mankind as a whole had not yet emerged from the prehistory of thought. The cerebrally literate — we lack an adequate term — are, in proportion to the mass of humanity, few. The capacity to harbor thoughts or their rudiments is universal and may well be attached to neurophysiological and evolutionary constants. But the capacity to think thoughts worth thinking, let alone expressing and worth preserving, is comparatively rare. Not very many of us know how to think to any demanding, let alone original, purpose. Even fewer of us are able to marshall the full energies and potential of thought and of directing these energies toward what is called "concentration" or intentional insight. An identical label obscures the light-years of difference between the background noise and banalties of rumination common to all human existence (as it is perhaps also to that of primates) and the miraculous complexity and strengths of first-class thinking. Just beneath this eminent level there are the many modes of partial understanding, of approximation, of involuntary or acquired error (the physicist Wolfgang Pauli's devastating phrase about false theorems: "they aren't even wrong").

A culture, a "common pursuit" of mental literacy, can be defined by the extent to which this secondary order of reception, of the subsequent incorporation of first-order thought into communal values and practices, is or is not widespread. Does seminal thought enter schooling and the general climate of recognition? Is it picked up by the inner ear, even if this process of audition is often stubbornly slow and fraught with vulgarization? Or are authentic thinking and its receptive valuation impeded, even destroyed (Socrates in the city of man, the theory of evolution among fundamentalists) by "unthinking" political, dogmatic, and ideological denial? What murky but understandable mechanism of atavistic panic, of subconscious envy fuels the "revolt of the masses" and, today, the philistine brutality of the media which have made the very word "intellectual" derisive? Truth, taught the Baal Shem, is perpetually in exile. Perhaps it should be. Where it becomes too visible, where it cannot shelter behind specialization and hermetic encoding, intellectual passion and its manifestations provoke hatred and mockery (these impulses intertwine with the history of anti-Semitism; Jews have often thought too loudly).

Can top-gear thinking be learned? Can it be taught? Drill and exercise can strengthen memory. Mental focus, spells of inwardness and concentration can be deepened by techniques of meditation. In certain Oriental and mystical traditions, in Buddhism for example, this discipline can attain almost unbelievable degrees of abstraction and intensity. Analytic methods, stringent formal consequentiality can be imparted and refined in the training of mathematicians, of logicians, of computer programmers and chess masters. To prevent children from learning by heart is to lame, perhaps permanently, the muscles of the mind. Thus there is much in cerebral skills, in developed receptivity and interpretation which can be heightened and enriched by teaching and practice.

But so far as we know, there is no pedagogic key to the creative. Innovative, transformative thought, in the arts as in the sciences, in philosophy as in political theory, seems to originate in "collisions," in quantum leaps at the interface between the subconscious and the conscious, between the formal and the organic in a play and "electric" art of psychosomatic agencies largely inaccessible both to our will and to our comprehension. The empowering media can be taught — musical notation, syntax and metrics, mathematical symbolism and conventions, the mixing of pigments. But the metamorphic use of these means toward novel configurations of meaning and mappings of human possibility, toward a *vita nuova* of belief

and feeling, can neither be predicted nor institutionalized. There
is no democracy to genius, only a terrible injustice and life-threat-
ening burden. There are the few, as Hölderlin said, who are compelled to catch lightning in their bare hands.

This imbalance, along with its consequences, the maladjustment
of great thought and creativity to ideals of social justice, is a ninth
source of melancholy *(Melancholie)*.

10

French and German grammar help. They allow us to elide the
preposition between the verb "to think" and its object. We are not
constrained to think "about" this or that. We can "think it" immediately, without interposition. *Das Leben denken* ("to think life"); *penser
le destin* ("to think destiny"). The force of this idiom is seductive.
But it posits, inescapably, the epistemological uncertainty or duality which I referred to previously. Does the grammatical immediacy
point to some mode of solipsism, to the supposition that the objects of thought are the dependent product of the act of thinking
(as in Kant)? Or does the elision of any intermediate term autho-
rize the belief that the object of thought has autonomy, that at certain levels of unimpeded focus human thought-acts do penetrate,
do fully grasp that which they conceive or conceive of — the difference between these two marking precisely the alternative paths
which philosophy has taken in the West? French and German grammatical fusions leave the issue of idealism as against realism open.
Characteristically, English usage enforces a choice. It internalizes a
fundamental, robust empiricism. The world is "thought about,"
not "thought" in some mirroring motion of transcendental au-
tism. Everyday French and German do communicate this com-
mon-sense option. *Je pense à, ich denke an.* But philosophic and poetic discourse, notably from Master Eckhardt to Heidegger, enlists
the possibility of symbiosis. This, perhaps, is the differentiation between philosophic-linguistic mentalities, between conventions of
perception on either side of the Channel or between the European
continent and North America (Emerson being an eminent exception). Here also is the locus of certain elemental untranslatabilities.

The "prime numbers" which thought addresses are constants,
circumscribing our humanity. They are or ought to be supremely
obvious. What is it "to be" and is it not, as Heidegger urges, the es-

sential task of thought "to think (about) being"? To discriminate between multiple phenomenal existentiality and the facticity of things on the one hand and the concealed core of the essence of being (*Seyn*) itself. Why is there not nothing — Leibniz's resounding challenge — should be the concern of thought-acts as primordial, as original, i.e., arising out of our origins, as is human life itself. Can we, *contra* Parmenides, think, conceptualize nothingness? It may be that every attempt to "think death" — a lamentably awkward phrasing in English — to think consequently about death, is a variant on this enigma of nullity. Innumerable creeds, mythologies, fantasies of transcendence are elaborations of thought-experiments which bear on death. Zero, our being made a vacuum, is to most of us "unthinkable" in both the emotional and logical sense of the word. From this stems the manifold architecture of myth and metaphor (many metaphors are concentrates of myth). Itself in perpetual motion and activity, human thought seems to abhor emptiness. It generates archetypally more or less consoling fictions of survival. Like a frightened child whistling, shouting in the dark we labor to avoid the black hole of nothingness. We do so even when the resulting scenarios are insultingly puerile and mere kitsch (those Elysian pastures and celestial choirs, those seventy-two virgins awaiting the martyrs for Islam).

Both spheres of thought, that of being and that of death, have been interpreted as subspecies of the never-ending efforts of the human intellect, of mortal consciousness, to think about, to "think" God. To attach to that monosyllable credible intelligibility. Plausibly, *homo* became *sapiens,* and cerebral processes evolved beyond reflex and bare instinct when the God question arose. When linguistic means allowed the formulation of that question. It is conceivable that higher forms of animal life skirt the realization, the mystery of their own deaths. The matter of God looks to be specific and singular to the human species. We are the creature empowered to affirm or deny the existence of God. We had our spiritual beginnings "in the Word." The fervent believer and the categorical atheist share an understanding of the issue. The hovering agnostic does not deny the question. The simple claim "I have never heard of God" would be felt to be absurd. Existence and death, as these pertain to "God," are the perennial objects of human thought where that thought is not indifferent to the enigma of human identity, to our presence in some kind of world. We are — the famous *ergo sum* — in so far as we endeavor to "think being," "non-being" (death), and the relation of these polarities to the presence or absence, to the anthropomorphically phrased life or death of God. The partial recession of this concern from public and private affairs in the developed technocracies of the West, a recession antagonistic to the angry tides of fundamentalism, pervades our current political and ideological situation. A tolerant agnosticism demands ironic maturities, "negative capabilities" as Keats called them, difficult to muster. The savage simplifications of fundamentalism, be they Islamic or southern Baptist, are on the march.

The fact remains, overwhelmingly: whatever its stature, its concentration, its leap across the crevasses of the unknown, whatever its executive genius of communication and symbolic enactment, thought gets no closer to apprehending its primary objects. We are not an inch nearer to any verifiable solution to the quandary of the nature or purpose, if any, of our existence in this probably multiple universe, to a determination of the finality or not of death, and to the possible presence or absence of God, than were Parmenides or Plato. We might be further off. The attempts to "think," to "think through" these questions toward some sanctuary of justifying, explicative resolution have produced our religious, philosophic, literary, artistic, and, to a large extent, scientific history. The effort has engaged the most powerful intellects and creative sensibilities in the human race — a Plato, a Saint Augustine, a Dante, a Spinoza, a Galileo, a Marx, a Nietzsche, or a Freud. It has bred theological and metaphysical systems of fascinating subtlety and suggestive proposal. Our doctrines, poetry, art, and science before modernity have been underwritten by the urgent questioning of existence, mortality, and the divine. To abstain from this questioning, to censor it would be to cancel out the defining pulse and *dignitas* of our humanity. It is the vertigo of asking which activates an examined life.

In the final analysis, however, we get nowhere. However inspired, "thinking being," "thinking death," "thinking God" end in more or less ingenious, far-ranging, or semantically resourceful pictures — one might even say "verbiage." So far as any substantive yield goes, the aboriginal dance around the totem pole and Aquinas's *summa,* Voodoo and Plotinus on emanations, act out, communicate myths which have between them more than accidental analogies. No proof is forthcoming. Indeed the history of successive attempts to prove immortality or the existence of God amount to one of the more embarrassing chronicles in the human condition. The agility of thought, its inexhaustible propensity to narrative, leads to the humiliating, almost maddening conclusion that "anything goes." For uncounted millions, God combs His white beard and Elvis Presley is risen. No refutation is axiomatically possible. The verifiability, the falsifiability of the sciences, their triumphant progress from hypothesis to application, constitute the prestige and the increasing domination they exercise in our culture. But in another sense, these also make up their sovereign triviality. Science cannot give an answer to the quintessential questions which possess or ought to possess the human spirit. Wittgenstein noted that point insistently. It can only deny their legitimacy. To inquire about the nanosecond prior to the Big Bang is, we are didactically assured, an absurdity. Yet we are so created that we *do* inquire, and may find Saint Augustine's conjecture far more persuasive than that of string theory.

It is immensely difficult to imagine what our maps of the mind — and the totalities which it inhabits — what our alphabet of recognitions would be like if the problem of God came to lose its meaning. No "death of God" rhetoric, no erosion of organized religion in the supermarkets of the West, come near to an eclipse of the possibility of God internal to our consciousness. Up to the present, atheism has been fiercely busied with God. If even that negative engagement receded from any serious awareness, the pure and applied sciences could, presumably, continue their advance. Whether the humanities, in the largest sense, could do so is not clear (it is the genius of Beckett to find allegoric expression for precisely this uncertainty). Meanwhile, it is not theological or philosophic argument which draws thought to the very limits of its indispensable, ever-renewed "dead ends." It is, I believe, music, that tantalizing medium of revealed intuition beyond words, beyond good and evil, in which the role of thought as we can grasp it remains deeply elusive. Thoughts too deep not so much for tears but for thought itself.

It may well be that Sophocles said it all in the choral ode on man in *Antigone*. Mastery of thought, of the uncanny speed of thought exalts man above all other living beings. Yet it leaves him a stranger to himself and to the world's enormity.

Sadness, *eine dem Leben anklebende Traurigkeit,* tenfold.

HELEN TWORKOV

Just Power

FROM *Tricycle*

IMAGINE LEAFING THROUGH a pamphlet or perhaps a monthly magazine and coming across a guide to good behavior with advice that included the following:

> Put on an ever-smiling countenance.
> Do not move furniture and chairs noisily.
> Do not open doors with violence.
> Take pleasure in the practice of humility.
> Always strive to learn from everyone.
> Speak with moderation, gently.
> Express yourself with modesty.

For many contemporary Westerners the assumption that this advice was intended for women probably runs so deep as to go undetected. Maybe your imagination has already leaped ahead to the idea that this could be a list of idealized feminine virtues of the Victorian era; or a set of guidelines for prim boarding-school girls of the 1940s; or perhaps a compendium of traits that the feminists of the 1970s rejected in favor of male behavioral models. But in fact, these behaviors were extolled in *The Way of the Bodhisattva,* a seminal text by the great Buddhist sage Shantideva, and delivered to his fellow — all male — monastics at Nalanda University in eighth-century India.

Throughout Buddhist history the enlightened masters have advocated behavior — such as the quintessential bodhisattva ideal of putting others before oneself — that progressive women today can easily associate with a legacy of oppression. And yet, with the world in such perilous straits, and in light of recent patriarchal and god-sponsored warfare, these behavioral archetypes have ramifications that, like the teachings themselves, expand far beyond gender. Putting down the cultural baggage, however, is easier said than done.

A thirteenth-century Zen teaching points to how the mind variously refracts the same object, and offers us a way to approach this issue:

> First mountains are mountains.
> Then mountains are not mountains.
> Then mountains are mountains again.

This saying, first attributed to Ch'an master Ch'ing-yuan, has itself been refracted through many interpretations and differing doctrinal schemes. In the first line, "mountains are mountains" can convey a conventional view of reality based on accepted, collective, perceptual norms. The second line expresses a deliberative remove from convention, in which "mountain" is understood to be a construct of the human imagination, devoid of any independent meaning or existence. In the third line, when once again "mountains are mountains," there remains only the pure, unfiltered view, neither constructed nor deconstructed, beyond acceptance or denial, beyond the duality of relative and absolute.

Using this Zen teaching as a lens through which to view Buddhism's prized attributes — those that many Western women associate with oppression — we first see a mountain of human attributes classically associated in the West with the feminine: gentleness, modesty, speaking softly, humility, equanimity, altruism, consideration, obedience, generosity. With the second line we can deconstruct the cultural reality to uncover the myth of normalcy. Here, we are forced to consider that the cultural ideal has often been a very poor fit with the actual experience of women's lives, that living a life of duty to one's family, husband, children can be accompanied by tightly harnessed feelings of anger, inadequacy, and humiliation. Here the attributes appear as external masks, so that, say, generosity masks greed, kindness masks anger, obedience masks servility. In this view, not even *women* embody the so-called female virtues: mountains are not mountains, and women, as defined in the first line, are not women, any more than the traits they exhibit are virtuous. In the third and final line, the mountain appears again to represent the same attributes we see in the first view, but now, generosity is *just* generosity itself; obedience is *just* obedience — with no subtext, no gender, no psychology, and no history. *Just* obedience, *just* modesty, *just* humility — beyond female and male, beyond oppressor and oppressed.

It's important to note that the above traits do not actually lie outside of constructed values, and in this way, do not reflect Zen teachings represented in the third line. Just the same, Shantideva identifies these attributes as those most appropriate for the followers of the Buddha; they are conditioned behaviors allied with taming the ego. By supporting liberation from self-centeredness, they help create possibilities for engaging in the sacred nondual dance of interdependence beyond relative and absolute.

American women have come a long way through hard-won ideological battles and changes in our educational and legal systems. All these efforts have significantly altered the way we live and have increased possibilities for women. There's a lot more work to be done, but I think that we've come far enough to ask ourselves not only how we can increase opportunities but also what we are going to use them for. The commitment to equality without attention to its application threatens to leave us emulating the flawed system we fought so hard to change. The shift that we're seeking is not a lateral gender move from, say, George Bush to Condaleezza Rice, although in some quarters, this is precisely what is happening. Consider, for instance, that the commanding officer at Abu Ghraib was a woman, as were two of the six US soldiers charged with sadistic abuses at the prison. For many of us in the West, the photographs of Abu Ghraib, and in particular, the one of PFC Lynndie England holding an Iraqi prisoner on a leash, reinforce the necessity of rethinking women's strategies for equality; as well, they intensify the need for a whole new experience of what power might look and feel like from an enlightened perspective.

For half a century, in the name of gender and religious equality and values, American women and American Buddhist leaders have beaten a path from the cultural margins toward the center, as if the center itself held the key to the kingdom. At this point in history, to continue in that direction without examination seems foolish, if not dangerously destructive. We're challenged to do no less than formulate another view of power, or to adopt one more consistent with our Buddhist values. Returning to Shantideva, his injunction to "remain like a log" provides an apt image around which we might initiate a discussion about enlightened views of power.

Remaining like a log is not an action the American military would associate with the exercise of power. Yet Shantideva uses the phrase again and again to depict internal strength. For Buddhist practitioners who have struggled mightily to overcome the dominance of ego, "remaining like a log" can suggest new definitions of control, of dominion, and of power.

> When the urge arises in the mind
> To feelings of desire or wrathful hate,
> Do not act! Be silent, do not speak!
> And like a log of wood be sure to stay. (5.48)

Shantideva advocates restraint, discipline, and nonreactivity. He speaks of taming, training, and subjugating one's own ego. The invitation in Buddhist practice is to yoking, or leashing, one's own mind, not another being's.

Considering this nontraditional view of power, it's perhaps not surprising that when Buddhism entered into the margins of American culture, gender played a pronounced role. In the 1950s we see two distinct streams of attraction to dharma: one was almost all male, the other almost all female. We have an intellectual interest catalyzed primarily by the books of D. T. Suzuki and Alan Watts, and championed by the Beat poets. But, with few exceptions, this interest did not extend to practice. The Beat scene was pervasively male, and for all its attraction to Eastern philosophies and its pungent and theatrical critiques of the United States, it enshrined the ethos of rugged cowboy individualism as much as Hollywood Westerns.

At the same time — the late 1950s — the first Zen retreats were held in the United States. Photographs reveal that almost all the participants of these first Zen retreats were middle-aged women. Taking the time to sit down, keep quiet, and "do nothing" was apparently a very unmanly activity, despite the fact that of all the Buddhist traditions, Zen strikes many as being archly masculine. But Japanese Zen came packaged with the so-called Zen arts, such as tea ceremony and flower arranging. And in the United States, appreciation for art (not making art — that was male) was considered a woman's domain. The refined aesthetics of Japanese Zen went a long way toward legitimizing Zen in this country, and particularly among women. So there was a period when the Beat scene — which definitely popularized Zen — was as solidly male, with its aggressive homoeroticism and its legendary chauvinism, as the Zen retreat scene was female. It would be another few years, and not without the advent of the counterculture, before Zen retreats would have equal numbers of men and women.

The counterculture of the 1960s derived from opposition to the culturally sanctioned Vietnam War. But there was also a division within the counterculture into spiritual and political. The spiritual wing was characterized by, as Timothy Leary famously put it, "turning on, tuning in, and dropping out." A lot of these people, including myself, are those who — if we got lucky — found our way to Buddhism.

Both the political and spiritual wings of the counterculture were characterized in part by defying gender stereotypes. While some feminists experimented with decidedly male forms, the spiritual wing embodied a feminized form. Both men and women who dropped out were wearing long hair, loose, braided, beaded; both genders were wearing jewelry and the slogan of that time which best encapsulates this feminization was "Make Love, Not War."

From within this sphere of the dropout counterculture, Buddhism began to attract young Americans new to dharma. Rejecting the compromised glory of the Vietnam War, many identified with the Vietnamese (and Buddhist) victims of American aggression. So, in completely monolithic, relative, and reductive terms, the hippie movement, which includes convert Buddhism, looks very feminine compared to the conventions of the mainstream middle class.

Through the 1970s, we see the growth of several big Zen centers, and we have the development of the Vipassana community in Barre, Massachusetts. And by the early seventies, we begin to see an influx of Tibetan teachers. We see equal numbers of men and women students, but almost all male teachers and a disproportionate number of men with organizational authority.

I started my own Buddhist studies with Tibetan teachers. Then, in 1981, I moved into the Zen Community of New York, where every morning we chanted the names of our "ancestors," which happened to be eighty generations of Zen patriarchs. What was more subtle and difficult to apprehend was that "the ideal Zen student" — in whatever body, male or female — looked a lot like a classic old-fashioned version of a gentleman's perfect wife.

Particularly in the Tibetan and Zen scenes you had, more often than not, an authoritative male teacher surrounded by students who were, more often than not,

> Soft-spoken
> Deferential
> Subservient
> Modest
> Respectful
> Receptive
> Smiling
> Willing
> Passive
> Without strong views or opinions

Now, it so happens that we see very similar kinds of behavior in people, and particularly in women, with issues of low self-esteem, or with very entrenched neurotic patterns of worthlessness that fit together perfectly with identifying oneself as the servant. And, as it happens, there were a lot of students who, with issues of low self-esteem and/or abuse, were very comfortable with a continuation of certain neurotic behaviors, especially if that meant they were upheld as ideal Buddhist students. This, not surprisingly, became a source of great confusion. After all, we know that the quintessential core of Mayahana Buddhism is putting others before oneself. And that historically the quintessential work of womanhood was — and in many parts of the world still is — to put the needs and wants of husband, in-laws, parents, and children first. Thousands of texts present this bodhisattva principle, but to quote Shantideva again:

> With perfect and unyielding faith,
> With steadfastness, respect, and courtesy,
> With modesty and conscientiousness,
> Work calmly for the happiness of others. (5.55)

And so it is that if I want contentment,
I should never seek to please myself.
And likewise, if I wish to save myself,
I'll always be the guardian of others. (8.173)

We know that to embrace unenlightened female forms may affirm individual and collective patterns of abuse and low self-esteem. If we continue to look at them as expressions of male dominance, then, of course, we will wish to abandon them. Yet to reject
these qualities is to reject the teachings of the Buddhas. If we trust
that they are gender-free Buddhist values, then we may be able to
use them to help frame a distinctly different value system.

By the mid-1980s, Buddhist women began looking at their own
practice centers through the feminist lens, describing women's situations in terms of what we did not have: the absence of authority,
the lack of equality. But there was something else going on in the
women's movement as it continued a quieter trajectory from the
chaos of the 1970s through the 1980s. Impelled in part by President Reagan's aggressive nuclear arms buildup and Strategic Defense Initiative — dubbed the "Star Wars" defense by the popular
press — and by a widespread awareness of environmental devastation, some political voices in the women's movement proposed traditional "female" qualities as critical to pulling the world back from
the brink — qualities such as compassion, deep listening, nurtur-
ing, serving. They identified the so-called weaknesses of women as
the very strengths that the planet most needed to survive. Yet while
this ideology can infuse a context for change, without an internal
shift, and one that goes far beyond the issues of gender, its effect
will — and has — remained limited.

Within a decade, young women became openly antagonistic to
the feminism of the baby boomer generation. "Feminism" itself became a dirty word, and the feminists of the 1960s were faulted for
advocating a male value system at the expense of female-identified forms. Rather than engage in literal and symbolic bra burning, young women retained the quest for equal opportunities but
dressed up in Victoria's Secret. The quieter feminism of the 1980s,
which advocated an embrace of female-identified behavior, did not
get much play, either. And consequently the very nature of power

itself was not questioned. At the same time, the ground for change has been tilled. And the rise of patriarchal fundamentalism and of religious militarism is so untenable that perhaps the time is right to make real shifts in how we understand power.

Perhaps the unmasked politics of fundamentalism, economic domination, and the loathsome consequences of unbridled greed have descended to such horrific lows that, however unwittingly, they can spawn a new story, or uncover an unborn dream by which we can navigate the realities of where we are, who we are, and who we wish to be.

Is it possible to imagine that power might be defined by presence of mind; that the more one is no longer controlled by compulsions, addictions, patterns, habits, the more power one has to act in service of wisdom and compassion? What if we said that power is internal freedom, that power is the capacity for choice? Can we — women *and* men — stand the heat of appearing to be passive, of remaining like a log? Can we imagine, compassionately, that in our society this might be much more difficult for men than for women?

Following 9/11 there was never a possibility of not bombing Afghanistan. It wasn't just the president and the politicians who disallowed nonaction; the mindset of the American people demanded retaliation. I use this example not to suggest that inaction in this particular case would have been a more enlightened strategy, but to suggest that "strategy," or any form of intelligent, wise consideration, was made impossible by the blinding thirst for revenge. A primitive, dualistic response — however easy it was to explain — ruled the day. Remaining like a log is not a political position. It is neither passive nor pacifist. Rather it describes a state of mind capable of making wise decisions, unplugged from the emotional charge of compulsive reactivity. Remaining like a log describes a mind that has options, one that is not merely being jerked around by selfish responses to external circumstances and that can therefore serve a larger reality with clear, cool insight.

In my own experience, Buddhist practice is indescribably difficult. I know of nothing in this world that is more challenging than the Buddha's invitation to an enlightened way of life. I don't think that the actual process of transformation from a selfish, self-oriented, me-first person into a bodhisattva of wisdom and compassion who consistently puts others first is any easier for one sex than it is for the other. Yet my hope for all those living on the American sidelines — such as women and Buddhists — is that we use our compromised status to our best advantage; that we capitalize on our experiences and strengths and training to investigate alternatives to conventional views of power. Perhaps it is worthwhile to figure out what it takes — and what kind of power is required — to "remain like a log."

JOHN UPDIKE

Angel Bones

FROM *The American Scholar*

Next to the statue-laden cathedral of Rheims,
the bishop's palace has become a museum
containing many stones cast down by wear,
bombardment, renovation, and the rare
   too-thunderous Te Deum.

Huge saints and angels, retired from the weather,
stand tall above us. Their visages were carved
to show a soul — a face of grace above the wars,
the plagues, the congregational stench of masses —
   to worshippers they dwarfed.

Now chips and missing chunks give proof these hulks
on loan from Heaven fell prey to earthly harm,
for limestone, being soft to sculpt, breaks easily.
Look here! — a sheared and fractured flank reveals
   a tiny shell, distinct, intact,

from vanished, darkling, long pre-Christian seas.
The pious masses, milling underneath
and looking up to holy largeness, lacked
the science to deduce from this small clue
   what mighty absence it might mean.

ROBERT LOUIS WILKEN

The Church's Way of Speaking

FROM *First Things*

WHEN SAINT AUGUSTINE abandoned the teaching of rhetoric in
Milan to enroll for baptism, he asked Saint Ambrose, the bishop of
Milan, what to read in the Scriptures "to make me readier and fitter
to receive so great a grace." Ambrose told him to read the prophet
Isaiah. Augustine took his advice, but as soon as he took the book
in hand he was perplexed by what he read. "I did not understand
the first passage of the book," he writes, and he thought "the whole
would be equally obscure." So Augustine laid it aside, as he explains, "to be resumed when I had more practice in the Lord's style
of language."

In dominico eloquio — it is an arresting phrase. For the Christian
reader Isaiah is a demanding and difficult book once one strays beyond the familiar passages cited in the New Testament or commonly read in Christian worship (Isaiah 9 at Christmas, Isaiah 53
during Holy Week). To the uninitiated, the first chapter is particularly daunting with its arcane oracles against Judah and Jerusalem:
"Ah, sinful nation, a people laden with iniquity, offspring of evildo-
ers, sons who deal corruptly. They have forsaken the Lord, they
have despised the Holy One of Israel."

For someone like Augustine, formed by the poetry of Virgil and
the philosophy of Plotinus, the opening verses must have seemed
embarrassingly parochial, taken up as they are with the fortunes of
the ancient Israelites centuries earlier. Words such as "sinful nation," "holy one of Israel," "daughter of Zion," "new moon and Sabbath" would have sounded alien, and anthropomorphisms like "I
will vent my wrath on my enemies" or "turn my hand against you"
would have offended his cultivated spiritual sensibility.

Yet Augustine called Isaiah's language "the Lord's style of language," and he recognized that if he were to enter the Church he would have to learn this new tongue, hear it spoken, grow accustomed to its sounds, read the books that use it, learn its idioms, and finally speak it himself. He had to embark on a journey to acquaint himself with the mores of a new country. Becoming a Christian meant entering a strange and often alien world.

In the early Church, catechumens were received at the great vigil of Easter, beginning on Saturday evening where the creed was "handed over." As Bishop Ambrose realized, there was more to becoming a Christian than putting the creed to memory and being instructed in the "mysteries." Christian catechesis meant learning the distinctively Christian language formed by the Scriptures. And among the books of the Bible, Isaiah was preeminent: an evangelist as well as a prophet, according to Jerome.

The "faith" is not simply a set of doctrinal propositions, creedal affirmations, and moral codes. It is a world of discourse that comes to us in language of a particular sort. And language, as we discover when we study a foreign tongue, is not simply an instrument for ideas, beliefs, and sentiments. Language defines who we are; it molds how a people think, how they see the world, how they respond to persons and events, even how they feel. Thinking and understanding, like memory, are not solitary acts; they are social, wedded to the language we share with others. If we forget how to speak our language, we lose something of ourselves. "What is pronounced strengthens itself," the Polish poet Czeslaw Milosz once wrote. "What is not pronounced tends to non-existence."

But the language of a people or a country is not the only kind of language. There are also languages within languages. Just as there is a language proper to biology or to medicine, so there is a language proper to Christianity. Our beliefs, our moral convictions, and our attitudes are carried by very specific words and images. Words, not ideas, bring into focus with compactness and intensity what is honored and cherished. They are the indispensable carriers of the Church's faith as it is handed on from generation to generation.

Think, for example, how many terms Christians use in a distinctive way: Father, Son, Spirit, faith, hope, love, grace, sin, mercy, repentance, forgiveness, image of God, flesh, kingdom, lamb of God, suffering servant, righteousness, see (as in "blessed are the pure in

heart, for they shall see God"), know (as in "know the truth"), believe, truth (as in "I am the truth"), creation, "male and female he
made them," passion (as in the Passion of Christ), the face of God,
Kyrie eleison. And that is not to mention the many place names
with extra meaning: Jerusalem, Mount Zion, Egypt, Galilee, Sinai,
Carmel, Damascus, the Mount of Olives, Bethlehem, Nazareth,
Golgotha. Or the names of persons: Abraham, Isaac, Jacob, Sa-
rah, Rebecca, Moses, Samuel, David, Solomon, Isaiah, Paul, James,
Mary, Mary Magdalene, Peter.

All of these words come from the Scriptures, for the basic lexicon of Christian speech is the Bible. Indeed, with some few exceptions — the Greek term *homoousios* (one in being with the Father)
in the Nicene Creed being one example — the distinctively Christian vocabulary is almost wholly drawn from the Bible. Though
Christians may speak English or Spanish or Arabic or Russian, they
nevertheless use another language, a language within their native
language, that is uniquely and recognizably Christian.

Consider the difference between the phrase "Happy Easter" and
"Christ is risen. He is risen indeed. Alleluia." The one is the language of our society, the other the Church's speech. Or take the
words "nature" and "creation." The first is the conventional term in
our society to refer to the world of plants and animals and mountains and oceans — what we call the "natural world." "Creation" is
the term used by the Bible and Christians to point to a Creator and
the world as ordered and purposeful. Instead of revered ancestors,
Christians speak of saints. When we are speaking of Christ's birth,
we speak of the Incarnation.

Even some of our prosaic terms are unique: we have a "pope"
rather than a "president"; we say "bishop" instead of "governor";
and we say "council" or "synod" instead of "convention." Christians
even have a unique term to refer to the community to which they
belong: "Church."

There is a *consuetudo loquendi ecclesiastica,* Augustine said — the
Church's customary way of speaking. As an example, he gave the
word "martyr," the term used by Christians for what the Romans
call *vir,* or "hero." Recall the opening words of the *Aeneid,* the
great Roman epic. *Arma virumque cano* — "Arms and the man I
sing": of the making of war and of a hero. The term *vir* had a vener-

able history in Latin, and from one perspective it seemed fitting for the martyrs. But Augustine thought Christians should avoid it and use a distinctively Christian word for their valor. The word "martyr" bore overtones that were absent from "hero," and "hero" carried connotations that would be offensive to a Christian martyr.

"Martyr" was, of course, a biblical term meaning "witness," and it is used with a specific sense in the Book of Acts. Again and again, the disciples are called "witnesses of the Resurrection" — people who knew Christ during his earthly sojourn and to whom the risen Christ appeared. Accordingly a martyr is one who knows Christ and bears witness in death to the living Lord. By comparison the term *vir* seemed colorless and anemic when applied to such faithful and courageous witnesses to the faith. In a sermon on the celebration of the martyrdom of Cyprian, Saint Augustine highlighted another term used by Christians for the martyrs. *Natales,* dates of birth, designated the days of martyrdom:

> Today we celebrate the birthday of the most glorious martyr, Cyprian. This expression, *natales,* is regularly employed by the Church in this way, so that it calls the precious deaths of the martyrs their "birthdays." This expression, I repeat, is regularly employed by the Church, to the extent that even those who do not belong to her join her in using it. Is there anyone to be found, I ask you, and I do not mean just in this city of ours, but throughout the whole of Africa and the regions overseas, and not only any Christian, but any pagan or Jew, or even heretic, who does not call today the birthday of the martyr Cyprian?
>
> Why is this, brothers and sisters? What date he was born on, we do not know; and because he suffered today, it is today that we celebrate his birthday. We would not celebrate that other day, even if we knew when it was. On that day he contracted original sin, while on this day he overcame all sin. On that day he came forth from the wearisome confines of his mother's womb into this light, which is so alluring to our eyes of flesh; but on this day he went away from the deep darkness of nature's womb to that light, which sheds such blessing and good fortunes upon the mind.

Another suggestive example is the Latin word *passio,* "passion." It occurs in 1 Thessalonians, "that each one of you know how to take a wife for himself in holiness and honor, not in the passion of lust like heathens who do not know God." Augustine judged this translation unacceptable because "passion" was the word used for Christ's suffering and death. "In the Church's customary way of speaking," he said, the term "passion" is not used in a pejorative sense (as in the phrase from 1 Thessalonians — the "passion of lust"). It should be reserved for the suffering of Christ and the martyrs. Latin-speaking Christians also used *altare* rather than *ara*, the conventional Latin term for "altar." For "pray," they preferred *orare* to *rogare*, the more common Roman word.

Augustine even thought that Christians should avoid the Roman names for the days of the week — Monday, *dies Lunae*, meant the moon's day; Wednesday, *dies Mercurii*, the day of Mercury. "We do not like this practice," says Augustine, "and we wish Christians would amend their custom and not employ the pagan name." And then he adds: "Christians have a language of their own that they can use." Augustine preferred the simple numeration of days — first, second, third — a practice that is kept to this day in the Latin breviary (*feria prima, feria secunda*, etc.).

The faith, then, is embedded in language. It is not a set of abstract beliefs or ideas, but a world of shared associations and allusions with its own beauty and sonority, inner cohesion and logic, emotional and rhetorical power. The Church's way of speaking is a collection of the words and images that have formed the thinking and actions of those who have known Christ. The faith they confessed cannot be divorced from the words they used, nor the words uprooted from the lives of their speakers. Christian thinking is inescapably historical.

Christian speech is not primarily the technical vocabulary of Christian doctrine: "substance," "essence," "one person and two natures," "prevenient grace," "atonement," "transubstantiation." It is the language of the Psalms, the stories of the patriarchs, the parables of the gospels, the moral vocabulary of Saint Paul's epistles. Though Christians became comfortable with the philosophical vocabulary of the cardinal virtues ("prudence, justice, fortitude, and temperance"), their native language for the virtuous life comes from Saint Paul who spoke of "fruits of the Spirit": "love, joy, peace, patience, kindness, goodness, faithfulness, gentleness, self-control." In using the Church's language, we learn to live together as a community, to breathe in harmony. We learn to think the Church's thoughts, share its loves, and live by its precepts.

One of the most beautiful words in the Christian lexicon is "hyssop," as in the fifty-first psalm's "purge me with hyssop, and I shall be clean." This is a term we only hear when reciting the Psalms. In Christian speech, "hyssop" has overtones of repentance and forgiveness, and calls to mind the beautiful seventeenth verse of the psalm: "A humble and contrite heart God will not despise." Nothing is more characteristic of Christian life than repentance.

Another is the term "patience." About A.D. 200, Tertullian, the first Christian to write in Latin, prepared a little treatise called *de patientia*, "On Patience." Cyprian and Augustine also wrote works with that title. Tertullian observed that patience was not only a divine but a human virtue. The supreme example is Christ's Passion, an observation echoed by Augustine: "The Passion of our Lord is a lesson in patience." For Christians, patience is not only about endurance; it is about a hope grounded in the Resurrection. For Tertullian (himself an impatient man) it is the premier Christian virtue because it signifies a life oriented toward a future that is God's doing. Its distinctive feature is longing — not so much to be released from the ills of the present, but for the good to come. Even love, said Tertullian, cannot be practiced "without the exercise of patience."

"Mercy" is another beloved Christian word taken from the Bible. Saint Caesarius of Arles called it *dulce nomen,* "a sweet word." Some years ago, sitting in Christ Church at Oxford during morning prayer, I noticed on the stone floor medallions with the terms *justitia, prudentia, fortitudo,* and *temperantia,* representing the four cardinal virtues. But then I noticed that there was a fifth. When prayers had ended and I could make my way to the front, I found the fifth was *misericordia,* "mercy." Clearly the designers of the church thought that the cardinal virtues, inherited from the Greek philosophical tradition, were not complete without the addition of a distinctively Christian term. As early as the third century, recognizing the indispensability of the term *misericordia* for thinking about the Christian life, the Christian writer Lactantius chided the Stoic philosophers because they had no place in their moral vocabulary for the affections.

Without the distinctive Christian language there can be no full Christian life, no faithful handing on of the faith to the next generation. For that reason, the words that embody what we believe and practice — words given us by those in whom Christ was present — cannot be frivolously tampered with, translated into another idiom, or discarded. As Augustine taught us centuries ago, the appropriate metaphor for the Church is a city. Language is a defining mark of the Christian *polis*. And, like a city, the Church draws its citizens into a shared public life, one marked by its central cultic activity, the Eucharist, and by other rituals, such as Ash Wednesday, Palm Sunday, and Corpus Christi. The Christian society has its own calendar that sets the rhythms of the community's life, offices, institutions, laws, architecture, art, and music, its own customs and mores, history and memory.

One of the most significant features of the transformation of the Roman world in the fourth and fifth centuries was that Christianity occupied and then reoriented public space. The classical city with its *agora* and temples and theaters gave way to a new city plan with the church located at the center. With this Christianization of space came the sacralization of time as the Church's calendar marked the days for fasting and resting and feasting. In the early Middle Ages, when kings and their peoples embraced Christianity, conversion was more than adherence to a new set of beliefs. It brought about a change in public practice.

And yet, in modern times — particularly in the last hundred years — the Church has gradually given up this public face, relinquishing the public square to other rituals, other calendars, other architecture, and other languages. There has been an alarming decline in communal rituals and practices. The Church's way of life is being chewed up and spit out by the omnivorous secular society that surrounds us.

A telling example is the rise of the term "culture." We tend to use "culture" not of the Church but of the society in which we live. But the task of handing on the faith is not primarily a question of how "Christ" relates to "culture" but of how the Christian culture is to be sustained and deepened in the face of another culture that is increasingly alien and hostile. The Christ-and-culture paradigm implicitly assumes that the secular culture is the arbiter of meaning. Consequently, a high premium is placed on translation from one idiom to another. Translation, of course, is inevitable in any religious transaction, whether it be telling a story from the Bible to a child, explaining the sacraments to a convert, or preaching the gospel to a people who know nothing of Christianity. If, however, Christianity is a culture in its own right, the Church must insist on its own way of speaking. There must be translation *into* the Lord's style of language, bringing alien language into the orbit of Christian belief and practice and giving it a different meaning. More frequently, however, the task of handing on the faith is understood to mean rendering Christian language into the patois of modernity — even in liturgy, an area where one would expect the uniqueness and idiosyncrasy of the Church's way of speaking to be preserved.

Here, for example, is the prayer for Pentecost XI prior to the reforms of Vatican II: "Look mercifully upon our service, O Lord, I beseech you, that what we offer may be a gift acceptable to you and a support to our frailty" (*nostrae fragilitatis subsidium*). In the new version, it reads: "Look mercifully upon our service, O Lord, we beseech you, that what we offer may be a gift acceptable to you and an increase of our charity" (*nostrae caritatis augmentum*).

The alteration seems innocuous, and the reason given by the compilers reasonable: they wished to render the petition positive rather than negative, thereby making the Latin prayer more dynamic. But the result was the elimination of "frailty," a vivid word found in early liturgical texts and used for centuries. In its place comes "love," obviously a good Christian word, but one that focuses the prayer on the goal while ignoring what stands in the way — our "frailty." An important theological nuance is lost as a common expression replaces the more profound formulation.

Another example is the collect for the first Sunday of Easter: "O God, who unlocked for us the gate of eternity through your only begotten Son who conquered death, grant, we beseech you, that we who celebrate the solemnity of his resurrection may through renewal of the Holy Spirit, rise from the death of the soul" (*a morte animae*). The revised version reads: "through renewal of the Holy Spirit, rise in the light of life" (*in lumine vitae*).

The new version is not simply vacuous, but incoherent. What does it mean to "rise in the light of life"? The faithful are deprived of two precious Christian words, "soul" and "death," both biblical and central to Christian faith. More, the new version ignores a fundamental truth about Easter — for Easter is not only a celebration of Christ's Resurrection, but a time of interior renewal for the Christian, a truth that is expressed metaphorically in the phrase "rise from the death of the soul." The original version plunges the faithful into the deeper caverns of the spiritual life, where they struggle against the forces that hold them in bondage. The revision injects the fatuous language of New Age religion into the Church's worship.

Such changes are deliberate, an attempt to accommodate the words of the liturgy to "the modern mentality" (in the words of one of the revisers). The translators display an embarrassing lack of confidence in what Christians believe and practice. Some texts were judged "shocking for the man of today" and "difficult to understand" and for that reason were "frankly corrected." What we have here is a kind of inculturation in Western modernity. "Liturgy," insists Anscar Chapungco, one of the leading exponents of inculturation, "must not impose on culture a meaning or bearing that is intrinsically alien to its nature." What this represents, to borrow a phrase from John Milbank, is a kind of "policing of the sublime."

The unique gift of liturgy, Roman Guardini wrote in his *Spirit of the Liturgy*, is to "create a universe brimming with fruitful spiritual life." Liturgy does not "exist for the sake of humanity, but for the sake of God." If the Bible is the lexicon of Christian speech, then the liturgy is its grammar, a place to come to know and practice the Christian idiom and to be formed by it. For Augustine, the reciting of the Psalms was a way of making the words of the psalmist his own, and he talked about what the words of the Psalms "had done to me."

Paul Griffiths recently observed that one does not have to believe to make use of Christian language and ideas. In the last decades four European philosophers, all atheists, have written major works that draw on Christian thinkers: Terry Eagleton on Thomas Aquinas, Jean-François Lyotard on Augustine's *Confessions*, Alain Badiou on Saint Paul, and Slavoj Zizek on Christ's willing acceptance of suffering and death. None of these writers embraces the Church's theological views, but they exhibit a yearning for something more than modernity has to offer — and the only place to turn, finally, is Christianity, with its language, its mode of thinking, and its texts. "This should not surprise Christians," writes Griffiths. "Our intellectual tradition is long-lived, rich, and subtle, and any attempt by European thinkers to do without it is not likely to last."

The Bible and Christian ritual have always been alluring to outsiders. Think for example of Nikolai Rimsky-Korsakov's *Great Rus-*

sian Easter. Rimsky-Korsakov was not a Christian believer (he was probably a pantheist), but his *Great Russian Easter,* one of his most popular and stirring works, draws deeply on the liturgy and the Scriptures. Subtitled "Overture on Liturgical Themes," it is based on the *Obikhod,* a collection of Russian Orthodox canticles, biblical texts, and hymns. The piece is ablaze with colors and lights as well as brooding darkness, at once awesome, majestic, austere, and carnival-like, and it would not be possible without the Orthodox Liturgy.

Rimsky-Korsakov lived in nineteenth-century Russia, but even in our secular society and present music culture, contemporary composers draw inspiration from the Bible. An example is the new work by Jefferson Friedman, a young American composer, that received its world premier by the National Symphony Orchestra under the direction of Leonard Slatkin in the fall of 2004. With the improbable title *The Throne of the Third Heaven of the Nations Millennium General Assembly,* the orchestral piece is based on an unusual sculpture in Washington, D.C., created by James Hampton.

The sculpture depicts a throne chair flanked by an altar table, pulpit, offertory tables — in other words, by church appointments. To the left are objects referring to the New Testament, to the right objects referring to the Old Testament. Some are labeled with names from the Bible and Christian history — Adam and Eve, the Virgin Mary, even Pope Pius XII. Drawing on the Book of Revelation, Hampton wished to depict the Second Coming of Christ. In his brief work Friedman tries to convey not only the aesthetic power of the sculpture but also Hampton's religious vision and a feeling of awe before the throne.

For too long Christianity has relinquished its role as teacher to society. Instead of inspiring the culture, it capitulates to the ethos of the world. The Church must rediscover herself, learn to savor her speech, delight in telling her stories, and confidently pass on what she has received. Only then can she draw people away from the coarse and superficial culture surrounding us into the abundance of life in Christ. "Walk about Zion," sings the psalmist, "go round about her, number her towers, consider well her ramparts, go through her citadels; that you may tell the next generation that this is God, our God for ever and ever."

This is not a new strategy but one that has marked Christianity from the beginning. Origen of Alexandria was the most brilliant Christian apologist during the first three centuries of the Church's history. His most famous work is a debate with Celsus, a Greek philosopher who had lived seventy years earlier. In his book titled *True Doctrine* Celsus had written: "Greeks are better able to judge the value of what the barbarians [meaning the Christians] have discovered." Celsus believed that the truth of Christianity should be measured "by the criterion of a Greek proof."

Origen, too, had been trained in the Greek intellectual tradition. But he rejected Celsus's assumption that the Church's faith should be measured by an alien standard. The truth of the gospel, Origen insisted, is to be judged by a "proof that is peculiar to itself, and this is more divine than Greek argument." This, said Origen, is what Saint Paul was describing when he spoke of a "demonstration of the Spirit and of power."

This is a strategy to be commended in our own time. Let the Church call attention to what is peculiar to herself, not to presumed notions about what is meaningful or intelligible or relevant to contemporary society. A robust Christian witness can only be forged by drawing on the fullness of Christ, as known through the Spirit in the Church.

C. K. WILLIAMS

Marina

FROM *The New Yorker*

As I'm reading Tsvetayeva's essays,
"Art in the Light of Conscience,"
stunning — *"Art, a series of answers
to which there are no questions"* —
a tiny insect I don't recognize
is making its way across my table.
It has lovely transparent wings
but for some reason they drag behind
as it treks the expanse of formica,
and descends into a crack.

*"To each answer before it evaporates,
our question"*: composed in Paris
during the difficult years of exile.
But which of her years weren't?
This at least was before the husband,
a spy, an assassin, went back,
then she, too, with her son,
to the Soviet madhouse, back.
*"This being outgalloped by answers
is inspiration."* Outgalloped!

Still lugging its filigreed train,
the insect emerges: fragile, distracted,
it can't even trace a straight line
but it circumnavigates the table.
Does it know it's back where it began?

Still, it perseveres, pushing
courageously on, one inch, another.
"Art . . . a kind of physical world
of the spiritual . . . A spiritual world
of the physical . . . almost flesh."

One daughter, dying, at three,
of hunger, the other daughter,
that gift of a sugar-cube,
in her mouth, drenched with blood . . .
"A poet is an answer . . . not to the blow,
but a quivering of the air."
The years of wandering,
the weary return, husband betrayed,
arrested, daughter in a camp . . .
"The soul is our capacity for pain."

When I breathe across it,
the bug squats, quakes, finally flies.
And couldn't she have flown again,
again have been flown? Couldn't she,
noose in her hand, have proclaimed,
"I am Tsvetayeva," and then not?
No, no time now for "then not."
But *"Above poet, more than poet . . ."*
she'd already said it, already sung it:
"Air finished. Firmament now."

FRANZ WRIGHT

East Boston, 1996

FROM *The New Yorker*

I

Armed Conflict

Snowy light fills the room
pronouncing itself

softly. The telephone ringing

in the deserted city —

On the Bus

It's one thing when you're twenty-one,
and I was way past twenty-one.
With unshaven face half concealed in the collar
of some deceased porcine philanthropist's
black cashmere rag of a coat,
I knew that I looked like a suicide
returning an overdue book to the library.
Almost everyone else did as well,
but I found no particular solace in this;
at best, the fact awakened some diverting speculations
on the comparative benefits
of waiting in front of a ditch to be shot
alone or in the company
of others, and then whether one would prefer

these last hypothetical others
to be friends, family, enemies, total
or relative strangers. Would you hold hands?
Or would you rather like a good *Homo sapiens*
monster employ them
to cover your genitals?
What percentage would lose bowel control?
And given time restrictions —
and assuming some still had the ability to move —
would ostracism result? Anyway,
I knew the rules on this bus.
No eye contact: the eyes of the terrified
terrify. Look
like you know where you're going,
possess ample change to get there,
and don't move your lips when you talk
to yourself: the destroyed
and sick, the poor, the hungry
and the disturbed estrange.
The badly dressed estrange, even,
and that is uncalled for. The degree
of one's power to estrange will increase
in direct proportion to the depth
of need for others. Do not cry.
This can only bring about, on the one hand,
an instant condition of banishment
from the sole available companionship or,
on the other, a *near*–
fatal beating (one more disappointment).
Just follow the simple instruction
if you ever come here.
It's easy to remember — any idiot can do it.
Don't cry,
the world has abandoned us.

Night Walk

The all-night convenience store's empty
and no one is behind the counter.
You open and shut the glass door a few times

causing a bell to go off,
but no one appears. You only came
to buy a pack of cigarettes, maybe
a copy of yesterday's newspaper —
finally you take one and leave
thirty-five cents in its place.
It is freezing, but it is a good thing
to step outside again:
you can feel less alone in the night,
with lights on here and there
between the dark buildings and trees.
Your own among them, somewhere.
There must be thousands of people
in this city who are dying
to welcome you into their small bolted rooms,
to sit you down and tell you
what has happened to their lives.
And the night smells like snow.
Walking home, for a moment
you almost believe you could start again.
And an intense love rushes to your heart,
and hope. It's unendurable, unendurable.

Solitary Play: Minnesota, 1961

In a clearing in the cornstalks, in light
November snow it was suggested
that I fire
on that muttering family of crows.
I complied
and watched as those big ruffled shadows
rose from the ground, scattered and vanished
in the direction of barren
border trees, commencing
to speak all at once
in hysterical tongues.
All except for one,
deceased.
I turned it over with my boot.
The eyes stared

at the sky, the minute
snowflakes falling into them.
Its beak was partly opened.
It was then I vomited a little.
This achievement was the last thing I'd expected
when they dug up the old .22
for my afternoon's amusement
and banishment. I was just eight, but I swore
then and there
my career as death was finished.
The ground was hard but I considered
going back to the house for a shovel;
it did not seem wholly implausible
that I might turn around to find
my victim limping after me,
and I ended up walking *away* from the house
for an hour or so.
Later on I cried and told my mother.
She comforted me, as I knew perfectly well she would.
In her opinion I was not to blame.
It was that gun. And besides,
she was certain crows had their own heaven.
I was off the hook.
My crow was much better off now.
That's what she thought.

Home Remedy

You could call someone
where it's still early.

Go out and look at the stars
shining
in the past.

Or open the Joachim Jeremias to the densely printed
page, its corner folded
for some reason
not yet remembered

before you set the clock.

You have to set the clock —
for a moment that doesn't exist yet
or one that has already passed, interestingly
symbolized by the identical numeral.

The friendly medications are beginning
to kick in: the frightening
objects
emitting the faint nimbus

of their reality, slowly
returning
to normal,

if this had been an actual emergency.

II

The long silences need to be loved, perhaps
more than the words
which arrive
to describe them
in time.

Reparations

The day's coming
when I will no longer consider
my mere presence inexpiable.
I will place my hand in that flame
and feel nothing.
I will ask nobody's forgiveness again.
Or I will just go
among people no more —
I may writhe with
remorse in the night, but
the operation must be
undertaken by
me, anesthesialess.

No one must be asked to relinquish
a grievance that can't be removed
without further destruction, it may be
it is lodged in who he is now
like a bullet in a brain
whose removal might only worsen its change.
The forgiveness! I know it
will be freely offered
or it won't, and that is all —
and no one may bestow it
on himself.
If it is to come
it will come of itself like a separate
being,
a mystery, working
unseen as a wind causes still
leaves or water to move once again.
And hide me in the shadow of Your wings.

Let the heart be moved again.

GENIE ZEIGER

20, 40, 60, 80

FROM *The Sun*

Yet, do thy worst, old Time. — William Shakespeare
— for Robyn Oughton, 1949–2003

I READILY CONFESS: I do not relish aging. As I close in on the age
of sixty, I can't understand how life's waters, pure and rushing,
have so mysteriously carried me here; how the moon keeps on with
its rhythms and the sun rises and falls and the days pass faster and
faster as I use up my allotment of breaths and move toward death. I
think: *Twenty, forty, sixty, eighty.* Both my parents died when they
were eighty; 75 percent of my life is probably gone. Where did
it go?

I remember once walking with my son along Boston Harbor near
a famous fish restaurant, but I can't remember the name of the
place. (Another aspect of aging.) I was about thirty-five at the time,
and my son was ten, and as a huge truck passed us, the driver stuck
his head out the window and whistled enthusiastically at me. What
was I wearing? Probably a miniskirt. What was my hair like? Probably long and dark and parted down the middle. As the truck's exhaust briefly swirled around us, Josh muttered, "I can't believe that
jerk. I wish I could slam him one."

I was touched and amused by my son's chivalrous impulse,
whereas the whistle left me feeling simultaneously flattered and an-
noyed. Who'd hoot at a woman when she clearly had her son in
tow? Was Josh upset by his mother's sexuality? Was it an Oedipal
scene? I have no idea, but I remember the incident well.

Now I'm mostly invisible to men, unless they're seventy or older.

"I don't feel invisible at all," one woman my age replied when I mentioned this. "I was never noticed before," she said. "It's you pretty ones who get to suffer this time."

Recently I went to a bar with my husband and a friend to listen to jazz. The place was smoky and jam-packed, our drinks long in coming. Our friend whispered loudly, "There's so-and-so!" — only he said the name of a famous writer — and nodded toward a schlumpy-looking man in a trench coat, moving slowly toward the bar. The writer took off his coat, laid it over a stool, and sat down on it. He was quickly handed a beer by a plump young bartender. Then the writer lit a cigarette and began to stare at me as I scrunched defensively next to my husband. I was, I confess, vaguely flattered even to be noticed by such a famous writer, and his rheumy eyes made me see myself in a more literary fashion. But, God, he was old!

How can one accept — let alone enjoy — aging in a culture where God is twenty-five; where advertisements are filled with twenty-somethings in halter tops and tight T-shirts, unless the ad is for a drug to treat incontinence, high blood pressure, or elevated cholesterol? What about the wisdom of age? What about endurance? What about the beauty of a face etched by years that were not always easy? Show me anyone over fifty who has not known tragedy, and I'll show you Icarus about to lose his wings and plunge into the sea. Maybe angels will arrive, maybe a medevac, maybe death.

So here I am walking down the only real long corridor there is, sometimes wanting to sing and dance, but often whining as I'm pushed in opposite directions: from behind by two dead parents, encouraging, "It's fine, it's fine"; from ahead by a thirty-five-year-old daughter, saying, "You're young. You can't die, Mom. You're my hero, and if you die, I'll never get over it." But it's not death that's the devil; it's the decaying body, the kind of deterioration my own mother faced in her long years of Parkinson's and dementia.

Recently my husband and I bought long-term-care insurance, to stave off nursing-home hell. And, at last, we've written our wills. My husband, thirteen years younger than I, acts as if he is going along for the ride. "Why don't you catch up?" I sometimes yell at him. He smiles and is silent; what can he say? And so I hold my husband, and he holds me, and I hold what life I have left in my arms like a child, trying to comfort it, make it laugh. But sometimes it feels like a real job.

"Oh, you're young," Gordon, the eighty-year-old man I like to sit next to in synagogue, says to me. I have no idea how to respond to this. Should I sing hallelujah? Thank God for the good life I've had? Gordon is a beautiful old soul with the face of a kindly god. Sometimes I feel an impulse to sidle up to him, thigh to thigh, turn that face to mine, and kiss him hard on the lips, but I'm afraid I'd give him a heart attack.

I had no fear whatsoever of kissing my friend Robyn, who, at fifty-four, was stricken with cancer. It started in her lungs and then spread just about everywhere else within two years, despite chemotherapy (the details of which I heard almost daily). During her illness, I laughed and wept with her, and did as many things for her as she would allow. We often held hands and talked above the racket of her three parakeets.

The last time I took Robyn to do errands — the drugstore, the pet store, the market — she marveled, "Oh, my God, Genie, you can just get up and go and do all that. It's amazing. Do you have any idea?" I paused for a moment and considered. Then I brought Robyn home, helped her switch over from a portable oxygen tank to the larger tank in her living room, kissed her once on each cheek, got back into the car, and drove past the familiar landscape that I could barely imagine existing without her in it.

Now that she's dead, I keep wondering where she is, although I've visited her grave twice. I could swear she was in the barred owl that flew over my head in the woods a month after her death and then sat in a tree about twenty feet from me and stared. I hadn't seen a barred owl since the winter before my mother's death, seven years earlier, when one had perched outside our kitchen window week after week. Now there was this bird, and there I was, my heart fractured by Robyn's departure. The owl watched me steadily, taking my grief into its black eyes. Then off it flew, and I walked back home.

I'm lucky to have come this far in life before losing a good friend. "What does it feel like?" someone in her forties asked me. "It feels hard and empty," I told her. What I didn't say is that sometimes, beneath this hard emptiness, there is a sense of flight, of wings spread, of chest and heart holding more love than before.

There is the knowledge that my heart won't ever seal up as tight again, and the real, earned understanding that we all are dying. I've already been blessed with six more years than Robyn had.

When Robyn and I walked down the street together talking, I never noticed whether men looked at us. I didn't care, and Robyn helped me not to care, with her bulky winter hats and the little red cap she wore to cover her baldness.

Middle-aged people shrink, crease, fade, and, if they're lucky, slowly lose the desire to be noticed, the way we once lost our childhood taste for Necco Wafers or Pez. My desire to be seen is gradually being replaced by the desire to see: the faces of those I love, the cardinal in the bush, the socks of the woman with MS who swims at the Y.

"Great socks," I tell her as I change for my workout.

"Thanks," she says. "Now that I'm older, I'm going for wilder, especially in the sock department."

I think of Robyn's strange hats.

As we continue talking, this woman says she's fifty-eight and can't wait to turn sixty. *I can't believe she's younger than I am,* I think as I go off to blow-dry my hair so it won't fall flat.

When I return, no one else is in the locker room. Robyn and I met here three times a week, every winter, for twelve years. Grief suddenly hits again. Packing up my things, I begin to cry. I walk out past a few people, averting my wet eyes. Outside, the late-afternoon sky glows pink over the red-and-white Toyota sign and the bare November trees. *Beauty and pain are sisters,* I think. *Aging and death are sisters. Robyn and I are sisters.* I can't see Robyn as she was, but I see something akin to her in this sky. Part of me, I believe, will never die. But I wonder if I will always miss, just a little, being the young woman who drew stares from strangers walking down the street.

A few weeks before Robyn's death, my husband and I went to see Wynton Marsalis perform at a small club. Bill and I sat about four feet from the stage, and Bill, who loves music more than he loves me (although he might deny this), was entranced, transported, gone from his body and taken up into pure sound the way prophets and poets claim we ecstatically dissolve into light at the end.

I kept looking at my husband. Bill's a serious guy, not quick with words, which he respects too much to misuse, aware as he is of their often-paltry ability to hold truth — unlike the long note from Marsalis's trumpet, that sound emitted from a gleaming piece of metal, its mouthpiece surrounded by those wide lips and miraculous, triple-jointed cheeks. I felt Bill's spirit undulating above his strong, erect body, utterly lost to flesh. Then the blue of his eyes caught the brown of mine for a second, and he leaned toward me and whispered, "I could die now." My eyes moistened, and I wanted so badly to believe that this joy was what had come for Robyn; that it's what will come for us all in the end.

Contributors

Notable Spiritual Writing of 2005

Contributors

Rick Bass is the author of twenty-one books of fiction and nonfiction, including *The Diezmo, Colter: The True Story of the Best Dog I Ever Had,* and *Where the Sea Used to Be.* His stories have been awarded the Pushcart Prize and the O. Henry Award.

Wendell Berry is the author of many books including *The Way of Ignorance: And Other Essays, Blessed Are the Peacemakers: Christ's Teachings of Love, Compassion, and Forgiveness,* and *Given: Poems.*

Peter J. Boyer has been a staff writer at *The New Yorker* since 1992. His stories have been included in the anthologies *Best American Crime Writing* and *Best American Science Writing.* As a correspondent for the PBS documentary series *Frontline,* he has won a Peabody Award and an Emmy.

Scott Cairns is a professor of English at the University of Missouri and the author of many books of poetry, including *The Theology of Doubt, The Translation of Babel, Figures for the Ghost, Recovered Bodies,* and, most recently, *Philokalia: New & Selected Poems.*

Michael Chabon's books include *The Final Solution: A Novel of Detection, Summerland,* and *The Amazing Adventures of Kavalier and Clay* (Pulitzer Prize for fiction, 2001).

Mark Doty's most recent book of poems is *School of the Arts.* A new prose work, *Dog Years,* a meditation on the relationship between people and canines, will be published in 2007. He lives in New York City and teaches every fall at the University of Houston.

Brian Doyle is the editor of *Portland* at the University of Portland in Oregon. He is the author of *The Wet Engine: Exploring the Mad Wild Miracle of the Heart, Spirited Men: Story, Soul, and Substance,* and other books.

Anthony Esolen is a professor of English at Providence College and a contributing editor to *Touchstone* magazine. His most recent work includes a three-volume translation and edition of Dante's *Divine Comedy.* He and his family attend Sacred Heart Roman Catholic Church in West Warwick, Rhode Island.

Malcolm Gladwell, a staff writer at *The New Yorker,* is the author of *Blink* and *The Tipping Point.*

Peter J. Gomes, an American Baptist minister, is the Plummer Professor of Christian morals and Pusey Minister in the Memorial Church at Harvard University. He is the author of *The Good Book: Reading the Bible with Mind and Heart, The Good Life: Truths That Last in Time of Need, The Backward Glance and the Forward Look,* and other books.

Mary Gordon is the author of numerous books of fiction and nonfiction, including a biography of Joan of Arc. Her most recent book is *Pearl.* She has won a Lila Acheson Wallace Reader's Digest Award, a Guggenheim fellowship, and an O. Henry Award for best short story. She teaches at Barnard College.

Rochelle Gurstein is the author of *The Repeal of Reticence: America's Cultural and Legal Struggles over Free Speech, Obscenity, Sexual Liberation, and Modern Art.* Her essays on intellectual history, aesthetics, and contemporary social and political matters have appeared in *The New Republic, Salmagundi, Raritan,* and other "little magazines."

Sam Hamill was editor of Copper Canyon Press from 1972 to 2004. He is the author of more than forty volumes of poetry, poetry in translation, and essays, including, most recently, *Tao Te Ching: A New Translation* and *Almost Paradise: New and Selected Poems and Translations.*

Jessie Harriman's writings have appeared in *Portland, North Dakota Quarterly, River Teeth,* and *Clackamas Literary Review.* She lives and works in Iowa City.

Edward Hoagland has published nineteen books of fiction and nonfiction, most recently *Compass Points: How I Lived* (Pantheon, 2001) and *Hoagland* *on Nature: Essays* (The Lyons Press, 2003). He sold his first novel in 1954 and is finishing his fifth novel this year.

Miles Hoffman is the violist and artistic director of the American Chamber Players and the music commentator for National Public Radio's *Morning Edition*. He is the author of *The NPR Classical Music Companion: Terms and Concepts from A to Z.*

Linda Hogan is a poet, a storyteller, a playwright, a novelist, an environmentalist, and a writer of short stories. She received a Lifetime Achievement Award from the Native Writers' Circle of the Americas. Her novel *Mean Spirit* was a Pulitzer Prize finalist and winner of the Oklahoma Book Award for fiction.

Charlotte Innes won the first prize in poetry in the Windows V contest (2003) in Los Angeles.

Alan Jacobs is a professor of English at Wheaton College and author of *The Narnian: The Life and Imagination of C. S. Lewis.*

Corby Kummer, a senior editor of *The Atlantic Monthly,* is the author of *The Pleasures of Slow Food* and *The Joy of Coffee.*

Thomas Lynch, a funeral director, is the author of *The Undertaking* (1998 American Book Award), *Booking Passage: We Irish and Americans,* and other books.

Charles Martin's verse translation of Ovid's *Metamorphoses* was cowinner of the 2004 Harold Morton Landon Award from the Academy of American Poets.

Wilfred M. McClay holds the SunTrust Chair of Humanities at the University of Tennessee at Chattanooga.

Richard John Neuhaus is editor in chief of *First Things* and the author, most recently, of *Catholic Matters: Confusion, Controversy, and the Splendor of Truth.*

Katherine Paterson is the author of many books, including *The Same Stuff as Stars, The Great Gilly Hopkins* (National Book Award, 1979), and *Bridge to Terabithia* (Newbery Medal, 1978).

V. Penelope Pelizzon is an associate professor of English at the University of Connecticut. Her first book, *Nostos,* won the 2001 Norma Farber First

Book Award from the Poetry Society of America and the Hollis Summers Prize.

Matthew Power writes frequently for *Harper's Magazine, Men's Journal, Popular Science,* and other periodicals.

Louis Simpson received the Pulitzer Prize for poetry in 1963. His most recent book is *The Owner of the House: New Collected Poems 1940–2001.*

George Steiner is the author of *Lessons of the Masters, Real Presences, After Babel, Language and Silence,* and other works of cultural and historical criticism. Among his works of fiction are *The Portage to San Cristobal of A. H.* and *Anno Domini.*

Helen Tworkov is the founding editor of *Tricycle* and the author of *Zen in America.*

John Updike's novels have won the Pulitzer Prize, the National Book Award, and the National Book Critics Circle Award. His most recent poetry collection is *Americana.*

Robert Louis Wilken is the William R. Kenan, Jr., Professor of the History of Christianity at the University of Virginia and the author of *The Spirit of Early Christian Thought* and other books.

C. K. Williams is the author of *Collected Poems, The Singing: Poems* (National Book Award, 2003), and other works. He was awarded the Pulitzer Prize for poetry in 2000.

Franz Wright is the author of *God's Silence, Walking to Martha's Vineyard* (Pulitzer Prize, 2004), and other books of poetry.

Philip Zaleski is the editor of *The Best American Spiritual Writing.* His most recent books are *Prayer: A History* and *The Book of Heaven* (both with Carol Zaleski).

Genie Zeiger is the author of two memoirs and three books of poetry, the most recent being *Radio Waves.* She lives with her husband, Bill, in western Massachusetts, where she has led writing workshops for the past twenty years.

Notable Spiritual Writing of 2005

GARY ANDERSON,
  "How to Think About Zionism," *First Things*, April

TIM BASCOM,
  "Chasing Charles Wesley," *Western Humanities Review*, Fall
MICHAEL BEHE,
  "Scientific Orthodoxies," *First Things*, December

STEPHEN CARTER,
  "The Weight of Priesthood," *Dialogue*, Fall
WILLIAM C. CHITTICK,
  "Spirit, Body, and In-Between," *Parabola*, Fall

GRETEL EHRLICH,
  "The Future of Ice," *Shambhala Sun*, January
ROBERT ELLSBERG,
  "Five Years with Dorothy Day," *America*, November 21

NORTHROP FRYE,
  "Reconsidering Levels of Meaning," *Christianity and Literature*, Spring
DEREK FURR,
  "Afterlife," *Fourth Genre*, Spring

NATALIE GOLDBERG,
  "New Century," *Creative Nonfiction*, November

AMY LAURA HALL,
  "Better Homes and Children," *Books & Culture*, November/December
DON HAYNES,
  "Going to Chimayo," *Portland*, Autumn

HEATHER KING,
  "Paradise Found," *The Sun*, July

SUMI LOUNDON,
   "I Married a Monk," *Shambhala Sun*, September

NANCY MAIRS,
   "I Will Hear God," *Notre Dame*, Winter
ALISTER MCGRATH,
   "The Twilight of Atheism," *Christianity Today*, March

DAVID NEFF,
   "Naming the Horror," *Christianity Today*, April
MICHAEL NOVAK,
   "Johannis Paulus Magnus," *American Spectator*, May

ROBERT A. ROSENSTONE,
   "My Wife the Muslim," *Antioch Review*, Spring
HANNAH ROSIN,
   "Can Jesus Save Hollywood," *The Atlantic Monthly*, December

OLIVER SACKS,
   "Recalled to Life," *The New Yorker*, October 31
CURTIS SMITH,
   "We Care!" *Mississippi Review*, October
HUSTON SMITH,
   "Reasons for Joy," *Christian Century*, October 4
THEA SULLIVAN,
   "Trying," *The Sun*, October

NORMAN WIRZBA,
   "Time Out," *Christian Century*, July 12

Introducing our newest addition to the BEST AMERICAN *series*

THE BEST AMERICAN COMICS 2006. Harvey Pekar, guest editor, Anne Elizabeth Moore, series editor. This newcomer to the best-selling series — the first Best American annual dedicated to the finest in graphic storytelling and literary comics — includes stories culled from graphic novels, pamphlet comics, newspapers, magazines, mini-comics, and the Web. Edited by the subject of the Oscar-nominated film *American Splendor*, Harvey Pekar, the collection features pieces by Robert Crumb, Chris Ware, Kim Deitch, Jaime Hernandez, Alison Bechdel, Joe Sacco, Lilli Carré, and Lynda Barry, among others.

ISBN-10: 0-618-71874-5 / ISBN-13: 978-0-618-71874-0 $22.00 POB

Alongside our perennial favorites

THE BEST AMERICAN SHORT STORIES® 2006. Ann Patchett, guest editor, Katrina Kenison, series editor. This year's most beloved short fiction anthology is edited by Ann Patchett, author of *Bel Canto*, a 2002 PEN/Faulkner Award winner and a National Book Critics Circle Award finalist. The collection features stories by Tobias Wolff, Donna Tartt, Thomas McGuane, Mary Gaitskill, Nathan Englander, and others. "Story for story, readers can't beat the *Best American Short Stories* series" (*Chicago Tribune*).

ISBN-10: 0-618-54351-1 / ISBN-13: 978-0-618-54351-9 $28.00 CL
ISBN-10: 0-618-54352-X / ISBN-13: 978-0-618-54352-6 $14.00 PA

THE BEST AMERICAN NONREQUIRED READING 2006. Edited by Dave Eggers, introduction by Matt Groening. This "enticing . . . funny, and wrenching" (*Cleveland Plain Dealer*) collection highlights a bold mix of fiction, nonfiction, screenplays, alternative comics, and more from publications large, small, and online. With an introduction by Matt Groening, creator of *The Simpsons* and *Futurama*, this volume features writing from *The Onion*, *The Daily Show*, *This American Life*, Judy Budnitz, Joe Sacco, and others.

ISBN-10: 0-618-57050-0 / ISBN-13: 978-0-618-57050-8 $28.00 CL
ISBN-10: 0-618-57051-9 / ISBN-13: 978-0-618-57051-5 $14.00 PA

THE BEST AMERICAN ESSAYS® 2006. Lauren Slater, guest editor, Robert Atwan, series editor. Since 1986, *The Best American Essays* has annually gathered outstanding nonfiction writing, establishing itself as the premier anthology of its kind. Edited by the best-selling author of *Prozac Diary*, Lauren Slater, this year's "delightful collection" (*Miami Herald*) highlights provocative, lively writing by Adam Gopnik, Scott Turow, Marjorie Williams, Poe Ballantine, and others.

ISBN-10: 0-618-70531-7 / ISBN-13: 978-0-618-70531-3 $28.00 CL
ISBN-10: 0-618-70529-5 / ISBN-13: 978-0-618-70529-0 $14.00 PA

THE BEST AMERICAN MYSTERY STORIES™ 2006. Scott Turow, guest editor, Otto Penzler, series editor. This perennially popular anthology is sure to appeal to mystery fans of every variety. The 2006 volume, edited by Scott Turow, author of the critically acclaimed *Ordinary Heroes* and *Presumed Innocent*, features both mystery veterans and new talents, offering stories by Elmore Leonard, Ed McBain, James Lee Burke, Joyce Carol Oates, Walter Mosley, and others.

ISBN-10: 0-618-51746-4 / ISBN-13: 978-0-618-51746-6 $28.00 CL
ISBN-10: 0-618-51747-2 / ISBN-13: 978-0-618-51747-3 $14.00 PA

THE B·E·S·T AMERICAN SERIES®

THE BEST AMERICAN SPORTS WRITING™ 2006. Michael Lewis, guest editor, Glenn Stout, series editor. "An ongoing centerpiece for all sports collections" (*Booklist*), this series stands in high regard for its extraordinary sports writing and top-notch editors. This year's guest editor, Michael Lewis, the acclaimed author of the bestseller *Moneyball*, brings together pieces by Gary Smith, Pat Jordan, Paul Solotaroff, Linda Robertson, L. Jon Wertheim, and others.

ISBN-10: 0-618-47021-2 / ISBN-13: 978-0-618-47021-1 $28.00 CL
ISBN-10: 0-618-47022-0 / ISBN-13: 978-0-618-47022-8 $14.00 PA

THE BEST AMERICAN TRAVEL WRITING 2006. Tim Cahill, guest editor, Jason Wilson, series editor. Tim Cahill is the founding editor of *Outside* magazine and a frequent contributor to *National Geographic Adventure*. This year's collection captures the traveler's wandering spirit and ever-present quest for adventure. Giving new life to armchair journeys are Alain de Botton, Pico Iyer, David Sedaris, Gary Shteyngart, George Saunders, and others.

ISBN-10: 0-618-58212-6 / ISBN-13: 978-0-618-58212-9 $28.00 CL
ISBN-10: 0-618-58215-0 / ISBN-13: 978-0-618-58215-0 $14.00 PA

THE BEST AMERICAN SCIENCE AND NATURE WRITING 2006. Brian Greene, guest editor, Tim Folger, series editor. Brian Greene, the best-selling author of *The Elegant Universe* and the first physicist to edit this prestigious series, offers a fresh take on the year's best science and nature writing. Featuring such authors as John Horgan, Daniel C. Dennett, and Dennis Overbye, among others, this collection "surprises us into caring about subjects we had not thought to examine" (*Cleveland Plain Dealer*).

ISBN-10: 0-618-72221-1 / ISBN-13: 978-0-618-72221-1 $28.00 CL
ISBN-10: 0-618-72222-X / ISBN-13: 978-0-618-72222-8 $14.00 PA

THE BEST AMERICAN SPIRITUAL WRITING 2006. Edited by Philip Zaleski, introduction by Peter J. Gomes. Featuring an introduction by Peter J. Gomes, a best-selling author, respected minister, and the Plummer Professor of Christian Morals at Harvard University, this year's edition of this "excellent annual" (*America*) gathers pieces from diverse faiths and denominations and includes writing by Michael Chabon, Malcolm Gladwell, Mary Gordon, John Updike, and others.

ISBN-10: 0-618-58644-X / ISBN-13: 978-0-618-58644-8 $28.00 CL
ISBN-10: 0-618-58645-8 / ISBN-13: 978-0-618-58645-5 $14.00 PA

THE BEST AMERICAN GOLD GIFT BOX 2006. Boxed in rich gold metallic, this set includes *The Best American Short Stories 2006*, *The Best American Mystery Stories 2006*, and *The Best American Sports Writing 2006*.

ISBN-10: 0-618-80126-X / ISBN-13: 978-0-618-80126-8 $40.00 PA

THE BEST AMERICAN SILVER GIFT BOX 2006. Packaged in a lavish silver metallic box, this set features *The Best American Short Stories 2006*, *The Best American Travel Writing 2006*, and *The Best American Spiritual Writing 2006*.

ISBN-10: 0-618-80127-8 / ISBN-13: 978-0-618-80127-5 $40.00 PA

 HOUGHTON MIFFLIN COMPANY www.houghtonmifflinbooks.com